GREECE & ROME STU

DEDICATION

The first volume in a projected series 'Greece & Rome Studies' is dedicated to the memory of R. D. Williams, the author of the first issue, *Virgil*, in the *Greece & Rome* series, New Surveys in the Classics.

GREECE & ROME STUDIES

VIRGIL

Edited by
IAN McAUSLAN
and
PETER WALCOT

Published by
OXFORD UNIVERSITY PRESS

on behalf of
THE CLASSICAL ASSOCIATION
1990

Oxford University Press, Walton Street, Oxford OX2 6DP

Oxford   New York   Toronto
Delhi   Bombay   Calcutta   Madras   Karachi
Petaling Jaya   Singapore   Hong Kong   Tokyo
Nairobi   Dar es Salaam   Cape Town
Melbourne Auckland
and associated companies in
Berlin Ibadan

Oxford is a trade mark of Oxford University Press

Published in the United States
by Oxford University Press, New York

British Library Cataloguing in Publication Data
Virgil. – (Greece and Rome studies)
1. Poetry in Latin. Virgil. critical studies
I. McAuslan, Ian   II. Walcot, Peter   III. Classical
Association   IIII. Series
871'.01
ISBN 0-19-920166-8 (Hbk)
ISBN 0-19-920170-6 (Pbk)

Library of Congress Cataloging in Publication Data
Virgil / edited by Ian McAuslan and Peter Walcot.
p.   cm. — (Greece and Rome studies)
1 Virgil—Criticism and interpretation.   I. McAuslan, Ian.
II. Walcot, Peter.   III. Classical Association (Great Britain).
IV. Series.
PA6825.V47   1990   89—27447
873'.01—dc20
ISBN 0-19-920166-8 (Hbk)
0-19-920170-6 (Pbk)

Typeset by Latimer Trend & Company Ltd
Printed and bound in
Great Britain by Biddles Ltd,
Guildford and King's Lynn

CONTENTS

EDITORIAL NOTE

This is the first volume in what is hoped will be a continuing series, collecting together *Greece & Rome* articles published on a particular author or theme.

IMITATION AND THE POETRY OF VIRGIL

By GUY LEE

Imitation, in the sense of the conscious adaptation and transference of an idea, a phrase, or a passage, from one poetical context to another, was a recognized procedure of ancient poetry, as it still is of modern. It is however a difficult art and on occasion, as we shall see, the re-working of alien material, though it may be poetically successful, is none the less achieved at some cost of clarity, accuracy, or literal truth.

Virgil, a scholar poet or *doctus poeta* if ever there was one, and therefore more conscious than most poets of particulars in the wide range of tradition behind him, employed the technique of imitation pervasively; so the shortest cut to a precise identification of the individual quality, the *timbre*, of his poetry ought to be to compare a few passages from his work with their originals in various earlier poets.

I

βοτὰ χίλια βόσκω ...
τυρὸς δ' οὐ λείπει μ' οὔτ' ἐν θέρει οὔτ' ἐν ὀπώρᾳ,
οὐ χειμῶνος ἄκρω· ταρσοὶ δ' ὑπεραχθέες αἰεί.
συρίσδεν δ' ὡς οὔτις ἐπίσταμαι ὧδε Κυκλώπων.

Theocritus, *Idyll* 11.34 and 36–8

I feed a thousand beasts ...
Cheese fails me not, neither in summer nor in autumn,
not at winter's end ...
I know how to pipe as none of the Cyclopes here.

mille meae Siculis errant in montibus agnae.
lac mihi non aestate nouum, non frigore defit.
canto quae solitus si quando armenta uocabat
Amphion Dircaeus in Actaeo Aracyntho.

Virgil, *Eclogue* 2.21–4

A thousand ewe lambs of mine roam on Sicilian mountains.
Fresh milk fails me not in summer, not in the cold.
I sing what he was used to if ever he called the cattle –
Amphion the Dircaean on Actaean Aracynthus.

In Theocritus the Cyclops Polyphemus lists his good points for the benefit of the sea-nymph Galatea. Virgil varies three of them and applies them to a different character, the shepherd Corydon, in love with his master's favourite Alexis, and thus turns the contrast between land-monster and sea-nymph into one between self-styled country bumpkin and city-bred boy, making the love homo- instead of hetero-sexual.

But in what sense can Corydon the slave own a thousand ewe lambs?

Not in the straightforward literal sense but in the extended sense in which, say, a trainer might talk about the owner's horses as 'my horses'. But even in this sense Corydon's claim is an exaggeration, for 'a thousand ewe lambs' outbids Polyphemus by four or five to one and adds up to an enormous flock if you include the unmentioned but still inevitable ram lambs, hoggets, ewes, wethers, rams, etc. No wonder, says the pedant, these lambs roamed about on the Sicilian mountains if Corydon had to cope with them all single-handed.

Corydon's claim as a singer also goes one or two better than Polyphemus, who was content to be the best piper among his brother Cyclopes; but the exaggeration is perhaps less than in the matter of the size of his flock, for Amphion after all had been brought up among shepherds. But what lies behind the sonorous and romantic line 24 with its dense mythological allusions? Most probably yet another Greek original, in hexameters or elegiacs: first, because the line is virtually a Greek dactylic hexameter written in Roman characters; secondly, because Propertius, some twenty-five years later, tells the story of Antiope, Amphion's mother, in elegiac couplets and here again Amphion the singer appears in connection with Aracynthus (3.15. 41–2):

> uictorque canebat
> paeana Amphion rupe, Aracynthe, tua.

> and victorious
> Amphion sang the paean on thy crag, Aracynthus.

A common source in Greek poetry is the likeliest explanation of the Virgilian and Propertian allusions. But this Greek line is a very grand one to put into the mouth of Corydon the humble shepherd whose love-song is described at the beginning of the *Eclogue* as *incondita* or 'uncouth'.

I hope the reader will not feel that I have exaggerated Virgil's exaggerations here but will agree that they really are there. Their presence is the main point I want to make about this passage. Of course this raises questions about the character of Corydon: is it consistent? do his words fit in with his state of mind? Various answers can be given to these questions but I am not concerned with them. Suffice it to say that the answers are by no means as simple as those that can be given to the same questions about the character of Polyphemus.

II

> Saepibus in nostris paruam te roscida mala
> (dux ego uester eram) uidi cum matre legentem.
> alter ab undecimo tum me iam acceperat annus,
> iam fragilis poteram a terra contingere ramos.

Eclogue 8.37–40

Inside our fence I saw you as a little girl (I was guide
to you both) gathering dewy apples with mother.
The second from the eleventh year had then just received me,
I could just touch the brittle branches from the ground.

The first two lines are based on another passage from the *Cyclops*
of Theocritus (*Id.* 11. 25–9):

ἠράσθην μὲν ἔγωγε τεοῦς, κόρα, ἁνίκα πρᾶτου
ἦνθες ἐμᾷ σὺν ματρὶ θέλοισ᾽ ὑακίνθινα φύλλα
ἐξ ὄρεος δρέψασθαι, ἐγὼ δ᾽ ὁδὸν ἁγεμόνευον.
παύσασθαι δ᾽ ἐσιδών τυ καὶ ὕστερον οὐδ᾽ ἔτι πᾳ νῦν
ἐκ τήνω δύναμαι.

I fell in love with you, lass, when first
you came with my mother wanting to pick hyacinths
from the mountain and I led the way.
And having seen you, from that day until now
I cannot stop.

But Virgil's adaptation has a remarkable particularity and conveys a
sense of strong emotion. Theocritus' 'mountain' becomes 'our fence',
'hyacinths' turn into 'dewy apples'; moreover there is the precise detail
of the boy's age and the striking line about his just being able to reach
the brittle branches. One is tempted to guess that we may have here
a memory of Virgil's own boyhood. Why, otherwise, was it necessary
to be so mathematical? To establish puberty? But might not a more
conventionally poetical line which ended, say, with the words *lanugine
malas*, 'my cheeks with down', have done the trick?

And yet, despite their memorable particularity, lines 37–8 exhibit
characteristics of a kind not uncommon in imitations. For example,
Virgil has left out the important word 'first', a word so important that
his translators E. V. Rieu and C. Day Lewis have supplied it for him.
Again, *dux ego uester eram* is not such a natural fit as its Theocritean
original, and *matre* is not clear. Whose mother? 'My mother' would
not need to be shown the way to 'our' orchard, therefore probably
'your mother'; for *uester* would seem to contrast with *nostris*, as
Professor Wendell Clausen has pointed out to me. On the other hand
if his guiding consisted in pointing out to them where the best apples
were, then 'mother' could be 'my mother'. This 'particular' vagueness
is perhaps typical of Virgil, and it is no disadvantage here – the poetic
effect of the passage is undeniable; nevertheless in comparison with
its source it is unclear.[1]

III

Felix qui potuit rerum cognoscere causas
atque metus omnis et inexorabile fatum
subiecit pedibus strepitumque Acherontis auari.

Georgics 2.490–92

> Happy he who could get to know the causes of things
> and threw under foot every fear and inexorable fate
> and the noise of avaricious Acheron.

As Munro in his note on Lucretius 1.78 makes clear, Virgil is here alluding to Lucretius and has constructed the three lines out of his memory of various passages in the *De Rerum Natura*, a poem which he must have known extremely well. The point that concerns us now, however, is not the kaleidoscopic character of a poet's memory but the force of the metaphor *subiecit pedibus*, 'threw under foot'. The words are adapted from Lucretius 1.78:

> quare Religio pedibus subiecta uicissim
> obteritur, nos exaequat uictoria caelo,

> Wherefore Religion thrown under foot in her turn
> is trodden down; the victory levels *us* with heaven.

Now the word *uicissim*, 'in turn', implies that the victory of Epicurus involves the reversal of a previously existing state of affairs; and going back in Lucretius' poem to the beginning of this famous passage we find that state of affairs vividly described:

> Humana ante oculos foede cum Vita iaceret
> in terris oppressa graui sub Religione
> quae caput a caeli regionibus ostendebat
> horribili super aspectu mortalibus instans ... 62–5

> When Human Life before his eyes lay foully prostrate
> on earth, crushed under the weight of Religion,
> who showed her head from the quarters of the sky
> with hideous aspect standing over mortals.

Religion is personified as a monstrous being with head in the sky and feet trampling on human life; there is also in the last line in *super instans* a probable allusion to an etymology of the word *super-stitio*, an etymology which may perhaps have suggested to the poet the idea of Religion as an evil Genie oppressing humanity from above.[2]

Returning to Lucr. 1.78–9, we notice how *Religio pedibus subiecta* reverses *Vita iaceret/ ... graui sub Religione*, how *obteritur* corresponds to *oppressa*, and how *nos exaequat uictoria caelo* looks back to 64–5. Everything fits and has the fullest meaning. But observe how tame the metaphor *subiecit pedibus* has become in Virgil, how relatively pointless it is unless one remembers, as Virgil doubtless means one to do, the Lucretian original. The two words derive their force from the primary passage. But even so the metaphor is less forceful and vaguer than in Lucretius because the abstract noun *metus* is not really personified (*inexorabile* personifies *fatum*), and because there is a slight awkwardness in treading on a noise, even though *strepitum Acherontis* can be regarded as a rhetorical figure for *strepentem Acheronta*, for Acheron if it exists is in the Underworld and the Underworld is under our feet anyhow.

IV

Huc omnis turba ad ripas effusa ruebat,
matres atque uiri defunctaque corpora uita
magnanimum heroum, pueri innuptaeque puellae
impositique rogis iuuenes ante ora parentum.

Aeneid 6.305–8

Hither the whole crowd rushed in confusion to the banks,
mothers and husbands and bodies discharged from life
of great-souled heroes, boys and unwed girls
and young men laid on pyres before the faces of parents.

We are in the Underworld with Aeneas and the Sibyl, watching the ghosts flocking to the ferry over the river Styx. Virgil here seems to be prepared to put up with one or two minor inconveniences for the sake of compensating advantages. How can the crowd rush to the banks when there is only one river and they are all on the same side of it? Surely not for the crude metrical reason that *ripam effusa* would not scan, but perhaps because the so-called poetic plural gives a touch of epic distinction to language that without it is not above the level of historical prose? Significant, though, that the logical disadvantage did not worry him. Similarly the periphrasis *defunctaque corpora uita/ magnanimum heroum* has the disadvantage of suggesting that 'shades', *umbrae*, are corporeal and tangible and sets up an unwanted antithesis between '*bodies*' and '*great-souled*'. But this phrase too has an epic, perhaps an Ennian, grandeur which Virgil must have felt outweighed the slight logical complications. Again, is there not a certain awkwardness in the idea of young men laid on pyres rushing anywhere? But we are now some distance from the verb *ruebat* and perhaps for a Roman the past participle here would have had a pluperfect feeling about it. Anyhow, the gain of this celebrated line is in the climax it makes to the pathos of the second group of three, the immature: 'boys and unmarried girls and young men laid on pyres before the faces of their parents' – something that had happened only too often, we may guess, in the civil wars of the first century B.C. and something too that looks forward to the figure of Marcellus later in this book.[3] The first group of three is not particularly pathetic; mothers and husbands and heroes discharged from life are mature, and indeed the words *defuncta uita* may contain a suggestion of fulfilment, like *defunctus honoribus*.

Virgil is re-working a famous passage from Homer's *Nekyia*, or Book of the Dead (*Odyssey* 11.36–41):

αἰ δ᾽ ἀγέροντο
ψυχαὶ ὑπὲξ ᾿Ερέβευς νεκύων κατατεθνηώτων.
νύμφαι τ᾽ ἠΐθεοί τε πολύτλατοί τε γέροντες
παρθενικαί τ᾽ ἀταλαὶ νεοπενθέα θυμὸν ἔχουσαι
πολλοὶ δ᾽ οὐτάμενοι χαλκήρεσιν ἐγχείῃσιν,
ἄνδρες ἀρηΐφατοι βεβροτωμένα τεύχε᾽ ἔχοντες.

They gathered together,
souls out of Erebos of dead corpses,
brides and young bachelors and much-enduring old men
and tender virgins with spirit new to grief,
and many pierced by bronze-tipped spears,
men battle-slain, wearing bloodied armour.

Homer begins with the pathos of the unfulfilled – 'brides and young
bachelors' – youth, but full-grown, female and male, newly married
and still unmarried. He continues with the pathetic contrast of old age
and immaturity, the contrast between old men whose life has been hard
and their old age painful, and unmarried girls whose first experience
of grief is their own death. He ends with mature men who have sought
glory in war, not heroes but casualties, their armour not shining, not
κλυτά or παμφανόωντα, as armour often is in the *Iliad*, but 'bloodied',
βεβροτωμένα, a striking Homeric *hapax legomenon*. Is there not here
a hint that the heroic ideal is unsatisfactory? And in the passage as
a whole do we not feel that life is tragic? The pathos in Virgil is less,
despite his introduction of 'young men laid on pyres before the faces
of their parents'. For he has provided a glimmer of light in the simile
that follows – in those sunny lands to which the birds flock in the chill
of the autumn (*Aen.* 6.310–12). And he has introduced the family at
the beginning and the end: *matres atque uiri* for Homer's 'brides and
young bachelors' and *parentum* as last word. A Roman does not face
life alone; he is part of a close-knit family group, and one feels that
the family is safe; for although the first of the dead to appear are mothers
and husbands and the last are the young men burnt on the pyre before
the eyes of their parents, those parents themselves are still alive.[4]

                                    V

Sicut aquae tremulum labris ubi lumen aenis
sole repercussum aut radiantis imagine lunae
omnia peruolitat late loca iamque sub auras
erigitur summique ferit laquearia tecti.

                                              Aeneid 8.22–5

Just as when from bronze basins of water quivering light
struck back by sun or radiant moon's image
flits abroad over all places and now under the airs
rises up and strikes the panels of the highest ceiling.

This simile, describing the swift and shifting thoughts of Aeneas at a time of danger, is complicated and perplexing – in fact quite a mind-teaser, but an entertaining one to try to work out. We probably need not decide whether *aquae* goes with *labris* or *lumen*; though we have to translate it with one or the other in English, in Latin why should it not go with both? *Labris* itself may be a poetic plural (*auras* certainly is) and refer to a cauldron or container of some kind (as at *Aen.* 12.417) or it may be a true plural and refer to the basins of a fountain (cf. Pliny, *Epist.* 5.6.20). We are not told that the water is in motion, as it has to be if the reflected light is to flit about. Perhaps a fountain playing in a peristyle or cloister is the best idea, and this would also explain why the light at one moment seems to be outside (*sub auras*) and at the next inside, flickering on a type of ceiling only found in the houses of the rich (*laquearia*). Syntactically lines 22–3 admit the alternative possibility that *labris aenis* is local ablative and that *sole* means 'from the sun'. 'The moon's image' (as James Henry argues in his *Aeneidea*) most likely means the moon's shape, but one can hardly avoid thinking at the same time of the moon's reflexion in the water. In short, Virgil seems to have gone out of his way to avoid making things clear. It is a reasonable inference from this passage that he prefers them to be imprecise. The inference becomes more probable still when we compare his Latin with the Greek original on which it is based, Apollonius, *Argonautica* 3.755–9:

> πυκνὰ δέ οἱ κραδίη στηθέων ἔντοσθεν ἔθυιεν,
> ἠελίου ὥς τίς τε δόμοις ἐνιπάλλεται αἴγλη
> ὕδατος ἐξανιοῦσα, τὸ δὴ νέον ἠὲ λέβητι
> ἠέ που ἐν γαυλῷ κέχυται, ἡ δ' ἔνθα καὶ ἔνθα
> ὠκίῃ στροφάλιγγι τινάσσεται ἀίσσουσα.

Her heart pounded madly in her breast
as in houses a sun-gleam leaps
upward from water newly poured in basin
or pail perhaps; hither and thither the gleam
in swift whirl is shaken, darting.

Here the only slight obscurity is στροφάλιγγι, which could be taken to refer to the moving water – 'by swift eddy'. But the word would be an exaggerated one to apply to water slopping in a pail, whereas it fits the twists and turns of the reflected light perfectly. Otherwise all is clear and precise: we are indoors, the water has just been poured and is therefore moving – in basin or pail, homely items representative of ordinary life perhaps, of the solid reality in which the dazzling but mercurial phenomenon of love occurs.

Conington's note is worth quoting: 'It must be owned that the com-

parison is more pleasing when applied ... to the fluttering heart of
Medea than to the fluctuating mind of Aeneas.' The interesting thing
is that in *Arg.* 3.767–71, shortly after this simile, Apollonius describes
Medea as reviewing the courses of action open to her and as unable
to decide between them. It looks as though this may have suggested
to Virgil his new application of the simile.

VI

Nec plura effatus saxum circumspicit ingens,
saxum antiquum ingens, campo quod forte iacebat,
limes agro positus litem ut discerneret aruis;
uix illum lecti bis sex ceruice subirent,
qualia nunc hominum producit corpora tellus.

Aeneid 12.896–900

Nor uttering more he looks round at a huge stone,
a huge old stone which lay by chance on the plain,
a boundary placed on a property to settle litigation for the fields;
twice six picked men would hardly support it on their neck,
such human bodies as earth produces now.

Again a complicated passage. *Agro* means both 'in a field' and 'on a
property' (I have taken it as ablative, but it could perhaps be dative).
In the next half of the line Virgil is extending the meaning of the word
discernere, as can be seen by consulting *Thesaurus Linguae Latinae* sub
voc. 1305, 21–2; *litem ut discerneret aruis* taken literally would mean
'to separate litigation from the fields', and so it appears to have been
taken in the fourth century A.D., e.g., by Tiberius Claudius Donatus
in his *Virgilian Interpretations*, who paraphrases it as *ut lites possi-
dentibus tolleret*. But the use of *discerno* in this context brings in the
ghost of *decerno* and then the phrase can be translated as above. Again,
what does *ceruice subire* refer to? We cannot reasonably suppose that
the twelve men are putting their shoulders to the stone and trying to
raise it from the ground that way. They must be carrying it somehow;
cf. *Aen.* 2.707–8, *ergo age, care pater, ceruici imponere nostrae./ipse subibo
umeris.* But we have to guess how the twelve 'undergo' the stone. Are
they carrying it like a coffin on their shoulders? If so, how did they
get it up? Clearly Virgil does not care. We are not to ask that sort
of question – there is no time to, anyhow, if we are attending to the
movement of the story. But on this occasion let us pause and break
the spell of the narrative and we shall find that the spellbinder has
here conflated and re-worked two passages from the *Iliad*:

(i) 21.403–5

ἡ δ' ἀναχασσαμένη λίθον εἵλετο χειρὶ παχείῃ
κείμενον ἐν πεδίῳ μέλανα, τρηχύν τε μέγαν τε,
τόν ῥ' ἄνδρες πρότεροι θέσαν ἔμμεναι οὖρον ἀρούρης.

But she (Athene) drawing back seized with stout hand a stone
lying on the plain, black and rough and great,
which earlier men placed to be boundary of a field.

(ii) 12.447–9

τὸν δ' οὐ κε δύ' ἀνέρε δήμου ἀρίστω
ῥηιδίως ἐπ' ἄμαξαν ἀπ' οὔδεος ὀχλίσσειαν,
οἷοι νῦν βροτοί εἰσ'.

This (i.e. the stone Hector has picked up) not two men, best of the people,
would easily lever on to a wagon from the ground,
such as mortals are now.

There are no problems here; everything is clear and credible. We notice
once more how Virgil has intentionally made things more difficult,
or if you like, much less obvious. In his re-working he enlarges and
syntactically complicates the idea of the boundary-mark; similarly he
contracts and technically complicates the idea of the men lifting the
stone, at the same time as he multiplies their number by six. The
multiplication is not to be regarded as totally arbitrary or entirely
hyperbolical, but as a not unreasonable estimate of the human degenera-
tion that has occurred between Homer's time and Virgil's – a conserva-
tive estimate if you compare it with Horace *Odes* 3.6.45–8:

damnosa quid non imminuit dies?
aetas parentum peior auis tulit
nos nequiores, mox daturos
progeniem uitiosiorem!

VII

Ac uelut in somnis, oculos ubi languida pressit
nocte quies, nequiquam auidos extendere cursus
uelle uidemur et in mediis conatibus aegri
succidimus . . .

Aeneid 12.908–11

And as in sleep, when listless repose presses
on eyes at night, we seem ineffectively to want to stretch out
eager runnings and in mid-efforts feebly
collapse . . .

As Conington puts it, 'the hint for this simile' comes from *Iliad*
22.199–201 and 'the rhythm and language recall Lucr. 4.453 ff.'. In
the passage from the *Iliad* Hector is running away from Achilles and
neither hero can gain ground on the other:

ὡς δ' ἐν ὀνείρῳ οὐ δύναται φεύγοντα διώκειν.
οὔτ' ἄρ' ὁ τὸν δύναται ὑποφεύγειν οὔθ' ὁ διώκειν.
ὡς ὁ τὸν οὐ δύνατο μάρψαι ποσίν, οὐδ' ὃς ἀλύξαι.

And as in a dream one has no strength to pursue one who flees,
neither has that one strength to flee away from him nor he
to pursue, so he (Achilles) could not catch him (Hector) on foot
nor could the other escape.

Virgil has taken over the general idea of this bare and poorly expressed
comparison, to use it in a corresponding context in his epic – the duel
between Turnus and Aeneas that brings the *Aeneid* to a dying close.
But his memory of the passage from Lucretius has enabled him to give
it detailed and unforgettable life. Here is the Lucretian passage:

> denique, cum suaui deuinxit membra sopore
> somnus et in summa corpus iacet omne quiete,
> tum uigilare tamen nobis et membra mouere
> nostra uidemur, et in noctis caligine caeca
> cernere censemus solem lumenque diurnum.

> Again, when sleep has tied down the limbs with sweet
> slumber and the whole body lies in utmost repose,
> then nevertheless we seem to ourselves to be awake
> and to move our limbs, and in night's blind darkness
> we reckon to see the sun and the light of day.

The effect of this passage, which occurs in a discussion of the reliability of sense-impressions, depends in part on paradox and antithesis:
thus, in the last two lines *noctis* and *diurnum, caligine* and *lumen, caeca*
and *cernere* are cleverly opposed in a sort of chiasmus. This feature
disappears almost entirely in Virgil, apart from the contrast between
languida quies and *auidos cursus* in lines 908–9. But the unusual rhythm
of Lucretius' line 456 – *nostra uidemur, et in noctis caligine caeca* –
re-appears in Virgil's line 910 – *uelle uidemur, et in mediis conatibus
aegri* – where the three words *uidemur et in* at precisely the same point
in the hexameter prove the connection with Lucretius beyond a doubt.
Their effect, however, in the new context is quite different. In
Lucretius *et membra mouere/nostra uidemur* conveys a sense of vigorous
and unimpeded movement, whereas the Virgilian adaptation suggests
vigorous effort that fails. The significance of the words *nequiquam
auidos extendere cursus/uelle uidemur, et in mediis conatibus aegri/
succidimus* in the mind of the reader as he reads them aloud to himself
has an almost physical reality about it, product of verbal connotation
plus these particular combinations of metrical ictus and word accent,
caesura and diaeresis, vowel and consonant, and of the changing
tensions of vocal chords, tongue, and lips that are needed to pronounce
them. This is one of the mysteries of poetry and the factors on which
it depends are too many and complicated to permit of explanation. The
best one can do, perhaps, is to say, for example, that the correspondence
of metrical ictus and word accent in the last two feet of 909 and the

first two of 910 combines with the alliteration of *u* to re-inforce the
sense of effort contained in the prose meaning of the words, while the
weak caesuras in the first and second feet of 910 reinforce the sense
of frustration, of failed effort.

Imitation often involves an element of rivalry, and so 'Longinus' in
his essay *On the Sublime* 13.2 pairs *mimesis* with *zelosis*. The imitator
in re-working his memorable original tries to be equally memorable
himself and in the attempt is apt to extend or enlarge the original idea
and sometimes to exaggerate it. One can see this principle clearly at
work in the couplet that opens Johnson's *The Vanity of Human Wishes*,

> Let Observation, with extensive view,
> Survey mankind from China to Peru ...

when Juvenal at the beginning of *Satire* 10, Johnson's model, had
written,

> Omnibus in terris quae sunt a Gadibus usque
> Auroram et Gangen ...
>
> In all the lands which are, from Gades far as
> Aurora and the Ganges ...

The world was bigger in Johnson's time, so China and Peru could
pointedly replace Gades and Ganges, with the added difference that
Observation surveys from east to west whereas Juvenal moves the
opposite way.

So in our examples Virgil writes, not of two men levering a stone
on to a wagon, but of twelve men carrying it on their neck (VI); not
only of reflected sunlight but of reflected moonlight too (V); not of
much-enduring old men but of young men laid on pyres (IV); not of
trampling on religion but of trampling on fears and fate and the noise
of Acheron (III); not of falling in love with a girl at first sight, but
of falling in love with a little girl at sight in one's thirteenth year (II);
not of a thousand beasts but of a thousand ewe lambs.

Such extensions of an idea sometimes also involve an extension of
idiom or meaning: thus *uidi* in the sense of *primum uidi* (II); *strepitum
Acherontis* for Lucretius' *metus Acherontis* (III); *repercussum* of reflected light and *imagine lunae* of the shape of the moon (V); *litem ut
discerneret aruis* (VI); *auidos extendere cursus* (VII).

Accordingly the imitation tends to be more complicated than its
original and may contain minor obscurities. How are the twelve men
carrying the stone (VI)? Is *imagine lunae* the moon's reflection or not,
and is *sub auras* outside or inside (V)? How can a corpse be a ghost
(IV)? How can you tread on a noise (III)? When you see someone

picking apples how can you be their guide (II)? If you are a poor slave how can you own a thousand ewe lambs (I)?

But the reader may well feel that the time has come to sweep aside these quibbles. After all we are not discussing logical prose but poetry, and Virgil – who but Robert Graves and the emperor Caligula would deny it? – is one of the world's great poets. 'Total accuracy' (Longinus again – 33.2) 'is apt to be small-minded; in great works, as in large fortunes, some things ought to be disregarded.' Virgil's poetry remains poetry even under the hypercritical microscope, and the risky attempt must now be made to articulate briefly some of its characteristics, using the evidence of these comparisons.

Where Homer describes a stone as 'black and rough and great', appealing directly to two of the senses, Virgil describes it as 'huge ... ancient and huge', which is vaguer, grander, more obviously emotive (on the principle of *omne ignotum pro magnifico*) and plays on the reader's imagination.

Where Apollonius talks of pouring water into a bucket and Homer talks of leverage and wagons, Virgil avoids the banausic detail, brings in a mysterious moon and a coffered ceiling, replaces practical machinery with degenerate man-power whose puny strength is a measure of the magnificent muscle of the age of heroes. Grander again, more opulent, and more romantic, idealizing the distant past and the ancestors.

The Cyclops boasts of his beasts and of piping better than his fellows; Corydon of his ewe lambs and the songs Amphion sang in a world of literary legend. Corydon is here no realist, but a sentimental dreamer bewitched by the incantation of poetry.

And there is much of Virgil in Corydon: he too knows the songs of Amphion, has heard the music of the lyre on Aracynthus, can lull the critical reason to rest with vivid and haunting combinations of words and sounds and rhythms, and awaken the reader's imagination to unusual life.

> Sicut aquae tremulum labris ubi lumen aenis
> sole repercussum aut radiantis imagine lunae
> omnia peruolitat late loca ...

Granted that all is not immediately or even finally clear, none the less it is surprisingly vivid; one can see the quivering light and feel the unsteadiness of the water, just as one can see a small boy reaching up and feel the stretch and strain of it in the second half of that line from the eighth *Ecologue*:

> iam fragilis poteram a terra contingere ramos.[5]

NOTES

1. For the combination of literary echoes and personal memories in T. S. Eliot's *Marina* and *Burnt Norton* see Helen Gardner, 'The Landscapes of Eliot's Poetry', *Critical Quarterly* 10 (1968), 323–4.

2. Servius on *Aeneid* 8.187: 'secundum Lucretium superstitio est superstantium rerum, id est caelestium et diuinarum quae super nos stant, inanis et superfluus timor.' He appears to be referring to our passage.

3. The point is made by Egil Kraggerud in his *Aeneisstudien* (Oslo, 1968), p. 73.

4. Virgil must have liked lines 306–8, for he repeats them verbatim from *Georg.* 4.475–7, a context describing how the ghosts came (*ibant*) from the depths of the Underworld to hear the song of Orpheus.

5. I am grateful to Mr Renford Bambrough, Mr Robert Coleman, Mrs Patricia Easterling, and Professor David West for criticisms. For further discussion of imitation the interested reader is referred to *Allusion, Parody and Imitation* (University of Hull, 1971), a published lecture by the present writer, and to David West and Tony Woodman (edd.), *Creative Imitation and Latin Literature* (Cambridge, 1979).

CORRIGENDA (1989)

Page 1 line 17
  For ὀπώρα read ὀπώρᾳ

Page 3 line 7
  For ἠράσθην read ἠράσθην

Page 3 lines 7–8
  For ἀνίκα πρᾶτου ἦυθες read ἀνίκα πρᾶτον ἦνθες

Page 3 line 8
  For θέλοιἀ read θέλοισ'

Page 3 line 10
  For πᾳ read πᾷ

Page 6 line 3
  For ἠΐθεοί τε πολύτλτοί read ἠΐθεοί τε πολύτλητοί

Page 6 line 4
  For ἔχουσαι read ἔχουσαι·

Page 6 line 5
  For ἐγχείησιν read ἐγχείησιν

Page 6 line 6
  For ἀρηΐφατοι read ἀρηΐφατοι

Page 7 line 28
  For ὠκίη read ὠκείη

Page 8 line 41
  For πακεί read παχείη

Page 8 line 43
  For ῥ̆ ἄνδρες read ῥ' ἄνδρες

Page 9 line 39
  For ὀνείρω read ὀνείρῳ

Page 9 line 41
  For ὀ read ὁ

THE DEATHS OF HECTOR AND TURNUS

By DAVID WEST

This article is an attempt to throw light on Virgil's narrative of the death of Turnus by comparing it to Homer's narrative of the death of Hector. It will begin with a summary of these two episodes.

In *Iliad* xxii. 136–7 Hector panicked at the approach of Achilles and ran away. Achilles pursued him like a mountain hawk pursuing a dove. They passed the windswept fig tree and the washing troughs, and ran three times round the walls of Troy, not for a tripod or any other such prize but for the life of Hector. Zeus and Athena discussed the fight and agreed that Hector must die. And all the time Achilles was pressing Hector hard like a hound pursuing a fawn, and heading him off from the walls of Troy. Achilles kept up the pursuit, Hector kept running away—it was an endless chase in a dream. Zeus then put their two fates in the balance. Hector's sank. Apollo deserted him. Athena came down disguised as Hector's brother Deiphobus and persuaded Hector to stand and face Achilles. Achilles threw his spear. Hector dodged it. Hector threw and his spear rebounded from the centre of Achilles's shield. Athena gave Achilles back his spear and Hector called on Deiphobus to hand him another. But there was no Deiphobus and Hector knew he was doomed. He charged Achilles with sword drawn. Achilles picked his spot. Hector was wearing the armour he had stripped from the body of Patroclus and Achilles struck at the gap between shoulder and neck, at the jugular vein. They exchanged a couple of speeches and Hector died. To sum up, the duel consists of a pursuit; a conversation of the gods; the weighing in the balance; and the final battle.

The duel of Aeneas and Turnus in *Aeneid* xii. 697–952 is more complex. The huge Turnus and Aeneas, as large as Athos, Eryx, or Appenninus, ran towards each other, threw their spears, and then clashed shield to shield. They were like a pair of bulls. Jupiter weighed their fates in the balance. Turnus rose to strike but his sword broke in mid blow. He fled like a stag from a hound begging his men to hand him his sword while Aeneas told them what would happen if they did. Five times they ran round in one direction, five times in another, not for any trivial prize in sport but for the life-blood of Turnus. Juturna, disguised as Metiscus, Turnus's charioteer, gives Turnus his sword; Venus frees Aeneas's spear from the sacred olive stump where it has stuck. The two warriors confront each other. Jupiter and Juno discuss the battle and agree the terms on which the Trojans may settle in Italy. Jupiter sends down one of the Furies to frighten Juturna from her brother's side. Turnus tries to throw a rock, but his strength fails him and like a man in a nightmare he can do nothing he tries to do. Aeneas throws his spear, which makes a noise like artillery or thunder. He wounds Turnus and stands over him. Turnus appeals for pity. Aeneas sees Pallas's baldric, strikes Turnus in the breast, and Turnus dies.

There are some differences in the organization of the elements in these two duels. Homer has pursuit, then battle; Virgil has first battle, then pursuit, then battle. Why does Virgil add this passage at arms at the beginning (701–32)? At the beginning of *Iliad* xxii the Greeks have driven the Trojans like deer into the walls of Troy. Only Hector has stayed outside the walls to confront Achilles. Priam sees him and pleads with him to come within the walls to protect Troy and save his old father from having his head and beard and private parts torn to pieces by the dogs at his own street door. Then Hecuba bares her breast for her son to see and pity her. With some difficulty Hector decides to reject their appeals and hold his ground. Achilles appears, the bronze glowing on his body. Hector begins to tremble, panics, and runs away. It is all passionate, particular, and credible—a brave man overcome by fear. And Virgil could not use it. Turnus has been running away from Aeneas for more than three books already. If at this long-deferred confrontation he turned and ran away again, it would be a disastrous anticlimax. But there is more to it than the logistics of the narrative. Homer can afford to depict Hector in panic because Hector's courage is beyond all question. The courage of Turnus is not so securely established. It is true that he has always had justification for avoiding Aeneas (divine intervention in Book x, military tactics in Book xi), but if he cracked here, his credit would collapse, and it would be no honour to Aeneas to conquer him. More than this, Turnus is the leader of the Latins. The war in Latium is amongst other things the prototype of the Social War (91–87 B.C.) in which Rome asserted her hegemony over Italy. The Latins in the *Aeneid* are amongst other things the prototypes of the contemporary Italian supporters of Augustus. Latins do not panic, do not lose face in the *Aeneid*. So this one change of organization in the Virgilian duel can be explained in three different ways, in terms of narrative, character delineation, and political purpose.

A second difference is the placing of the conversation of the gods. In Homer it comes in the middle of the pursuit. In Virgil it comes after the first battle and the pursuit, and just before the final battle. In making this change Virgil has forfeited a finesse in Homer's narrative. Without making an explicit point of it, Homer leaves it to be understood that the short conversation of the gods took place while the pursuit was going on. 'So these two ran round the city of Priam and the gods were all watching them and the father of gods and men began to speak' (165–7), resumed in twenty lines, 'Swift Achilles was keeping up his relentless pursuit of Hector'. The conversation comes in the middle of the pursuit but it does not *interrupt* the pursuit. Nobody could imagine that the men stopped running to let the gods talk and then started up again. In Virgil on the other hand the conversation of the gods occurs after Turnus has turned to stand his ground against Aeneas. In 790 they confront each other ready for battle. In 791 Jupiter addresses Juno. She replies. He replies. He then drives Juturna from her brother's side. Juturna utters a farewell speech, harping upon her lost virginity. She withdraws and it is 887 before we return to our heroes, *Aeneas instat*. What have they been doing during these exchanges? Is *anheli* (790) an attempt to integrate the narrative,[1] by suggesting that the human beings need ninety-six lines to get their breath back while the divine machinery catches up with the human narrative? Or have the gods the power to arrest the movement of time, or to cram their activities into minute particles of it? There is no need to ask such silly questions. The point is that Homer is swift and realistic. *Semper ad euentum festinat*, says Horace (*AP* 148). Virgil is slower, less realistic, less concerned with military verisimilitude, less soldierly.

A third, last, and most important difference in order between the narratives is that in Homer the conversation of the gods precedes Zeus's balancing act, whereas in Virgil Jupiter consults the balance before he converses with Juno. In Homer the balance scene is dramatically effective in its place. So far the duel has been entirely a chase, Achilles pursuing but unable to catch, Hector fleeing but unable to escape. Then, when they reached the springs for the fourth time, Zeus puts the two fates on the balance and Hector's sinks. Apollo leaves him and Athena goes down to stand by Achilles. This is effective for its sudden finality in a hitherto inconclusive scene. From this moment on (line 212) Hector is alone, there is no escape for him, although there is chilling dramatic irony in the fact that he does not know it till line 296. So much for the stark drama of the Homeric scene. What is the point of the weighing in its place in the *Aeneid*? None. Servius, it is true, says that the function of the episode is to show the decision of fate to gods and men, and this is repeated by Quinn (*Virgil's Aeneid* [Ann Arbor, 1968], 266 n. 2) but this makes poor dramatic sense in the context, and is not in the text of the *Aeneid*. Virgil does not disclose the decision of the balance, and could not do so without destroying his narrative sequence. If the gods knew the decision, that would stultify the subsequent conversation of Jupiter and Juno. If the watching armies knew, or if the reader knew, that would destroy the suspense of the narrative. Virgil takes over this scene because it is an impressive part of the Homeric narrative. It does not fit sensibly into the logic of his own.[2]

But if he has no reason to put the scene with the balance before the conversation of the gods, he has his own reason to put the conversation of the gods after the scene with the balance. Jupiter reads the riot act to Juno and she capitulates, like a true wife stipulating every inch of the way. Jupiter is amused and magnanimous. The terms of this matrimonial reconciliation are the conclusion of the argument of the *Aeneid* and the climax of the poem. It is dramatically effective to keep this back as late as possible. The death of Turnus that follows is the necessary consequence of the political settlement, the personal coda to the national epic.

The *Aeneid* provides a legendary prototype and authentication of the Augustan principate. But the model does not fit exactly. We may be willing to believe that Augustus is the linear descendant of Aeneas, but if the Romans are the descendants of the Trojans as Virgil would have us believe, why are they not called *Troiani* or *Teucri*? Why do they live in *Latium* amongst *Latini*? Why speak Latin and not Phrygian? Why wear the toga instead of Phrygian dress? Virgil foresees these objections and disarms them by the stipulations of Juno (823–5): 'Do not order the native Latins to change their ancient name and become Trojans or be called Teucri or change their language or their national dress.' Jupiter smiled quietly at his wife and granted all that and more. One of his formulations is particularly shrewd. *Faciamque omnis uno ore Latinos* (837) in its legendary context means that he is going to make the Trojans give up their language and speak Latin. But in the context of recent history in which the war against the Latins is a prototype and justification of the Roman hegemony over Italy, we should not forget that in the first century B.C. the Italians were giving up their own language in favour of Latin.[3] Jupiter's statement of Trojan destiny is here almost an apology, and a religious sanction, for the Roman hegemony of Italy—'you Italians are suffering from Romans what the Trojans long ago accepted from Latins. And this is in accordance with Fate and the will of the Gods.' This political purpose is an important element in the *Aeneid*, and wholly foreign to the *Iliad*. It accounts for Virgil's postponement of the conversation of the gods to form the climax and grand conclusion of the poem.

Our study of some differences in the organization of these two duels has suggested that in making changes Virgil has been guided by the logic of his own narrative and in particular by the requirements of his character delineation; that Homer has greater soldierly realism; that Virgil is interested in the impressive detail and in his political purpose.

Looking away now from differences in order, towards differences in detail, we shall try to confirm and develop these general observations. In Homer soldierly realism: Achilles bore down on Hector, looked like the God of War in his flashing helmet, brandishing over his right shoulder his terrible spear made from an ash tree from Mount Pelion and the bronze of his armour gleamed like a blazing fire or the rising sun. This is vivid and technically precise (in particular the brandishing of the spear over the right shoulder). The comparison to the God of War is the only touch of the supernatural. In the *Aeneid* the supernatural is everywhere. Whereas the spear of Achilles was cut on Mount Pelion (a factual statement), the weapon brandished by Aeneas was like a tree, *telum ingens arboreum*, 888 (and here we are beginning to move away from facts). *So*, the clash of shields in the *Aeneid* filled the aether (*ingens fragor aethera complet*, 724)— another hyperbole. *So*, Achilles's spear is said to have a heavy bronze head (μελίη χαλκοβάρεια, 328) but when Aeneas throws his fatal shaft (919), it is compared to three other noises ranging from the exaggerated to the impossible: it makes more noise than rocks shot by catapults in siege warfare, than the detonation of a thunderbolt, and it flew like a black whirlwind. *So*, as we have seen, Achilles is compared to the God of War as he bears down on Hector at the beginning of the duel, but that apart the stature of the heroes is not described. Virgil, on the other hand, provides data which enable us to calculate the height of Aeneas. He is said to be the size of Mount Athos 1935 m., Eryx 751 m., or Appenninus 2902 m., ascending to a climax in the only Italian mountain of the tricolon. Again Virgil is striving for effect and again he overtrumps Homer. This procedure is seen at its most mechanical when Turnus (899) lifts his rock. A dozen picked men could hardly get it up on their backs, 'one of these monstrous exaggerations', according to James Henry, ad loc., 'more suitable for the story of Jack the Giant-killer than the *Aeneis*, and which but too frequently bring Ariosto to our minds when we are reading the prince of Latin poets'.[4] Presumably Turnus's rock was too heavy for *twelve*, because the rocks thrown in the *Iliad* by Diomede, Hector, and Aineias (v. 302, vii. 445, xx. 285) are too heavy for two men to lift, as men are nowadays, and perhaps because the rock thrown by Jason in the *Argonautica* of Apollonius Rhodius is too heavy for *four* young men to lift even a little off the ground (iii. 1367). *So*, Achilles chased Hector three times round the walls of Troy whereas Aeneas and Turnus completed five circuits in one direction and five in the other (763–4)—no wonder they were out of breath at the end of it (790). And it seems even more than ten. In a recent article[5] it is argued that the similes of Virgil contain more calculated artistry than do those of Homer, and often interlock with their contexts by means of multiple correspondences both verbal and substantive. The author counted some twenty-six such correspondences between the pursuit of Turnus and the hunting simile (742–65), but he stupidly failed to notice that the ten circuits of Turnus are compared to the thousand or two thousand of the stag, and rendered more impressive by the comparison. *Quinque orbis explent cursu totidemque retexunt huc illuc*, gathers up *mille fugit refugitque uias*, from ten lines earlier. But what were they running round? Not the city of Laurentum. Aeneas deliberately leaves it to come to meet Turnus (698). The pursuit is taking place on level ground adjoining the city, in an open space between the walls and a marsh, hemmed in by a ring of Trojans. This explains *nunc huc inde huc incertos explicat orbis*, 743, 'he describes rough circles first in one direction, then in another'. They are *rough* circles (*incertos orbis*) because it is a pursuit in a complex curving pattern in an enclosed space, not the precise circuit of a city wall. And they change direction for a similar reason. Hector could not turn and go in the other direction because the wall was on one side of him and Achilles was at his heels. If he moved away from the wall to double back Achilles would cut him off from the gate (194–8). Turnus on the other hand is hemmed in by the armies and there is no reason why he should not jink and double back. He is therefore not restricted to a circular course, but free to run in any direction. So then Virgil has kept the motif of repeated orbital motion, but has augmented it from a function of three to a function of ten and associated it with a function of one thousand or two thousand. He makes his warriors run in circles to preserve the famous Iliadic motif, but to make their course plausible he allows them to run in rough circles. Hence *incertos* in 743. And hence the doubling-back *nunc huc inde huc*, 743, *huc illuc*, 764. By these many tiny adjustments Virgil marries the Homeric model to the requirements of his own context, and strives to make it more impressive.

And what were they running for? The answer to this question further extends our conceptions of Virgil's intentions. In Virgil (765) 'they were not competing at games for unimportant prizes (*ludicra* at games, *levia* unimportant; Quinn, 268 n. 3, is quite wrong to talk of 'a crazy race with ridiculous prizes'), but were struggling for the lifeblood of Turnus'. Virgil's negative is bare—'unimportant prizes at games'—he is not interested in what they are not running for. But Homer cares enough about such matters to say what the prizes were, and what the event was and even to develop a comparison to yet another competitive event. 'For they were not competing for an ox or a leather shield awarded as athletic prizes but they were running (at this point Virgil again tightens the screw, 'but they were struggling') for the life of Hector tamer of horses, like thoroughbreds rounding the turning-point at full gallop as they race for a great prize at a funeral games, a tripod say, or a woman.' A few minutes before the death of Hector, this glimpse of a rich life richly enjoyed by Hector tamer of horses is all the more tragic because Homer does not spell out the moral.

Similarly Homer has a tree, a windswept fig tree. The warriors pass it before they reach the springs where stood the troughs where the women of Troy used to wash their clothes in the days of peace. All of this is vivid, realistic, and saddening. Virgil too has a tree (766). But *this* tree was a sacred tree. The Trojans had not recognized its sanctity and had removed it to clear the ground for battle. As a punishment for this profanation, Aeneas's spear sticks in the tree and he cannot withdraw it. Venus frees it for him while Juturna is giving Turnus his sword. In Homer the domestic interlude and the impression of autopsy; in Virgil the violation of one deity and intervention of others, demonstrating the greater power of the divine support for Aeneas.

The soldierly realism of Homer is well illustrated by the spear casts (273–9). Achilles throws. Hector sees it coming and ducks. It goes over his head and he jeers at Achilles. 'A miss for the god-like Achilles? Has Zeus given you the wrong date for my death?' Now Hector throws and *his* spear *hits* Achilles's shield plumb centre. But it rebounds, 'and Hector was furious that his cast had been wasted'. This is not only plausible from a soldier's point of view but very effective dramatically. It reasserts Hector's prowess—his speed of reaction and his accuracy—and provides him with a welling-up of hope to be bitterly stanched in the next moment when he realizes that Deiphobus was in fact Athena luring him to his death. In Virgil, by contrast, the spear casts are barely noticeable. Donatus in fact does not notice them. Nor does Putnam (*The Poetry of the Aeneid* [Cambridge, Mass. and London, 1965], 189). 'Since there has never been any mention previously of Aeneas's use of a spear, one *seeks* another reason', he says, 'for the significance of the spear stuck in the olive tree', and he finds it in a symbolic interpretation. Unfortunately for this symbolism it explains the absence of that which is present. The spears *were* thrown, *coniectis eminus hastis* (711). That is all. They threw their spears at long range. Then they engaged shield to shield, *invadunt Martem clipeis*. We know nothing about the spear casts, whether they hit or missed, whether they were dodged or taken on the shield, who threw first. *Eminus*, at long range, suggests that they missed but nothing here is of interest at a soldierly level. Dramatically too, despite its rapidity, it is inferior to the Homeric spear casts. There is no temporary success, no moment of hope and exultation for the doomed warrior in the *Aeneid*.

There is one episode in the duel between Turnus and Aeneas for which there is no model in Homer's duel. Turnus (731) draws himself up to his full height and strikes with his sword. What happens? There is a long controlled pause for suspense in the Virgilian narrative noted by La Cerda, ad loc.:

corpore toto
alte sublatum consurgit Turnus in ensem
et ferit: exclamant Troes trepidique Latini
arrectaeque amborum acies, at perfidus ensis
frangitur in medioque ardentem deserit ictu,   (728–32)

and then we learn that it breaks in mid blow (*in medio ictu*). It looks as though it did not actually strike Aeneas or his armour but simply disintegrated in mid air. And yet in 713 it was already clashing on the sword of Aeneas and in 740 it seems to break on impact. The account is not quite clear, and it is not, from a soldierly point of view, credible. What stimulated Virgil to this invention? Again the answer lies in the supernatural. Virgil goes on to explain that at the beginning of the day's fighting Turnus in his excitement had grabbed Metiscus's sword instead of his own. This has served him well enough while he was harrying retreating Trojans, but the *mortal* blade split when it came to the arms which the *god* Vulcan had made for Aeneas (in 739–40 *dei* and *mortalis* are in active contrast). From a military standpoint this will not wear.[6] No soldier could go into battle with somebody else's sword without knowing it. No hockey player could walk out of the dressing-room with somebody else's stick. No golfer could draw a club out of the wrong bag without a shock to his system. Why has Virgil invented the 'wrong-sword' motif? The familiar answer is that the armour of Aeneas and the sword of Turnus were both made by Vulcan (xii. 90). If the Vulcanian sword had been allowed to clash on the Vulcanian armour Virgil would have been impaled on the horns of a scholastic dilemma. What happens when an irresistible weapon meets impenetrable armour? This explanation is confirmed by what happens later, after Turnus gets his own sword. It is not used. The divine weapon is never engaged in a losing battle. Turnus throws or tries to throw a rock.

A last example of Homer's keener interest in military matters is the death blow. The wounds sustained by Homer's heroes are often of interest to a fighting man. Cebriones is struck by a stone on the eyebrows breaking the bones so that the eyes drop out and fall in the dust before his feet (*Iliad* xvi. 738). Erymas receives a spear in the mouth; it goes up under the brain, splits the white bones, shakes out the teeth filling both his eyes with blood which spurts through his nostrils and gaping mouth (*Iliad* xvi. 345). Such clinical details are inconsonant with the dignity of Virgilian Epic.[7] In *Iliad* xxii. 321 Achilles is scanning Hector's body to pick the spot where he could best strike through the armour to get at the flesh. Hector was completely protected in the armour taken from the body of Patroclus except for a gap at the throat where the collarbone joins neck and shoulder—the quickest place to kill a man. The anatomy and physiology are sound and interesting to the military man, and once again intensely dramatic. It is not for nothing that we are reminded that Hector is wearing the armour he stripped from the body of Patroclus whom Achilles loved. Homer as usual makes no explicit comment. But this is not inert fact. At the end of the *Aeneid* Aeneas is wondering whether to save Turnus when his eye lights on the belt and baldric of young Pallas whom Turnus has killed. He burst into a *blazing* rage and sank his sword in Turnus's breast. But Turnus's limbs relaxed in *cold*[8] and his life reluctantly departed. Virgil has abandoned anatomy for psychology. Turnus's wound has no clinical interest. Virgil does not for instance trouble about Turnus's breastplate and shield (Heinze, 208, refers to line 925). It is the normal honourable death blow in the *pectus* which every first-line hero in the *Aeneid* receives (except for the unrespectable Mezentius who took it in the throat). The psychological element on the other hand is explicit and important. Homer states what was seen; Virgil what was felt. The hesitation of Aeneas, his inclination towards mercy is a vital manifestation of the character of his prototype of Augustus.[9] The tone of the Homeric motif is thus changed and put to Virgil's own purposes of developing our conception of Aeneas's character, of explicitly indicating emotional intensity and perhaps subserving the political function of the poem.

This analysis of the two death blows has ignored a Virgilian invention which has been praised for its military realism (*magnum poetae inventum*, Donatus 930). Turnus is wounded in the thigh, not in a vital part, so that he can plausibly survive to utter his final appeal. Homer has not been so careful. Hector manages to make two speeches to Achilles after he has been struck in the jugular. There is no doubt that Virgil is more realistic here than Homer; but the convention of battlefield conversation is so firmly established in Homer that it seems more like common civility than an implausibility in the narrative.

Apart from this detail, however, we find in Homer, to sum up, an interest in military matters, in wounds, in the technique of weaponry. Such detail in Homer is realistic and often charged with excitement and drama. Virgil is less concerned with such material, less observant, striving for impressive effects. His detail is not veristic, sometimes not credible, for example in the frequent attribution of supernatural powers to his heroes. Homer is interested also in ordinary life, in the washing of clothes for example and in funeral games, and the vivid evocations of such scenes have their pleasure and a peculiar power in their context—not that Homer draws any moral from them or explicitly points to any contrasts, but nevertheless (indeed to some tastes all the more) these scenes of peace add pathos to the scenes of war. Such scenes do not occur in the Virgil passage but instead Virgil adds his own register, the elevated, the sacral and religious (our purpose has not for example included the Juturna episode, 843–66), the imposing, the subjective statement of emotions all of which accord with and further his political purpose in writing this poem.

This comparison between the deaths of Hector and Turnus has been based upon the organization and content of the two narratives. It may be useful to append an arrangement of some of the key conclusions of Brooks Otis's similar comparison which is slanted rather towards stylistic analysis (*Virgil* [Oxford, 1964], 48–51). 'The relative continuity of grammatical subject, absence of traditional epithets, the abundance of words with a feeling tone, the deliberateness of the grammatical structure, the artful onomatopoeia ... receive their adequate explanation, when we note that they are all necessitated by Virgil's subjective method and attitude. Virgil is constantly conscious of himself inside his characters ... Nisus is a source of emotion, rather than a tangible human being in a tangible human environment ... Virgil's technique is far more deliberate and knowing than Homer's ... Homer achieves remarkable characterisation which sheds absolutely no light on his own feelings: the whole thing comes out in speeches and the bare recital of action.' There are also a few words of 'a chilly Scotch critic' which may round off the matter. 'The Iliad and the Odyssey are essentially epics of human life: the Aeneid is essentially the epic of national glory.'[10]

NOTES

1. So R. Heinze, *Virgils epische Technik* (Darmstadt, 1957), 235, 386.

2. R. S. Conway, *Bulletin of the John Rylands Library* xiii (1929), 272, argues that the Virgilian version is preferable in that it heightens the suspense. This looks like special pleading—like his general contention that the contest in Virgil is more even. G. N. Knauer, *Die Aeneis und Homer* (Göttingen, 1964), 288 believes that Virgil deliberately stops short because he is so close to Homer that his readers will take the Homeric conclusion for granted. But surely if we assume in a highly imitative literature that omissions are to be *sous-entendu*, chaos will supervene. If an element is omitted in imitation, we should rather assume that it was not wanted. For W. Kühn, *Götterszenen bei Virgil, Bibliothek der klassischen Altertumswissenschaften* N.F. 2. 41 (Heidelberg, 1971), 159, the point of the weighing episode is its finality. We now know that this is the moment of truth. The fates are sanctioning the cause of Aeneas. This is a valid comment on the episode of the balance, but no explanation of the omitted decision. See Heinze, 296, n. 2.

3. E. Pulgram, *The Tongues of Italy* (Cambridge, Mass., 1958), 264–8.

4. On such pejorative evaluations of Latin hyperbole E. Norden has some cautionary words in his commentary on *Aeneid* vi. 959 ff. For numerical increases see his note on 625 f.

5. D. West, *Philologus* cxiv (1970), 267–72. Since that article contains a detailed comparative analysis of the relevant similes, these are not studied here.

6. *Fama* is the standard warning for tall stories, e.g. in the third book 165, 294, 551, 578, 694.

7. See Heinze, 205–8.

8. For such contrasts in Horace see D. West in *Horace* (London, 1973), edited by C. D. N. Costa, 29–58.

9. A word on anti-Aeneanism. 'It is Aeneas who loses—leaving Turnus victorious in his tragedy, submitting to the forces of violence and irrationality which swirl around him, failing to incorporate the ideal standards proper for the achievement of empire' (Putnam, 193). 'We must condemn the sudden rage that causes Aeneas to kill Turnus. The killing of Turnus cannot be justified: this is beyond doubt the judgement expected of us' (Quinn, 273). These views represent a morality wholly foreign to heroic and to Augustan politics. Virgil evinces a pity for the victims of fate, but this does not mean that he disapproves of its instruments. Sensible assessments may be read in W. S. Anderson, *The Art of the Aeneid* (New Jersey, 1969), 90–100, and G. Binder, *Aeneas and Augustus* (Meisenheim, 1971), 146.

10. W. Y. Sellar, *The Roman Poets of the Republic: Virgil* (Oxford³, 1897), 324. The shivering Sassenach is W. Warde Fowler, *The Death of Turnus* (Oxford, 1919), 50.

SYMBOLISM IN VIRGIL:
SKELETON KEY OR WILL-O'-THE-WISP?

By J. A. RICHMOND

I

We read in the fourth book of the *Aeneid* that unhappy Dido, when Anna came to her as she lay dying,

> ter sese attollens cubitoque adnixa leuauit,
> ter reuoluta toro est ... (*Aen.* 4. 690–1).

Some ancient critic, feeling that there must be more than met the eye in this passage, explained that *ter* referred to the three wars that Rome was destined to fight against Carthage! I suppose that most modern readers, familiar with the scene in the sixth book, where Virgil says that Aeneas catching at the shade of Anchises

> ter conatus ibi collo dare bracchia circum;
> ter frustra comprensa manus effugit imago
> (*Aen.* 6. 700–1)

will feel that *ter* as used in the similarly pathetic passage about Dido is not to be explained on the basis of any symbolic reference to the Punic Wars, and will smile, or shudder, when they see this curious explanation. Servius, however, thought it worth recording (ad loc.), and his tolerance must be ascribed to a frame of mind used to seeking for meanings conveyed by symbols in the work of Virgil. I do not deny that there are symbols in Virgil, and that on occasion they play the part of a skeleton key in enabling us to approach Virgil's meaning. I believe, however, that the search for symbols, as conducted by many contemporary scholars, often becomes a chase after wills-o'-the-wisp. The purpose of the paper is to stimulate a dialogue, but—to use the Platonic terminology—a dialogue of a heuristic, not of an eristic nature.

I begin with a few definitions: *Allegory* is sustained metaphor, that is to say, the words used do not refer to their normal meanings, but to something else that they indicate darkly—as Demetrius (101) says, 'Allegory is like darkness and the night'.

Symbolism, however, is a concept that was not formulated by the ancient critics. It came into prominence in the eighteenth century, and appears first to have been clearly distinguished from Allegory by Goethe.[1] Words used by poets to convey their ordinary senses may also convey a second sense. Thus if Tityrus in the first *Eclogue* is really Tityrus, but at the same time is intended to suggest the person of Virgil himself to the reader, then we are dealing with a symbol. As Goethe expressed himself in rather oracular terms 'it is the thing, without being the thing, and still it is the thing'.[2] An analogy from painting may be clearer: a king depicted with a figure of Justice at his side is accompanied by an allegory; put, however, a sceptre in his hand, and he holds a symbol. Justice is a purely imaginary representation of an abstraction; a sceptre is a real thing, but represents one or more abstract ideas.

Thus in Virgil the description of Fama (*Aen.* 4. 173–88), and the account of the wonderful temple that Virgil will raise on the banks of the Mincius (*Georg.* 3. 13–39)[3] are examples of Allegory, not of Symbolism, as the descriptions are clearly not meant to be taken in any literal sense.

Though the ancients had no separate notion of literary symbolism, they were very familiar with the concept of Allegory and often used it. The literary critics and philosophers constantly recognize it. Thus the fables of Aesop were allegories which conveyed moral truths, and the philosophers who tried to reconcile disagreeable primitive religious concepts and crude mythological stories with a more advanced morality sought refuge in allegorical explanations.[4]

The critics and the philosophers used Allegory very often as a matter of choice: in the field of religion the use of Symbolism was frequently inescapable, even if no name were given to the device.[5] In particular, if the gods wished to communicate with men by means of an omen, they had little choice but to use symbols. Thus in the *Iliad*[6] the omen mentioned in the second book of a snake devouring both the mother bird and her eight offspring is intended to refer to an actual occurrence, which conveys by symbolism to Calchas, and through him to the Greeks, the message that Troy would resist the siege for nine years. Symbolism played a large part in religious ritual, e.g. the colours of the sacrificial victims had symbolic force, as had also the cutting and burning of the portion of the hair of the victims taken from between the horns. That prevalent branch of magic known to modern students as 'sympathetic' depended on the substitution of symbolic objects of those it was desired to affect by magic (cf. M. P. Nilsson, *Geschichte der griechischen Religion* 1[3] (München, 1967), 51).

The use of Allegory as a method of interpretation passed over to the Church Fathers, who made much use of it in Biblical exegesis.[7] Allegory was used in the Middle Ages in an attempt to show that the pagan authors had really set out to convey important moral truths and lessons in veiled language. The more remote scholars found the real thoughts of the ancient authors, and the more repugnant theologians and moralists found their sentiments on questions of religion and morality, the stronger was the temptation to explain away by allegorical interpretation all that was unwelcome. In Donatus we find the method already applied to Virgil, and the 70,000 verses of the *Ovide moralisé* written in the fourteenth century perhaps represent the high-water-mark of allegorical interpretation.[8]

Christianity made a rich use of Symbolism in ritual, but it was not until the latter half of the eighteenth century that symbolic interpretation began to play a dominant role in literary criticism. German critics developed a modern type of criticism which laid great stress on Symbolism (cf. R. Wellek, *A History of Modern Criticism, 1750–1950*, vol. i (London, 1955), p. 4). It was, perhaps, the related change of taste in German-speaking lands, whereby Virgil was regarded as an inferior imitation of Homer, that prevented the interpretation of Virgil on symbolic lines of criticism during the nineteenth century. Symbols, though occasionally referred to by Sainte-Beuve (if I am not mistaken)[9] and by Sellar[10] in their masterly works which advanced the study of Virgil on traditional lines in France and in Britain during that period, are not treated by them as a matter of any great significance, and are relegated to a peripheral position in their view of Virgil.

The dominance of the Symbolist Poets in France towards the end of the last century first affected contemporary literature in other languages, and then, after the usual delay, spread its influence through academic literary criticism.[11] Contemporaneously the scholarly work of E. Norden (especially his *P. Vergilius Maro, Aeneis Buch VI*[3] (Leipzig, 1927)) and of R. Heinze (especially his *Vergils epische Technik*[3] (Leipzig, 1915))—aided, no doubt, by the experience this century has had of *lacrimae rerum*—has restored Virgil to honour in German-speaking lands. The hour found the man: Viktor Pöschl in the two editions (1950 and 1964) of his *Die Dichtkunst Virgils*[12] hurled defiance at the rationalism which had directed literary criticism of the Classics, set out a partly intuitive doctrine of imagery and symbolism which he detected in Virgil, and has inspired a host of scholars to flood the learned world with articles and with books, in which, when they turned stones in Virgil, they found, if not the 'angels' wings' of Francis Thompson's poem, at least 'many-splendoured things'. I think it is fair to conclude from this mass of publications that Symbolism now occupies a predominant position in the contemporary criticism of Virgil's work. Dissentient voices, however, have been heard from time to time, which have questioned in reviews and in articles the methods and the assumptions of the hunt for symbols in Virgil and in other Latin poets,[13] and the president of the Classical Association in 1972 gave a large portion of his address to suggesting reasons why some scholars are less than enthusiastic in welcoming the subjection of the Augustan classics to the critical methods popular in the present century (L. P. Wilkinson, *PCA 69* (1972), 13 ff.).

II

In considering the works of Virgil, we may first of all settle on some common ground where all sides will readily admit that Virgil uses Symbolism. As already indicated, it is the religious field that offers the clearest examples. In the omen of the swans in the first book of the *Aeneid* (393 ff.) the twelve swans shown by Venus to Aeneas clearly represent the twelve ships that are missing but safe. In the twelfth book, however, the omen of the swan attacked by the eagle (247 ff.) presents some difficulties of interpretation. Have the gods allowed Juturna to send a fallacious omen, or is the interpretation an error on the part of Tolumnius, the augur? Some believe that the swan as the bird of Venus must stand for Aeneas or for the Trojans, as in the first book, and that the credit of the gods can be saved accordingly by attributing to Tolumnius the erroneous interpretation that equates Turnus to the swan (cf. F. J. Lelievre, *PVS* 11 (1971–2), 74–7, and W. S. Anderson, *CSCA* 4 (1971), 49–58). If this is correct we have a remarkable consistency between the two omens in the first and twelfth books. In my view Virgil makes it clear that Juno permits the sending of the false omen, and I cannot see that in doing so she needs defence any more than when she uses other questionable methods to thwart the destiny of Aeneas. The credit of the other gods is not involved.

Pöschl has drawn attention to a passage in the twelfth book of the *Aeneid*, where Turnus sees a tower, which he himself has built, enveloped in flames, and explains that the tower is a symbol of Turnus. As Wagner had already remarked, Turnus evidently sees in the destruction of the tower an omen of his own downfall, and implicitly he says as much in his speech to Juturna which follows (Pöschl, *Die Dichtkunst Virgils*[2] (Wien, 1964), p. 227 on *Aeneid* 12. 627 ff.; *Publius Virgilius Maro*[4], ed. Heyne-Wagner, 5 vols. (Lipsiae, 1830–41), ad *Aen.* 12. 676).

Servius (ad *Aen.* 5. 85) believes that the sevenfold coils of the snake that appear at the beginning of the fifth book of the *Aeneid* are an omen of the seven years the Trojans have spent in their wanderings, and that thus it may be concluded that their time of wandering is at an end. It is tempting to compare this scene with the omen in *Iliad* 2 of the bird and the eight fledglings, to which I have referred above. But it is remarkable, if Virgil did intend symbolism here, that the omen is not explained, or at least remarked upon, in the usual fashion. In my view Virgil would not be likely to include in his epic omens that do not guide (or misguide) the characters, but give the reader with gifts of augury an insight into the future events of the poem. It seems that critics who follow Servius in his interpretation of this passage are led astray.[14]

Magical symbolism is found especially in the eighth *Eclogue*, where, for example, the knots tied in the pieces of tnread are symbols of the knots of love (cf. *Theocritus*[2], ed. A. S. F. Gow (Cambridge, 1965), vol. II, p. 40), and in the fourth book of the *Aeneid*, where, again, for example, we have a symbolical effigy of Aeneas prepared for Dido's magical rites (cf. *P. V. M. Aeneidos liber quartus*, ed. A. S. Pease (Cambridge, Mass., 1935), on 507–21).

How far Virgil believed in the personal existence of his gods, and how far they may be considered allegories or symbols of natural forces is a particularly difficult question on which I am reluctant to express an opinion.[15]

A second field where Symbolism was well established in ancient times was in the language that poets used to refer to their own poetry and to its inspiration.[16] Poetry was closely connected with mythology and religion, and poetic inspiration was believed to be a direct gift of the gods. Pindar had already a wide range of metaphorical language to describe his poetic craft.[17] Callimachus,[18] it seems, extended the range of these metaphors, and under his influence the Roman poets[19] adopted them as readily recognizable symbols. Thus even so matter-of-fact a poet as Horace describes his metamorphosis into a swan (*Odes* 2. 20), that bird long associated with Apollo, god of poetry, which was believed to utter tuneful strains as death approached. This allegory of his poetic immortality can be understood only in terms of the metaphors current in Greek literature.

Virgil seems to allude to the symbol of the swan in the *Eclogues* (9. 36) when he makes the shepherd Lycidas say

> (uideor) argutos inter strepere anser olores.

According to Servius (ad loc.) *anser* conceals a hit at the contemporary poetaster Anser: it is also to be taken, I suggest, in its literal meaning as a metaphor for a tuneless poet. So *olores* plays its part as 'sweet-singing birds' opposed in the metaphor to the harsh-sounding 'goose, and also symbolizes 'true poets' who enjoy Apollo's inspiration. The same symbol is used a few lines above (*Ecl.* 9. 27–9) and also, if I am not misled, at *Georg.* 2. 198–9. The *laurus*, or bay-tree, constantly associated with Apollo, is a common symbol of poetry: Virgil in the *Eclogues* seems to extend this symbolism to use the *myrica*, or tamarisk, to signify bucolic poetry.[20] (Examples of this usage are to be found at *Ecl.* 4. 1–3, 6. 9–11, 8. 11–13, and 10. 13–15.)

A faint and subtle echo of these symbols is found in the sixth book of the *Aeneid* (658), when Aeneas finds that the chanters of the paean in Elysium spend their time 'inter odoratum lauris nemus'.[21] With considerable probability commentators have seen symbols of a poetic nature in references to shepherds and their activities at *Ecl.* 3. 111, 10. 16–17, and 10. 77.

Works of art had a long tradition of Symbolism in the ancient world.[22] Greek convention discouraged the representation of living persons on temples, and current events had to be alluded to by using mythological symbols. So when works of art are described in the *Aeneid*, we may feel it to be our duty to scrutinize them for hidden meanings. In the first book of the *Aeneid* Aeneas and Achates are examining paintings on a temple wall in Carthage, and see various episodes from the siege of Troy (455–93). The last of the scenes shows Penthesilea, that beautiful warrior queen, fighting among the heroes at Troy. Immediately the beautiful Dido appears surrounded by her Carthaginian warriors. It is hard to resist the conclusion that the juxtaposition is deliberate, and that the picture of Penthesilea alludes not only to the masculine role that Dido is playing, but also to the tragic death that Dido will suffer just as Penthesilea did. Turnus, in the tenth book of the *Aeneid*, strips from the dead Pallas a sword-belt which is embellished with the scene of the murder of the sons of Aegyptus by their brides, the Danaids. Again it is difficult to avoid believing that the untimely death of Pallas is hinted at by the death of the forty-nine young husbands (*Aen.* 10. 497–9).

A more difficult case is presented by the famous scenes on the temple doors at the beginning of the sixth book of the *Aeneid*. One detail—the picture of the labyrinth—has been the subject of much discussion.[23] Some scholars have invested it with profound significance as an emblem of the after-life and of the underworld. It is not easy to see, however, how the rest of the scenes on the doors can be referred to any symbolism. Nothing appears to parallel the death of Androgeos or of the Minotaur, and it would be rash to see Pasiphae as representing Dido, Ariadne as the Sibyl guiding Aeneas, or Daedalus and Icarus as an inversion of Anchises and Aeneas. If the labyrinth were mentioned in some more detail and held the last position in the series, as did Penthesilea, the consequent prominence might lend support to the idea that Symbolism was intended.

III

So far we have discussed probable, or at least possible, uses of Symbolism in Virgil. The late Professor Jackson Knight, for instance, suggests that the gods, gold, various numbers, certain places, storms, trees, the labyrinth, flowers, the community of bees, circles, underground passages and cavities, volcanoes, and so on, have a symbolic force in Virgil's poetry.[24]

Thus, in a long article (*AJPh* 87 (1966), 18–51), G. K. Galinsky finds in the eighth book of the *Aeneid* 'stone-symbolism', and much else besides. He writes: 'Rocks are lifted and fall down and thus symbolize, in Books VIII and XII, the ascendancy of Aeneas and his mission as well as the downfall of the demonic characters Cacus and Turnus', and further:

Primarily, however, Sisyphus' stone is a symbol of futility, of a task too big to be accomplished with success. The rock which Turnus hurls at Aeneas in XII and which falls short of its target has precisely the same symbolic connotations. To both Turnus and Sisyphus success is denied because they acted against the will of the gods (p. 34).

On the basis of this and of other similar alleged links it is asserted that the conflict between Aeneas and Turnus in the twelfth book is symbolized by the struggle between Hercules and Cacus in the eighth book. Other such 'links' indicate a relationship between *Aeneid* 6 and *Aeneid* 8, and support the view that *Aeneid* has a threefold structure. It is always difficult to prove a negative: in such cases I am content to take the attitude that we know of no reason to believe that Virgil used such symbolism, and must be content to throw the burden of proof on those who do.

A few examples may be discussed to show how the quest for symbols in Virgil is leading scholars to take a dangerously one-sided view of the poems. A recent book on the *Eclogues* in discussing Virgil's ninth *Eclogue* tells us that walking is an unusual activity in pastoral poetry (M. C. J. Putnam, *Virgil's Pastoral Art* (Princeton, 1970), p. 294). The further conclusion is drawn that this restless activity is a covert reference to the state of unrest in Cisalpine Gaul caused by the confiscations of the year 42 B.C. Walking possibly is an unusual activity in pastoral poetry, but earlier critics have been content to see in the walking of the ninth *Eclogue* no more than a natural result of Virgil's imitation of the seventh *Idyll* of Theocritus. As that *Idyll* has an atmosphere of content that well suits the harvest festival with which it concludes, it is not easy to accept that the walking it inspired Virgil to describe should be intended as a symbol of unrest in the ninth *Eclogue*.

That snakes play a prominent part in the action and in the imagery of the second book of the *Aeneid* is not to be denied. But that at one time they represent in that book symbols of treachery, and at another time symbols of divine help, seems to me to be just as improbable as the belief that the flames in the same book at one time represent death and destruction, and at another indicate the hope of escape and salvation for the Trojans.[25] One of the snake symbols of the second book has attracted special attention: Neoptolemus when about to slay Priam is compared by Virgil to a snake in the following simile:

> qualis ubi in lucem coluber mala gramina pastus,
> frigida sub terra tumidum quem bruma tegebat,
> nunc positis nouus exuuiis nitidusque iuuenta
> lubrica conuoluit sublato pectore terga
> arduus ad solem, et linguis micat ore trisulcis (471–5).

We may read in a recent article that 'the snake has cast its old slough, and is resplendent in its new skin, so Achilles is dead and the young Neoptolemus is gleaming with youth. There is nothing abstruse about this

(see B. M. W. Knox, *AJPh* 71 (1950), 394). The reader who does not
transfer this simile detail to the narrative is comatose.'[26] My pain at having
to admit that I am comatose is assuaged only by the consideration that
generations of scholars have suffered from the same defect. But can we be
sure that Virgil really meant all this? In the third book of the *Georgics* we
read about the danger of sleeping in the open during warm weather: the
snake comes forth from his hole

> cum positis nouus exuuiis nitidusque iuuenta
> uoluitur aut catulos tectis aut oua relinquens
> arduus ad solem, et linguis micat ore trisulcis (437–9).

The simile in the second book of the *Aeneid* is generally agreed to have
been inspired by the simile in *Iliad* 22:

> ὡς δὲ δράκων ἐπὶ χειῇ ὀρέστερος ἄνδρα μένῃσι,
> βεβρωκὼς κακὰ φάρμακ', ἔδυ δέ τέ μιν χόλος αἰνός,
> σμερδαλέον δὲ δέδορκεν ἑλισσόμενος περὶ χειῇ (93–5).

It seems to me then that the language used by Virgil can be accounted for
by the imitation of the Homeric simile which describes the snake coming
out of its hole in spring, and by the reminiscence of the passage in the
Georgics describing the snake in warm weather. The description in the
Georgics pretty clearly owes the phrase 'positis nouus exuuiis nitidusque
iuuenta' to Virgil's reminiscence of Nicander, *Theriaca* 137 f.,

> ... ὅτε ῥικνῆεν φολίδων περὶ γῆρας ἀμέρσας
> ἂψ ἀναφοιτήσῃ νεαρῇ κεχαρημένος ἥβῃ.

Neither in Nicander nor in the *Georgics* is there any question that the
words chosen to describe the renewed youth of the serpent allude in any
way to Neoptolemus—I do not think it at all probable that they do so in
the *Aeneid* either. Surely it is merely a coincidence that the snake has a
new skin, and that the name of Neoptolemus contains the Greek word for
'new'? No symbolism, in my view, is intended.[27]

When Virgil is describing in the fourth book of the *Aeneid* the departure
of Aeneas from Carthage,[28] he tells us that Aeneas, after the appearance of
Mercury with a command for instant departure, cut with his sword the
anchor cable of his ship and set sail. This is an unusual method of
departure, and it has been suggested that Virgil intended the sword with
which Aeneas thus severs his connection with Dido to form a symbolic
parallel with the sword Dido used to commit suicide, and so sever her
connection with Aeneas. Still, the reader was expected by Virgil to know
his Homer, and such a reader will at once recall the sword-stroke with
which Odysseus freed his ship when it lay in the harbour of the
Laestrygonians (*Od.* 10. 126–7). Is it necessary to go further?

Another article asks why Venus wore boots when disguised as a huntress she met Aeneas near Carthage (E. L. Harrison, *PVS* 12 (1972–3), 10–25). A simple critic might answer 'because, if you don't protect your legs, they will be torn by the underbrush, when you are hunting' (Pollux 5. 18; Grattius 338; Nemesianus, *Cyn.* 90). There are many representations in ancient art of hunters and of Diana herself wearing buskins. A shepherd in the seventh *Eclogue* promises a statue to Diana:

> Puniceo stabis suras euincta cothurno (32).

In an echo of this phrase Venus says to Aeneas

> Virginibus Tyriis mos est gestare pharetram
> purpureoque alte suras uincire cothurno (*Aen.* 1. 336–7).

What could be more natural? Aeneas is hunting; Venus disguises herself as a huntress, dressed like Diana; Aeneas takes her for a goddess hunting; she disclaims the honour by explaining that girls hunt in Africa and dress themselves in the hunting gear not usually worn by mortal women. To me it seems perverse for Harrison to write, 'He chose a booted rather than a sandalled figure for Venus' disguise, because this allowed him to introduce a tragic prologue with an ingenious combination of word-placing and dress-symbolism' (op. cit., p.21). As I understand the reference to dress-symbolism, it means that the cothurnus hints at tragedy, as it was the boot worn by the tragic actors, and thus introduces Venus' account of Dido's tragic history. This is ingenious, but I do not think the ingenuity is Virgil's.

Once one gets into a frame of mind that looks for the meaning of the *Aeneid* under rather than on the surface of the poem, it is possible to find strange things. Thus when the Trojans land at Cumae, at the beginning of the sixth book, one might be pardoned for thinking that they felt a certain confidence when one reads

> . . . iuuenum manus emicat ardens
> litus in Hesperium (5–6).

But no: a recent book on the *Aeneid* tells us that they have drawn up their boats stern foremost on the shore to be ready to make a quick departure, and evidently are very uneasy about the reception that awaits them.[29] A traditionalist like myself will object that the Trojans merely drew their ships up on the shore in the fashion that is described repeatedly in Homer. We can draw no more conclusions as to the state of mind of the Trojans from this detail, than we could if Virgil told us that they took supper on the shore at sunset: it was simply the thing to do in heroic circles.

IV

However, between these alternatives of acceptance and rejection we shall find a no-man's-land of doubt. Many will echo the confession of a distinguished American scholar (W. V. Clausen, *HSPh* 68 (1964), 147), who, when discussing how Anchises sends Aeneas to the upper world, admitted that, although it has been persuasively explained that the gate of horn was closed before midnight, and that hence Aeneas had to pass through the gate of ivory with the false dreams, nevertheless he has a sense 'which I cannot quite put into words, that Virgil was not merely telling the time of night'.

The golden bough is a feature concerning which explanations have been advanced in plenty to show how Virgil may have borrowed it from ancient rituals.[30] Again many scholars feel that whatever may be the source from which Virgil has borrowed, the golden bough must be a symbol of cardinal importance.

The eerie atmosphere—so suitable as a prelude to the sixth book— which characterizes the account Virgil gives at the end of the fifth book of the death of Palinurus has induced some to seek symbolism here, too (cf. Quinn, op. cit., pp. 158–9). In all such doubtful cases, and they are many, the conflicting interpretations suggested in modern times, and their slight correspondence with ancient views, must make one doubt whether we have much warrant for thinking we have arrived at Virgil's meaning through using the concept of Symbolism.

V

One can hardly leave this subject without discussing, however cursorily, the relationships in time of the *Aeneid*. In retrospect it constantly alludes to the Homeric poems, and in prospect it looks to Roman history, and especially to the age of Augustus. How far is there any symbolism in the poem to emphasize these relationships? It is true that the situation in Italy when the Trojans arrived is often compared to the war in Troy. Thus the Sibyl remarks that Turnus is an *alius Achilles*, and the taunts of Numanus in the ninth book draw attention to the recurrence of the Trojan misfortunes (*Aen.* 6. 89 and 9. 599 ff.). But, as Virgil set himself out to imitate the Homeric epic in subject and in treatment, it was inevitable that the reader should notice many parallels between Virgil and the earlier works. The events of the *Aeneid* recall the events of the Homeric poems, but I do not see how we can say that they symbolize them. Even to say that the relationship is 'typological' in the sense that the personages and events of the Old Testament may be said to be types of the personages and events of the New seems to me to be hardly correct.[31] I cannot see that Virgil thought that the personages and events of the Homeric poems in any way obscurely hinted at the destiny that was to be fulfilled in the *Aeneid*. However, when Virgil alludes to events in the Homeric or in the Cyclic poems to hint at what is yet to take place in the *Aeneid*, we may fairly claim that we are dealing with a kind of symbolism. When Aeneas sends the ornaments of Helen to Dido in the first book of the *Aeneid*, Virgil intends us, I think, to remember the ill omen that attends the gifts and to perceive an undertone of doom.[32] In the same way the picture of Penthesilea, which we have considered above, directs our minds to an event yet to take place (the death of Dido) and is symbolic, while the other pictures, which look back only, are not. It is true that Aeneas draws the lesson that he may expect sympathy from the Carthaginians, but the pictures do not in any way symbolize this sympathy.

Apart from symbols that look forward to events within the poem we may have a second kind of symbol that looks to events beyond the poem. This symbolism would resemble the symbolism of the myths in the *epinicia* of ·Pindar. There is the difference, however, that the Pindaric symbolism has reference to events discussed within the ode itself, but the symbolism we are here considering refers to events properly outside the epic. Virgil, of course, wrote his *Aeneid* with his own age and the glorification of Augustus very much in the forefront of his mind. On a number of occasions prophecy is used to make it clear that Augustus will lead Rome to the fulfilment of her destiny (esp. 1. 286 ff. and 6. 791 ff.; cf. 12. 821 ff., and Hor. *Odes* 3. 3. 57 ff.). Then, too, various Roman customs or episodes in Roman history are alluded to, as in the catalogue of Roman worthies at the end of the sixth book (756–866), the *Lusus Troiae* in Book 5 (esp. 596–603), the later buildings of Rome and the historical scenes on the shield of Aeneas in Book 8 (337–50 and 626–728). All these and many other references are made without the use of symbolism. In the fourth book we have a constant awareness of the great struggle that will take place between Rome and Carthage.[33] Consequently it seems probable that, when Virgil compares the confusion in Carthage on the occasion of the death of Dido with the confusion which would take place if Carthage or Tyre were captured, he has in mind the later capture of Carthage by the Romans, and sees in Dido's death a symbol of the fall of the city, or uses the simile as a symbol of the death of the queen (*Aen.* 4. 669–71).

Many have seen in Aeneas a symbol of Augustus.[34] I feel myself that, if Aeneas is presented as an ideal leader of the Roman people, and if Augustus was greatly admired by Virgil as a leader of the Roman people, it is inevitable that there should be a considerable resemblance between the two figures. It is hard to conceive that Augustus was not continually before the mind of Virgil as he wrote of Aeneas. I should be slower to assume that the reader was expected to think of Augustus as a mirror of the traits of Aeneas. In particular, if the rejection of Dido by Aeneas is intended to remind the reader of the rejection of Cleopatra by Octavian, it seems that Virgil largely defeated his own purpose by his sympathetic and tender portrayal of Dido, not to mention the human weakness and inhuman strength with which he endows Aeneas. In reliance on the curious verbal parallels found in the passage at the end of the eighth book describing the battle of Actium it has been argued that Virgil intends us to see in Aeneas and Dido symbols of Octavian and Cleopatra. The phrase used of Octavian at Actium

cum patribus populoque penatibus et magnis dis (*Aen.* 8. 679)

echoes the phrase used at the beginning of the third book to describe Aeneas setting out from Troy

cum sociis natoque penatibus et magnis dis (*Aen.* 3. 12)

and this echo seems to be reinforced some thirty lines on by the phrase describing Cleopatra

... pallentem morte futura (*Aen.* 8. 709)

which echoes the words applied to Dido at the end of the fourth book

... pallida morte futura (*Aen.* 4. 644)

Some believe that Virgil means us to understand that Octavian had right, fate, and the Olympian gods on his side just as surely as Aeneas had, and that Cleopatra, and by implication Antony, were doomed by fate and the gods just as inexorably as was Dido (cf. A. M. Guillemin, *Virgile* (Paris, 1951), p. 265). However, although Virgil had a remarkable fondness for repeating the scheme or verbal details of particular episodes or passages in his work,[35] it is difficult to be sure that he intended his readers to see significance in any particular repetition. Thus, to take only two passages already considered in this paper, it is hard to see what purpose Virgil could have had in the first book of the *Aeneid* for reminding his readers of the hunting boots of the *Eclogue*, and why in the snake simile describing Neoptolemus in the second book of the *Aeneid* he reminded his readers of the summer scenes of the *Georgics*. Even if there is symbolism in the passage at the end of the eighth book just considered, it seems very rash to extend it further.

Servius[36] informs us that Virgil, when he tells us that Priam lay on the shore, a headless and dishonoured corpse, alludes to the notorious fate of Pompey. Austin comments 'this may well be true'.[37] I find it hard to see why Virgil should allude to Pompey in this passage, and rather incline to think that the unexpected word *litore* and the somewhat awkward rhythm of *iacet ingens litore truncus* may indicate that Virgil is borrowing from some lost passage of an earlier poet—perhaps one that described the death of Priam on the shore, although Virgil represents him as slain in his own palace.[38]

The explicit antiquarianism in which Virgil indulges from time to time (e.g. the opening of the temple of Janus (*Aen.* 7. 601–15), or the allusions to family names at Rome (cf. R. D. Williams in his edition of *Aeneid V* (Oxford, 1960) on 117)) will, perhaps, render us less likely to credit the possibility that similar references are to be found hidden, so to say, in the poems.

VI

Lack of space precludes any discussion of the vexed question of how far the personages of the *Eclogues* conceal real persons: I can only state my personal view that Virgil is symbolized by Tityrus in *Eclogue* 1 and by Menalcas in 9 and at 5. 86 ff., and that this is all.

VII

As this is a discussion-paper it is hardly fitting that I should pronounce any very firm conclusions. However, the reader may like to see a summary of the positions I have taken, even if only to have them conveniently disposed for attack. I hold that Symbolism is a feature of Virgil's technique in (1) matters relating to religion and to magic (especially to omens), (2) references to poets and to poetry, (3) descriptions of works of art, (4) foreshadowing events in the poem or in Roman history, and (5) references to himself in the guise of shepherds in the *Eclogues*. If this is approximately correct, then in these cases we shall find in the concept of Symbolism a skeleton key. I have also given cases outside these areas, where, I believe, the concept of Symbolism has proved to be a dangerous will-o'-the-wisp luring scholars from the firm ground of traditional rational criticism and exegesis to treacherous morasses of ingenious but futile rationalization. Such, however, is the subtlety and the ambivalence of Virgil's work that in this field, no less than in others, there will always be plenty of debatable ground.[39]

NOTES

1. 'Jederman wird gestehen, dass hier [Goethe is discussing a painting] nicht an Allegorie zu denken sei. Es ist nach unserem Ausdruck ein Symbol', Goethe, *Werke* (Zurich, 1948–54), XIII. 868.

2. 'Es ist die Sache, ohne die Sachs zu sein, und doch die Sache', ibid.

3. L. P. Wilkinson, *The Georgics of Virgil* (Cambridge, 1969), p. 165, describes this as a 'remarkable symbolic vision of epic'.

4. 'Eine Geschichte der allegorischen Erklärung [of Greek Literature] ist dringend erwünscht', says M. Pohlenz, *Die Stoa*[2], II (Göttingen, 1955), 55. Cf. J. Tate, *CQ* 28 (1934), 105 ff., and J. Pépin, *Mythe et allégorie* (Paris, 1958), pp. 85–214.

5. The Augustan revival of early Roman religion made it difficult for the Romans to acquiesce in a literal interpretation of outworn religious practices; cf. K. Latte, *Römische Religiongeschichte* (München, 1960), p. 297.

6. *Iliad* 2. 308–19. It is not easy to define exactly what an omen is (E. Reiss, Pauly–Wissowa, *RE* xviii. i (1939), 352 ff.). I have in mind the kind of sign frequently found in the Homeric poems, where the symbolism is usually easily understood (cf. H. Stockinger, *Die Vorzeichen im homerischen Epos* (St. Ottilien, 1959), p. 165). In popular beliefs it is often impossible to understand why an omen has a particular meaning. See also B. Grassman-Fischer, *Die Prodigien in Vergils Aeneis* (München, 1966), p. 118 and bibliography.

7. On the allegorizing tradition applied in Alexandria to the Hebrew scriptures, cf. H. Chadwick in the *Cambridge History of Later Greek and Early Medieval Philosophy*, ed. A. H. Armstrong (Cambridge, 1967), pp. 137 ff., and Pépin, op. cit., pp. 215 ff.; Clement of Alexandria extended the practice to the exegesis of the New Testament (Chadwick, p. 180; Pépin, pp. 265 ff.).

8. D. Comparetti, *Virgilio nel Medio Evo*, rev. ed. by G. Pasquali (Firenze, 1943), vol. I, pp. 71 ff. and pp. 128 ff.; F. Robertson, *PVS* 6 (1966–7), 34–45; E. Coleiro, *PVS* 13 (1973–4), 42–53.

9. I do not think he actually uses the word 'symbole' or its derivatives. But the idea may be seen, e.g. in 'on peut dire que l'idée des guerres puniques, l'idée d'Anniba, plane sur la composition de *l'Énéide*' (C.-A. Saint-Beuve, *Étude sur Virgile* (Paris, 1857), p. 183) and in 'Énée, a dit énergiquement Gibbon, contient en lui le germe de tous ses descendants' (ibid., p. 86).

10. e.g. 'we may . . . recognise some symbolic meaning' in *Georg.* 1. 24–42 (W. Y. Sellar, *The Roman Poets of the Augustan Age: Virgil*³ (Oxford, 1908), p. 224).

11. 'We have come to equate "symbolist" with modern and to see the symbol as the sole instrument of the modern poet', B. Weinberg, *The Limits of Symbolism: Studies of Five Modern French Poets* (Chicago, 1966), p. 6.

12. The first edition was translated into English by G. Seligson under the title *The Art of Virgil: Image and Symbol in the Aeneid* (Ann Arbor, 1962).

13. e.g. A. La Penna, *DArch* 1 (1967), 220–44, and D. E. Eichholz, *G&R* 15 (1968), 105–12.

14 M. C. J. Putnam, *HSPh* 66 (1962), 233, inclines to this view, and R. D. Williams in his edition of *Aeneid I–VI* (London, 1972), ad loc., is prepared to consider it.

15. Cf. e.g. R. Heinze, op. cit., pp. 291 ff., on the one hand, with P. Boyancé, *La Religion de Virgile* (Paris, 1963), pp. 17 ff., on the other; personally I incline to the caution of C. Bailey, *Religion in Virgil* (Oxford, 1935), pp. 312 ff.

16. A comprehensive survey is a desideratum; cf. however, H. Maehler, *Die Auffassung des Dichterberufs im frühen Griechentum bis zur Zeit Pindars* (Göttingen, 1963), and A. Kambylis, *Die Dichterweihe und ihre Symbolik* (Heidelberg, 1965).

17. Cf. C. M. Bowra, *Pindar* (Oxford, 1964), pp. 3 and 230.

18. Cf. W. Wimmel, *Kallimachos in Rom* (Wiesbaden, 1960), pp. 103 ff. and 222 ff.

19. Cf. especially Propertius 4. 6. 1–10, and W. Eisenhut, *Hermes* 84 (1956), 121–8.

20. For an attempt to elucidate this symbolism, cf. C. Griffiths, *PVS* 9 (1969–70), 1–19a.

21. Verse 658. So too the suicides for love are placed in a wood of myrtle (sacred to Venus) at *Aen.* 6. 443. It is hardly more than a coincidence that the bay and the myrtle are found mentioned together at *Ecl.* 2. 54 ('et uos, o lauri, capiam, et te, proxuma myrte,/sic positae quoniam suauis miscetis odores'). As Conington notes, the two shrubs are constantly mentioned together. But cf. M. C. J. Putnam, *Virgil's Pastoral Art* (Princeton, 1970), p. 106, for a contrary view.

22. Cf. E. Fraenkel, *Horace* (Oxford, 1957), p. 282, and references there given: B. Snell, *Die Entdeckung des Geistes*³ (Hamburg, 1955), p. 397; and T. Hölscher, *Griechische Historienbilder des 5. und 4. Jahrhunderts v. Chr.* (Würzburg, 1973), p. 71, n. 332.

23. *Aen* 6. 27; cf. P. J. Enk, *Mn.* Ser. IV, 11 (1958), 322–30, and W. F. J. Knight, *Vergil: Epic and Anthropology*, (London, 1967), pp. 188 ff.

24. Knight, *Roman Virgil*² (Harmondsworth, 1966), pp. 206 ff. These views were developed with a wealth of uncritical learning by R. W. Cruttwell in *Virgil's Mind at Work* (Oxford, 1946).

25. Putnam, *The Poetry of the Aeneid* (Cambridge, Mass., 1965)—contrast pp. 40–1 with 20, 27, and 67; cf. also B. M. W. Knox, *AJPh* 71 (1950), 380 and 395. See R. R. Schlunk, *The Homeric Scholia and the Aeneid* (Ann Arbor, 1974), pp. 38 ff., for an attempt to show that the important part played by snakes in *Aeneid* 2 is a result of Virgil's knowledge of the view that was held by certain critics (cf. *Schol. bT ad Iliad.* 2. 316 (Erbse)) to the effect that the snake in the omen of *Iliad* 2. 303 ff., symbolized by its winding method of progression and by coiling round its prey the indirect route (Troy–Tenedos–Troy) by which the Greeks travelled to capture Troy. He thinks Virgil followed the scholiasts' sources in taking this symbol to signify 'the eventual sack of Troy, and especially . . . the devious means by which the Achaeans contrived to capture it', and

made it a dominant theme in *Aeneid* 2 for this reason. I do not find his argument convincing, but cannot discuss the problem here.

26. D. West, *JRS* 59 (1969), 42. R. D. Williams (ad loc. in his edition of *Aeneid I–VI* (London, 1972)), is more cautious: 'Perhaps too we may connect the renewed snake (*novus*) with the renewal of Achilles in Neoptolemus . . .'.

27. How much Virgil's simile in the *Georgics* owes to reminiscences of Nicander is explained by I. Cazzaniga, *SIFC* 32 (1960), 26–8, and by I. Gualandri, *Acme* 23 (1970), 149–51.

28. *Aen.* 4. 579–80. Cf. D. R. Bradley, *CPh* 53 (1958), 234–6, and K. Quinn, *Virgil's Aeneid* (London, 1968), p. 57, n. 1.

29. 'They turn the prows of their ships to face the sea (they must be ready for departure—who knows what may happen in this strange land?)', Quinn, op. cit., p. 161.

30. There is a full discussion by E. Norden on *Aen.* 6. 136. For more recent views, cf. R. A. Brooks, *AJPh* 74 (1953), 260–80.

31. Cf. G. N. Knauer, *Die Aeneis und Homer* (Göttingen, 1964), pp. 354 ff.

32. *Aen.* 648 ff. Cf. Austin on 650: '*ornatus . . . Helenae:* an ominous association: Virgil makes Aeneas seem extraordinarily insensitive, and the sinister character of the gift is further underlined in *inconcessos hymenaeos* (651).'

33. Cf. n. 9 supra, and R. G. Austin's edition of *Aeneid I* (Oxford, 1971), pp. ix ff., and references there given.

34. Cf. n. 9 supra, and also e.g. A. S. Pease, op. cit., pp. 23 ff. and 47 ff.; T. R. Glover, *Virgil*[7] (London, 1942), p. 166; and G. Binder, *Aeneas und Augustus* (Meisenheim am Glan, 1971).

35. A useful list may be found in Knight, *G&R* 13 (1944), 10–14.

36. Aen. 2. 557; cf. Servius ad loc.: 'Pompei tangit historiam. Quod autem dicit "litore", illud, ut supra (506) diximus, respicit quod in Pacuuii tragoedia continetur . . .', and ad *Aen.* 2. 506: 'alii dicunt quod a Pyrrho in domo quidem sua captus est, sed ad tumulum Achillis tractus occisusque est iuxta Sigeum promunturium . . .'.

37. In his note on *Aen.* 2. 557: he gives no reason why Virgil should have alluded to the fate of Pompey.

38. Cf. n. 36 supra, and the discussions by M. C. van der Kolf, Pauly-Wissowa, *RE* xxii (1954), 1888 ff., and by S. Stabryla, *Latin Tragedy in Virgil's Poetry* (Wroclaw, 1970), pp. 46–8 (Polska Akad. N.-Odd. w Krakowie: Prace Kom. Filol. Klas., Nr. 10).

39. A condensed version of an earlier draft of this paper was read as a discussion paper at the Triennial Joint Meeting of the Classical Societies at Oxford on 26 July 1975, and I am grateful for the criticism offered by a number of scholars on that occasion. They will, I trust, appreciate that it has not been practicable to take account of their views here. The preparation of the paper was greatly facilitated by the generous hospitality of the Institute of Classical Studies of the University of London which I enjoyed during May and June of 1975, and by the opportunity of discussing aspects of my views with scholars I met there (especially with Dr. N. Horsfall and Dr. A. Johnston).

ADDITIONAL NOTE (1989)

Mr. E. L. Harrison in the course of an article ('Snakes and Buskins', *Eranos* 77 (1979), 51–6) criticizing this paper points out two errors for which I apologize: (i) p. 31 line 18: the words 'in spring' should be omitted as I had confused the fennel of Nicander *Theriaca* 31 with the φάρμακα of *Iliad* 22. 94; and (ii) p. 32 line 11: 'Aeneas is hunting' should be replaced by 'Aeneas had hunted in the area on the previous day'.

THE GODS IN THE *AENEID*

By ROBERT COLEMAN

The supernatural forces at work in Vergil's epic narrative are succinctly presented in the opening lines – 'Italiam fato profugus Lauiniaque uenit | litora ... iactatus et alto | ui superum saeuae memorem Iunonis ob iram': far more prominently too than in Homer.[1] If the Stoic overtones that *fatum* carried in Augustan Latin were remote from the notion of a divine autocrat's arbitrary will, the wrath of Juno takes us back uncompromisingly to the Homeric world in which the seafaring Odysseus is perpetually harassed by Poseidon (*Od.* 1.20 etc.) and Hera is implacably opposed to Trojans (*Il.* 1.536 etc.), on account of the judgement of Paris and the abduction of Ganymede, which are explicitly mentioned in *Aen.* 1.26–8.

Divine interventions were a traditional staple of epic, conferring status upon the human events portrayed and evoking a world where gods and men were closer to one another.[2] The most famous statement of this effect is of course in Livy's preface:

quae ante conditam condendamue urbem poeticis magis decora fabulis quam incorruptis rerum gestarum monumentis traduntur ea nec adfirmare nec refellere in animo est. datur haec uenia antiquitati ut miscendo humana diuinis primordia urbium augustiora faciat, et si quoi populo licere oportet consecrare origines suas et ad deos referre auctores, ea belli gloria est populo Romano ut, cum suum conditorisque sui parentem Martem potissimum ferat, tam et hoc gentes humanae patiantur aequo animo quam imperium patiuntur.[3]

Now the status conferred by the presence of gods, if not the actual dramatic impact of the narrative, is obviously heightened if the reader holds or can be persuaded temporarily to adopt[4] some kind of belief in their existence. Where the narrative is linked causally to actual historical events that status may even be dependent on such belief.[5] The claim that Mars was a founding father of the Roman race becomes trivial if we cannot assent to any reality, even an abstract symbolic one, behind the name *Mars*. That Vergil's educated contemporaries, if they were disposed to religious belief at all, did interpret the gods whom they publicly worshipped in a symbolic way can be inferred from the demythologizing account of the traditional pantheon delivered by the Stoic Balbus in Cicero's *de Natura Deorum* 2.63–9.[6] There the gods are represented as personified instances of the beneficent divine order in Nature.[7] We cannot of course transpose Balbus's precise equations into the *Aeneid*, but symbolic modes of interpretation were open to poets as well as to philosophers.[8]

At the surface level, however, poets continued to present the traditional mythology of anthropomorphic gods. 'induti specie humana fabulas poetis suppeditauerunt', says Balbus (63) of his Jupiter-group. But if these myths remained the most effective poetic way of portraying a divine presence in human affairs, the use of anything more than a fragmentary personification inevitably detracted from the remoteness and sublimity of the gods.[9] In fact poetry finds a close parallel in popular piety, which in ancient as in modern times attributed favour, hostility, anger to its gods; so it is not accidental that Balbus concludes the sentence just quoted 'hominum autem uitam superstitione omni referserunt', implicitly distancing his theology from popular religion. For as representatives of a universal beneficent order Balbus's Jupiter, Juno etc. could never be hostile to mankind.[10] Men may come to harm through ignorance, neglect, or contempt of the divine plan but there is no place for supplications or placatory offerings – indeed for any of the multifarious rituals that abounded in Roman religion and were the basis of the contractual *pax deorum* on which the prosperity of Rome depended.[11] The reconciliation of polytheism with a more rational theology, by the very act of demythologizing the anthropomorphic mythology, dissociated it at once from the conventional piety and from the *fabulae poetarum*, for both of which a phrase like *saeuae Iunonis ob iram* still had a valid meaning and a live reality.

It is therefore no mere coincidence that Vergil brings together in the *Aeneid* the divine participation of earlier epic and the rites and customs current in Augustan religious practice. Roman piety was prefigured in the heroic age by the piety of Latins and Arcadians[12] and above all of the exiled Trojans. Aeneas, custodian of Vesta and the Penates of Troy, has a dual commission that is most un-Homeric: 'dum conderet urbem/inferretque deos Latio'.[13] The city is still not founded at the end of the poem but at least the gods are brought into Latium.

As in earlier epic Vergil's gods intervene in two general ways: by manipulating the external world and by influencing human reactions and decisions internally. The reader may know that storms and plagues are due to natural causes but will nevertheless accept and indeed welcome the symbolic representation of them as the work of hostile deities in the context of heroic events. Sudden storms and shipwrecks were a familiar hazard of Mediterranean sea-travel. But Aeneas like Odysseus was no ordinary seafarer; his fortunes have an importance far beyond himself and his companions, and the storms that harass him are no chance phenomena but the work of a deity. The same is true of the miracles that occur in the story: fatal blows warded off, a long-range spear guided unerringly to its target, a cloak of invisibility that enables the hero to escape notice. What might be put down to a happy accident in the field of battle is thus attributed to divine intervention. As a result the status of the human contestants is enlarged and a contrast established between the events of the heroic past and our own times.

In contrast to Homer, Vergil does not allow his gods to take part in the battle scenes, even though Roman legend itself provided a precedent in the intervention of the Dioscuri at Lake Regillus in 499 B.C.[14] But Vergil's gods, for all their anthropomorphic representation, are set apart from the human events that they seek to influence and are occasionally, as at 10.755–60, moved to pity from afar.

Internal motivation of human behaviour comes principally through dreams and visions, which are private experiences not even shared by those present with the recipient at the time. Oracles, portents, and prodigies represent an intermediate category: like storms and plagues they are not private experiences but belong to the external world. And yet like dreams and visions they affect the mind directly. Both groups of phenomena were recognized institutionally by contemporary Roman religion.[15]

The demythologization of internal motivations was already well advanced in Euripidean tragedy. Aphrodite, who appears in the prologue to *Hippolytus* as the vindictive Homeric goddess, is transposed once the drama is under way into an amoral impersonal force that works universally upon people's minds and when resisted – as it is by Hippolytus and Phaedra – destroys them. Even more striking is Hecuba's retort to Helen's protest in *The Trojan Women* that Aphrodite inspired her adultery: ἦν οὑμὸς υἱὸς κάλλος ἐκπρεπέστατος, / ὁ σὸς δ' ἰδών νιν νοῦς ἐποιήθη Κύπρις.[16] In *Argonautica* the divine interventions at this level merely anticipate what Apollonius is able to account for in psychological terms, as in the long description of Medea's falling in love, which begins with the visitation of Eros (3.275 ff.). Even her famous dream (616 ff.) is given no supernatural motivation.

If the gods were not to be either puppet-manipulators or redundant metaphors of psychological events, a new role had to be found for them. In order to discover what that role was, we may start by examining the various kinds of deity that appear in the poem.

Aeneas's mission was to bring gods to Latium. But of course Latium was not without gods of its own. A number are mentioned, all still worshipped in Vergil's time.

Faunus, *deus siluicola* and ancestor of Latinus (7.213) and Tarquitus (10.551), first appears at 7.81 ff., when the Latin king seeks enlightenment in his oracular grove. The wild olive in which Aeneas's spear sticks is *sacer Fauno* (12.766–7), and it is to Faunus and Terra that Turnus prays ten lines later.

Ianus bifrons, the picturesque god of gateways, and *Saturnus senex*, who had fled to Latium from the conquering Olympians (8.320), are both associated together at 7.180 and 8.357, where the Roman *Ianiculum* is derived from *Ianus*. The ceremony of opening and closing the gates of the god's temple is already established in Latium (7.610) and at 12.198 Latinus addresses his prayer to him along with Apollo and Diana.

The Italian gods show no hostility to the Trojan immigrants and it is in fact the local river-god Tiberinus who appears in a dream (8.30 ff.) to encourage Aeneas and announce the imminence of the portent which had been foretold by the Trojan Helenus to his compatriots when they called at Buthrotum (3.388 ff.). This is, perhaps significantly, one of the very few instances of an internal motivation that is not attributed to an Olympian god.

The Trojans too have their own specific deities. Cybele the Phrygian goddess is the recipient of Aeneas's prayer at 10.251–5, before he renews battle with the Italians. In the previous book (9.77 ff.) she had intervened to save the Trojan ships from arson, and a compliant Jupiter had transformed them into sea-nymphs. Just before Aeneas's prayer one of the nymphs, Cymodocea – the choice of name is emphatically un-Latin – appears to him, bringing a prophecy and an omen (10.225–249) which equally amaze and encourage him.

Far more important are Vesta and the Lares and Penates. For these are the gods that Aeneas brought with him from Troy to Latium.[17] Vesta first appears along with Fides in Jupiter's prophecy of the Roman future (1.292) but her Trojan origin is explicit in 2.293–6, when she and the Penates are entrusted to Aeneas by Hector's ghost.[18] It is to the *canae penetralia Vestae* and the Lar of Pergamum that Aeneas sacrifices after the appearance of Anchises's ghost (5.744), to the *canae penetralia Vestae, magni Penates* and the Lar of Assaracus that Ascanius calls when he sends Nisus in search of Aeneas (9.258–9).

The Trojan Penates[19] are prominent throughout the poem. They had a place of honour beside the great altar in Priam's palace (2.514) and, once entrusted to Aeneas by Hector, have a talismanic status, both reminding him of his mission and guaranteeing its safe fulfilment. Their appearance to Aeneas during the plague in Crete (3.148 ff.) is their one direct intervention in the poem. They appear to Aeneas during the night either in a dream or a vision,[20] and their obscure message *est locus Hesperiam* etc. (163 ff.) is quickly clarified by Anchises, when it is reported to him. Now Vergil could easily have introduced Anchises's explanation (182 ff.) as an afterthought: 'I've been pondering that oracle at Delos and I think we misunderstood it. For I recall there was an ancient tradition about the origin of our race, to do with

Dardanus ...' But in fact he does not. The change of plan is crucial for the mission of the Trojans; but we are left to infer that, if they had had nothing but their native wits to guide them, the Trojans would have been incapable of extricating themselves from their plight and the mission would have come to a premature and disastrous end. Not only does the intervention of the Penates confer status on the event; it also fills a gap in the aetiology of the heroes' decision-making.

One other detail is of interest here. For this is the only passage in the poem in which these Trojan deities are assimilated to the other gods and given an anthropomorphic embodiment; a detail not required by the fact that they address words to the hero. Aeneas recognizes them by their hair and faces (173–5).[21]

The significant repetition of lines and phrases is a familiar feature of Vergilian style (cf. *canae penetralia Vestae* above), and two particular instances involve the Penates. When Juno enlists the aid of Aeolus against the seaborne Trojans, she refers to 'gens inimica mihi .../ Ilium in Italiam portans uictosque penatis' (1.67–8). In 8.9 the Tiburtine Venulus is sent – unsuccessfully as it turns out (11.252–95) – to enlist the aid of the Argive Diomedes, now settled at Argyripa, against these same Trojans, who have followed him to Italy bringing with them their *uictos penatis*. In 3.12 Aeneas sets forth disconsolate over the sea from Troy 'cum sociis natoque penatibus et magnis dis'. The central scene on Aeneas's shield (8.679) shows Augustus sailing to victory at Actium 'cum patribus populoque penatibus et magnis dis'.[22] The gods defeated at Troy are to triumph in Italy before the poem is ended, and in the distant future the inauguration of the *pax Augusta* will complete the divinely ordained mission that began with Aeneas's journey into exile.

The gods whom we have considered thus far are all assigned specifically to either Italian or Trojan piety. Both groups were to be combined in the religion of the new city. Individually they may intervene now and then in the narrative but none of them has a sustained role in shaping events. In this respect they contrast with the Olympian group, familiar from the Homeric tradition.

Of the Olympians Neptune appears only in Trojan contexts. The Trojans are after all the seafarers of the story and Neptune's element is the sea. Moreover, as the Latin equivalent[23] of Poseidon he easily assumes Poseidon's Homeric role of Trojan patron. Laocoon was his priest at Troy (2.201) and, although his old anger at Laomedon's treachery finally prompted him (2.610, 5.810–11) to overthrow the walls he himself had built, he continues to be honoured by the Trojans and favourable to their voyage. Thus he is one of the deities to whom Anchises sacrifices on the receipt of Apollo's oracle at Delos (3.119) and it is from his altar in Sicily (5.640) that the women draw the fire brands to attack the ships. Although it is more from outraged vanity at Aeolus's encroachment on his prerogatives than from concern for the harassed Trojans that he moves to quell the storm (1.124 ff.), he readily complies with Venus's request for a calm passage from Sicily to Italy (5.779–863) and of his own accord provides favourable winds for the voyage past Circe's lands (7.23). On the shield of Aeneas he and Venus give a 'Trojan' weighting to the triad of Olympian deities supporting Augustus at Actium (8.699).

The third member of this group, Minerva, was not so tied. She has temples on both the Trojan citadel (1.479) and the coast of Calabria (3.531); and Aeneas can assume that olive branches worn by his men (7.154: *ramis ... Palladis*) will be immediately recognized by King Latinus as a sign of peace. Minerva had of course long been equated with the Greek Pallas Athena, who had been a patron of Diomedes and the Argive army in the Iliad and of Telemachus and his father in the *Odyssey*. The wooden horse was represented as a dedication to her (2.17, 31), the serpents that destroyed Laocoon make off to her shrine (2.226) and she is one of the deities whom Venus reveals to Aeneas presiding over the destruction of the city (2.615).

Ajax's sacrilege had subsequently turned her against the Greeks (1.39) and she shows no hostility to the Trojans in their journey.[24] The vain supplications of the Latin women at Minerva's temple in 11.475 ff. recall the vain supplications of the Trojan women to her depicted on the walls of Juno's Carthaginian temple at 1.479. She was to have an honoured place in Roman worship and it was the descendants of Aeneas who were destined finally to avenge the sacrilege of Ajax (6.840). Her presence at Actium with the two 'Trojan' gods perhaps symbolizes the reconciliation of ancient enmities.

Apollo, whose temple overlooked the victory at Actium and whose patronage Augustus recognized by building a new temple for him at Rome (8.704, 720), is naturally prominent in the poem. His worship is ubiquitous: he has an oracular cult at Troy (2.114), Dido's ill-omened sacrifice is offered to him among other gods (4.58), the bay tree in Latinus's palace yard is dedicated to him (7.62), he had guided Evander's exiled Arcadians (8.336) and the Etruscan Arruns seeks his aid as *sancti custos Soractis* even against his sister Diana's favourite Camilla (11.785). But it is with the Trojan wanderers that he is especially associated, continuing the patronage he had bestowed on Troy in the Iliad, and at 6.56 Aeneas addresses him as 'grauis Troiae semper miserate labores'.

His interventions in the external world are rare. In addition to the warning plague in Crete (3.137 ff.) the protection of Ascanius in Book 9 is of particular interest. The lad has just excited the Trojans by shooting Remulus (9.632–7) and is eager for the fight (661). But his companions restrain him and he takes no further part in the battle. Surely no divine initiative is needed to add to the protective concern that they show for their absent leader's son. Yet Apollo appears to Ascanius, disguised as Butes, only to be recognized by the Trojans as he departs (659–60). This warning intervention adds nothing to the motivation of events; what it does is to confer status on Ascanius's first martial exploit. Furthermore Vergil chooses this moment for the prophetic Olympian to reassert the glorious destiny of Ascanius's descendants: 'macte noua uirtute, puer, sic itur ad astra, / dis genite et geniture deos' (641–2).

It is by his prophetic guidance that the god helps the Trojans most in their wanderings. The oracle at Delos is greeted by a sacrifice to Apollo together with Neptune, Hiems, and the Zephyrs (3.119–20). Dido mentions similar prophecies elsewhere (4.345–6) and Helenus, having announced his own prophecy to the Trojans, concludes (3.395) 'fata uiam inuenient aderitque uocatus Apollo'. The only time that Aeneas invokes the god's direct intervention is when he is about to close with Mezentius (10.875), and to this we shall return.

In his representation of Diana Vergil draws on the whole complex of Greek and Italian associations that she had acquired in the Latin religious tradition. Thus in the famous simile at 1.498 ff. she is the majestic Artemis; at the start of Dido's magic rite she is invoked as the threefold Hecate, *tria uirginis ora Dianae* (4.511); the Trojan Nisus prays to the *nemorum Latonia custos* in the form of Luna (9.403–5). In the Italian half of the poem the specifically Latin title *Triuia* recurs: it is to *Triuiae lucos* that Aeneas is led by the Sibyl (6.13), the temple of Diana at Aricia is dedicated expressly to Trivia (7.764, 778),[25] and the Latin priest Haemonides serves Phoebus and Trivia (10.537).

Diana's only intervention is very Homeric in design and detail but is given a thoroughly Italian context. Unable to save her Volscian favourite Camilla from *fata acerba* (11.587), she promises to spirit away her body for burial in her native land (594) and to punish her killer Arruns.[26] In typical Olympian fashion she works through an agent, the nymph Opis, who on the completion of the undertaking (867) 'ad aetherium pennis aufertur Olympum'.

The Olympians who influence the course of events most of all are Juno, Venus, and Jupiter, who are, appropriately, most fully characterized.

Juno's hatred of Trojans, conceived long ago (1.27–8), is aggravated in the poem by the injury done by Trojans to her favourite city Carthage (1.15–16).[27] Mindful of this hostility, Aeneas is meticulous in observing the advice to honour her that is given by Helenus at Buthrotum (3.437–

8, 546–7) and by the god Tiberinus in Latium (8.60, 84), in both instances to no avail.

The ubiquity of her worship is made prominent. She is the patron of the Carthaginians and the first building completed by Dido's immigrant community is a temple in her honour, adorned with scenes of her latest triumph – over Troy (1.456 ff.) – which Aeneas with pathetic irony misinterprets (459–63). The queen addresses her hospitality-prayer to Juno along with Jupiter and Bacchus (1.731–4) and Juno is the chief recipient of her anxious sacrifice in 4.59.

The Italians too have their cults of Juno: she has a temple of which Calybe is priestess (7.419) and is the patron of Gabii (682–3) and protector of Turnus too, as he claims with tragic irony in 438–9. But devotion to the goddess brings no greater reward to her favourites than to her foes. Both Dido and Turnus are doomed to violent deaths, Carthage is left in disarray, the Italian opposition to Aeneas crushed and she herself is finally forced to put aside her anger and accept Jupiter's assurance that the new united community of Trojans and Italians at Rome will always hold her in high honour (12.838–41).

Her first intervention is a violent one in the external world, the storm that wrecks the Trojan fleet on the African coast. Unlike Poseidon in the *Odyssey*, who as sea-god could harass seafarers directly, Juno has to work through a lesser deity, Aeolus (1.50 ff.). The storm has grave consequences for the Trojans and so must be elevated above the mere vagaries of the Mediterranean climate, and that status is conferred by the divine initiative.

Two external interventions by Juno occur in Book 7. The Fury Allecto, enlisted as Juno's agent, crosses the scent for Ascanius's hounds during a hunt (475 ff.) and Silvia's pet stag is shot. Accidents often happen on hunting expeditions: one thinks of the hind carelessly shot by the Cretan shepherd in the Dido-simile of 4.69 ff. But once again nothing that contributes so critically to the story can be relegated to mere chance. Later in the book King Latinus, fortified against the rising war hysteria by Faunus's oracle (7.96–101), refuses to open the Gates of War; so Juno descends from heaven to open them herself (6.18 ff.). An accident? The gates had been insecurely fastened ... a sudden gust of wind ... No, the event is decisive and must therefore be attributed to the supernatural agency that is persistently working against the Trojans. Finally in 9.745 we have a purely Iliadic intervention. Pandarus's spear is 'miraculously' turned at the last moment and Turnus is unharmed. We often use this adverb as a facile synonym for 'luckily, fortunately', but a miracle it literally is here and it confers heroic status upon its beneficiary.

There are a number of instances of internal motivation by Juno.

While the funeral games for Anchises are taking place, the Trojan women are absent, alone on the shore mourning the lost patriarch and depressed at the thought of their never-ending sea-travel (5.604 ff.). Juno seizes the opportunity to send Iris to them disguised as one of them, and she inspires them to set fire to the ships. Nothing in their character or even in their present dispirited mood has indicated the possibility of such aggressive frenzy. Their behaviour is inexplicable in terms of ordinary human motivation and some extraordinary cause must be sought. A supernatural force has momentarily possessed them and that force can be none other than the deity constantly opposing Aeneas.[28]

In Book 7 Allecto's career of havoc begins with a vain attack on King Latinus (341 ff.). She is more successful with his consort Amata (373 ff.), who with her attendants is possessed by a seemingly Bacchant madness, *simulato numine Bacchi* (385). The queen was of course more promising material; for she had favoured Turnus as a prospective son-in-law (56–7), even though she must like Latinus have known the oracle (104–6).

Turnus himself might have seemed an easy target too. For like the African chieftain Iarbas (4.196 ff.), he has good cause for anger when an eligible bride has been snatched from him by an alien intruder.[29] However, when Allecto comes to him disguised as the old priestess Calybe, he dismisses her with a very Homeric – and very Roman – retort: 'bella uiri pacemque gerent quis bella gerenda' (7.444). Finally, assuming her own form, the Fury hurls her torch at him and he goes berserk: 'arma amens fremit, arma toro tectisque requirit; / saeuit amor ferri et scelerati insania belli, / ira super'. The war-hysteria is now under way in earnest.

Would Turnus have reacted so violently without Allecto's goading? We see too little of him before this to form much idea of his character[30] but there is no hint that he would be given to outbreaks of *furor* naturally, as Mezentius – and Aeneas – clearly are. In the speech rallying his terrified comrades after the metamorphosis of Aeneas's ships even the defiant *nil me fatalia terrent* (9.133), if it is not simply rhetoric for the occasion, can be read as the utterance of a man still not in possession of himself. For it was Juno who through Iris[31] inspired him to attack the Trojan camp in Aeneas's absence. The idea was reasonable enough strategically and Vergil could easily have motivated it in purely human terms. Instead he assigns it to divine intervention, implying that the goddess was constrained to keep up the pressure on Turnus, who, if left to himself, might have reverted to a more circumspect attitude.

After the Council of the Gods in Book 10 Juno is as much preoccupied with saving Turnus as with harassing Aeneas. At 10.606 ff. she is granted one last request by Jupiter to intervene directly in the battle. Creating a phantom of Aeneas (636–7), she lures Turnus on to a ship, sets it adrift (659–60) and so rescues him from danger. We may de-mythologize this easily enough: Turnus suffers a momentary hallucina-tion and the ship on which he finds himself accidentally drifts away taking him with it. But this is Turnus's last escape and the occasion is magnified by the divine intervention, which is effected in two stages: firstly at the internal level, since the hallucination is private to Turnus (though like other internal phenomena – dreams and visions – it has of course to be externalized in description); secondly at the external level by the act of cutting the ship adrift.

The incident is based on two Homeric interventions by Apollo, the rescue of Aeneas from Diomedes, who is left confronting a mere phantom (*Il.* 5.449 ff.), and the rescue of Hector from Achilles, when the Trojan hero is wrapped in a mist (*Il.* 20.443 ff.).[32] Like Diomedes and Achilles Turnus is deluded; like Aeneas and Hector he is saved. The incident underlines Turnus's Iliadic status. But Vergil also uses it to characterize him. For, when he comes to his senses, far from being grateful for the rescue he protests vehemently to Jupiter: 'omnipotens genitor, tanton me crimine dignum / duxisti et talis uoluisti expendere poenas?' (668–9). He is humiliated by the thought that he has deserted his men, trapped and helpless as they now are, and Juno has forcibly to restrain him from committing suicide or returning to the fray (680–88). To have left his comrades in the lurch and saved his own skin is the last thing Turnus would have done, if he had been in full possession of himself. The divine intervention that effects his rescue does so by compelling him to act out of character.

Juno's last intervention is at 12.134 ff. Having now exhausted the last concession from Jupiter, she can now promote her cause only through the agency of others. She appears to Turnus's sister the nymph Juturna, urging her to aid him now that *imparia fata* are closing in on him (149–51). It is perhaps a sign of her desperation that she treats the victim of one of her husband's amorous escapades so charitably (140–5). She leaves Juturna 'incertam et tristi turbatam uolnere mentis' (160) but obedient and ready to act like Iris as one of the goddess's supernatural agents (468 ff.), until she is put to flight by Jupiter's intervention (854 ff.). Vergil might well have explained Juturna's intrusion solely by her fears for her brother, but once again the impli-cation is that without Juno's instigation Juturna would not have acted as she did. Indeed the sister's intrusion marks the desperation of a hero who had once dismissed a woman with the words 'bella uiri pacemque gerent quis bella gerenda'.

If Juno's role is roughly comparable to Poseidon's in the *Odyssey*, Venus's corresponds to Athena's. She is of course, as Dido notes (1.618), the mother of Aeneas and unlike Juno she is worshipped only by the Trojans. Before setting sail Aeneas sacrifices to her and to the *diui auspices* (3.19) and at Eryx he founds a temple in her honour, dedicating the nearby grove to the memory of his father (5.759–61). It is perhaps surprising that Venus is not addressed in any of Dido's love-stricken rites (4.58–9, 510–11); but then Carthage is Juno's territory. More surprisingly Aeneas pays no homage to her at the site of Rome. The portentous sow is offered to placate Juno before his arrival (8.84–5); after the vision of the arms in the sky (520 ff.) he sacrifices with Evander to Hercules and the Arcadian Lar and Penates; and on receipt of the armour, including the great shield on which the goddess's presence at Actium (699) brings together her Trojan patronage in the poem and the mythical descent of the *gens Iulia*, he does nothing but gaze at it in uncomprehending wonder before taking it on his shoulders (729–31).

Venus's first interventions in the poem are immediately after the ship-wreck in Book 1 and Jupiter's reassuring prophecy. Aeneas of his own accord sets out with Achates to explore and Venus appears to him – but apparently not to Achates – in the guise of Diana (1.329).[33] It is rare for the Olympians to appear in person to mortals in the *Aeneid*; usually they communicate, as they intervene in events, through minor supernatural agents – Cupid, Iris, Allecto, Mercury. But of course the maternal relationship allows a special intimacy both here and in Book 8; indeed at 407–9 Aeneas reproaches her for having deceived him by the disguise. The effect of the encounter is remarkable. Aeneas at 208–9 was intensely dispirited, more so than at any time since the departure from Troy, but henceforth he proceeds with more confidence. The implication is plain. A sudden transformation of the hero occurs that cannot be explained in purely human terms; so a divine intervention is called upon to fill the gap in causation.[34] There follows a divine manipulation of the external world: Venus throws a mist around both the Trojans. How was it, we should otherwise have been tempted to ask, that they managed to enter Carthage and remain miraculously unobserved (*mirabile dictu*, says Vergil himself (439), forestalling our incredulity)? Venus provides the answer: she was responsible for the miracle.

Venus had already intervened to guide her son during the sack of Troy. Aeneas witnesses in horror the sacrilegious slaughter of Priam (2.550–3) at the very altar where Hecuba and her daughters had vainly sought refuge (515 ff.). Suddenly he recalls the danger that his own father, wife, and son are in, left alone in the house that he has recklessly deserted (559 ff.). But the sight of Helen seeking sanctuary in Vesta's temple distracts him to wild thoughts of vengeance.[35] His mother appears, to reproach him: 'quis indomitas tantus dolor excitat iras? / quid furis?' (594–5), and to recall him to his proper concern for his family, repeating Hector's exhortation (289–95) to flee. The implication is clearly that, left to himself, he would have abandoned himself to *furor*, as he does immediately after the death of Pallas in Book 10, when he slaughters the suppliant Magus (521 ff.) and Haemonides, the priest of Phoebus and Trivia, dressed in full ceremonial robes (537 ff.), and exults over the death of young Lausus (786 ff.), and above all in the final horrifying dismissal of Turnus's supplication at the end of the poem. No divine guidance is at hand to save him from himself on these occasions. But at Troy the divine intervention checks the *furor* that lies close to the surface of his character.

Reverting to Carthage, we come next (1.657–756) to the ruse that is Venus's response and the structural counterpart to Juno's initiative in causing the storm. Jupiter has already despatched Mercury to Carthage (297 ff.) to ensure a friendly reception for the Trojans, which they could not otherwise have expected in a town dedicated to Juno. But Venus, still suspicious of Tyrian treachery (661), decides to exploit her departmental power by inspiring Dido to fall in love with Aeneas, whom she has already (588–93) invested with a god-like beauty.

Now it is possible that, left alone, Dido would have fallen for Aeneas. In her welcoming speech she remarked on the similarity of their fortunes (628–9), and Anna at 4.39–44, by now preaching to the converted, advances good rational arguments in favour of Aeneas as a consort. But in fact there is not the slightest hint in Dido's opening speech or at any time before Venus's ruse that she is likely to fall in love with him. The ruse itself, when demythologized, has obvious psychological overtones. Cupid is sent to impersonate Ascanius. It is while Dido caresses the child (717–21) that the goddess's poison does its work and Aeneas's half-brother, disguised as his son, gradually overcomes her devotion to the memory of Sychaeus, the betrayal of which she later (4.552) comes to blame upon herself. Now the real Ascanius, image of his father (4.84–5), might well have had a powerful effect upon the childless Dido,[36] awakening her frustrated maternal instincts. The details of Vergil's text thus show that he could have motivated Dido in purely human terms. But while the attractions of the handsome foreign prince, the fellow-feeling for a refugee, the advantages of a male consort and the hope of children might explain why a queen could fall in love, they cannot account for the utter disintegration in her character that results from that love. The regal authority she had exercised when Aeneas first saw her is now gone. The description of her, following the Diana-simile, at 1.507–8 – 'iura dabat legesque uiris operumque laborem / partibus aequabat iustis aut sorte trahebat' – may well have sent shudders through Vergil's male-chauvinist readers, still haunted by memories of Cleopatra. But it reveals a woman totally in command of herself and her kingdom, not the sort of woman liable to be reduced to a total wreck for love of any man. The change is explicable only in terms of some external force that inspires her to act wholly out of character. Hence the aptness of the images that haunt her dreams (4.469 ff.): Pentheus and Orestes, both of them insane victims of divine power.

Juno is naturally cooperative and after Venus's lying words about Aeneas's future (4.110–2) she offers to solemnize the union: 'conubio iungam stabili ... hic hymenaeus erit' (126–7). On the day she causes the storm that drives the couple to the cave (160–2; cf. 120–1) and there presides as *pronuba* (166). No wonder Dido is deceived into believing she is legitimately married! Only the lightning flash and the wail of the nymphs at the nuptials (167–8) give warning that this is no joyous occasion but *leti ... malorum causa*.

By contrast no divine intervention is needed to awaken Aeneas's love. Indeed this was not at all part of Venus's design. *labefactus amore* he certainly is (4.395) but the love is quite spontaneous and there is no divine possession to destroy his reason. On the contrary he takes over the superintendence of the very building operations (260) which he had once gazed on so wistfully (1.437) and Dido's indisposition had now brought to a halt (4.86–9). Resplendent in the gear that Dido has given him, including a cloak embroidered by her own hand (261–4), he seems content in his role as consort and in the work of building a city, the only city that he is ever to be involved in building in the poem. It is perhaps the only time that we see him truly happy.

At this moment Jupiter intervenes, sending Mercury to remind the hero of his mission (cf. 229–36) and to speed him on his way. Mercury's speech to Aeneas skilfully plays upon the hero's prejudices and emotions: he begins with the taunting *uxorius*, contrasts the building of Carthage with the quest for the new Troy that Aeneas has forgotten and ends with an appeal to his sense of responsibility towards his son, 'quoi regnum Italiae Romanaque tellus / debetur' (275–6).[37] The speech contains all the ingredients out of which Vergil, had he so chosen, could have provided a spontaneous motivation for Aeneas's decision to leave Dido. His words to the queen in 354–9 reveal that he has already been reflecting very much on the lines of Mercury's argument even before the theophany. But there is no hint that these reflections or the appearance of the *turbida ... imago* of his father to him in dreams (351–3) would have moved him to forsake his new-found

happiness for the pursuit of his mission. It is precisely because he has
forgotten his own affairs (267) that he is so shattered by Mercury's
visitation: 'aspectu obmutuit amens / arrectaeque horrore comae et uox
faucibus haesit' (279–80).[38] There is no need then to doubt the sincerity
of his words to Dido in the underworld: 'inuitus regina tuo de litore
cessi. / sed me iussa deum . . .' (6.460–1). Vergil's narrative has demonstrated it. Aeneas's self-defence merely repeats what the poet tells us
in 4.393–6; and Jupiter, who has to drive him from his love, takes care
that his eyes and ears are closed to Dido's entreaties (331–4, 440–49).

In the affair both Aeneas and Dido act out of character, Dido in
the manner of her falling in love, Aeneas in the final suppression of
his love;[39] and this is indicated by the timing and nature of the intervention by the deities.

In Book 5 Venus's request to Neptune (779 ff.) provides again a
counter-balancing intervention, this time to Juno's attempt to fire the
ships. It is a critical moment in the story; for the Trojans are beginning
the last stage of the journey to Italy. Their previous attempt ended
in the shipwreck on the shore of Africa and Venus is apprehensive
of some further effort by Juno to thwart Jupiter's command and the
fates (784). Neptune reminds her of his loyal services to Aeneas at Troy
(803–4) and assures her of a calm voyage to Italy – at the price of one
life, 'unum pro multis dabitur caput' (815). Even a god must be paid.
The helmsman Palinurus is overcome by sleep and drowns (854 ff.).
When Aeneas meets his unburied shade on this side of the Styx
(6.337 ff.), he reproaches Apollo for having deceived him. (The
prophecy referred to is not recorded elsewhere.) Palinurus in reply
rejects the suggestion, adding 'nec me deus aequore mersit. / namque
gubernaclum multa ui forte reuolsum . . . praecipitans traxi mecum'.
Such accidents happen at sea. The contradiction of 5.815 is surely
deliberate and significant. A divine intervention will always appear,
unless it is accompanied by an overt sign, to be a chance event, unpredictable and inexplicable. Vergil gives us here an important clue
to the way in which we must interpret his divine machinery.

Conforming to the pattern of her earlier interventions, Venus's
prominence in the latter part of Book 8 follows close upon Juno's
machinations among the Italians in Book 7. First she sends a portent
to Aeneas and Achates, which lifts them from their mood of depression
(522–3), and this is followed by the presentation of the armour that
she has persuaded Vulcan to make for Aeneas. This is of course no
mere issue of new equipment. That could have been provided by human
agency. This armour like the set which the god had made at Thetis's
request for Achilles – a precedent recalled both by Venus (383–4) and
later Turnus (11.438–40) – will guarantee the hero's invincibility.

Moreover the scenes depicted upon the great shield represent the burden of destiny Aeneas must bear, *famamque et fata nepotum* culminating in the *pax Augusta*. Its importance both for the plot of the poem and for its ideology demands a divine initiative.

Her later interventions are all external and conform to the more Iliadic texture of the narrative in these books. Thus she protects Aeneas from a shower of arrows (10.331–2), heals his wounded leg in the battle (12.411 ff., though it still troubles in the final duel, 746–7) and releases his spear from the wild olive where it has been fixed by Faunus in response to Turnus's prayer (12.766–86), an instance of a superior deity upstaging a lesser one that would have delighted Homer's audiences. The frequency of these intrusions is proof of her mounting anxiety over the ultimate success and indeed safety of her son (cf. 10.46–50). On each occasion the incident can be demythologized very simply as 'a piece of unexpected and indeed inexplicable good luck'. But it is given an explication, and one that confers status upon the hero and his fortunes.

Finally Jupiter. Like Apollo and Juno he is worshipped universally. He has shrines in North Africa (4.199) and is patron of Anxur in Italy (7.799); the Arcadians believe in his presence on the Capitoline hill (8.353) and Evander prays to him (572–3). In Carthage Dido invokes him as a god of hospitality when she welcomes the Trojans (1.731). But he is also the father of the Dardanian race, as Ilioneus's speech to King Latinus relevantly recalls (7.219–20). Indeed he is the chief recipient of Trojan piety, for instance at 2.689, 3.116 (Anchises), 3.21, 5.687, 12.496 (Aeneas), 9.624 (Ascanius). Both the Trojan and Italian associations point forward to the Roman cult of *Iuppiter Capitolinus*, alluded to on Aeneas's shield (8.640).

But it is in close association with Fate that Jupiter's role in the poem is most clearly shown. The Vergilian concept of Fate is notoriously difficult to define. The Parcae, traditionally equated with the Μοῖραι, manufacture all that is fated to be ('extremaque Lauso / Parcae fila legunt' in 10.814–5), and both Juno (1.22–3) and Venus (5.796–7) acknowledge their superior power. Hence, although Jupiter administers the operations of Fate, the fates cannot be understood as emanating from him. It is true that in 3.375–6 Helenus declares that 'sic fata deum rex / sortitur uoluitque uices', apparently assigning to Jupiter powers that belong to the Parcae (*sic uoluere Parcas* in 1.22). But here as everywhere else it is important to distinguish the voice of the created character from the voice of the creating narrator. Helenus's exordium has a deliberate mood of 'impressive mystery'[40] and cannot therefore be taken as the poet's view of the relation between Jupiter and Fate. Moreover a clear counter-example is put into the

mouth of the god himself in the course of his angry outburst in 10.8–9:
'abnueram bello Italiam concurrere Teucris. / quae contra uetitum discordia?'[41] For the war must have been fated – the implication of
Jupiter's own words in 1.261–3 is clear enough – and yet it is equally
clearly contrary to the god's wishes. This situation is admittedly
unusual. In general Jupiter's expressed will is in accord with Fate's
decrees and he himself is as bound by those decrees as any of the divine
or human characters in the story.

A phrase like Dido's *fata Iouis poscunt* (4.614) is not conclusive even
for her own view of Jupiter and Fate. For it could mean the Fates
'ordained by Jupiter' or merely 'kept in his possession'. But most
probably, if we recall Aeneas's *mandata* in 357, it means simply 'the
decrees or pronouncements of Jupiter'. This last sense of *fata* (in fact
its oldest) is found frequently in the poem with a dependent subjective
genitive;[42] e.g. *fatisque deum defensus iniquis* (2.257) of the traitor Sinon
and *fatis Iunonis iniquae* (8.292) of Hercules's labours. In *Iouis imperio
fatisque* (5.784) from Venus's request to Neptune *fatis* could be either
'Fate' or 'the decrees of Jupiter'.

Sometimes Jupiter is represented as the active collaborator with Fate
or even as its agent, e.g. 'fata obstant placidasque uiri deus obstruit
auris' (4.440; cf. 651). But then so also is Juno, for instance in 1.30–2,
where her anger 'Troas ... / arcebat longe Latio multosque per annos /
errabant acti fatis maria omnia circum'. The wanderings are fated but
the precise course they take is due to Juno. Conversely while she is
responsible for the Trojans' presence in Africa, it is fated (299) that
they be received hospitably at Carthage. A close parallel to the coupling
of *fata* and *deus* in 4.440 is offered by Helenus's words at 3.379–80:
'prohibent nam cetera Parcae / scire Helenum farique uetat Saturnia
Iuno'.[43]

Prophets like Helenus are vouchsafed rather more knowledge of what
has been and is to be than the rest of us. The inability to discern the
patterns of Fate leads men to ascribe what happens to chance.[44] Hence
fata and *fortuna* or *casus* are closely associated on a number of occasions.
The Trojans who are *acti fatis* (1.32) are said by Venus to be *tot casibus
actos* (1.240). Nautes at 5.709 advises Aeneas 'quo fata trahunt retra-
huntque sequamur.[45] quidquid erit superanda omnis fortuna ferendo
est'. Evander links *Fortuna omnipotens* with *ineluctabile fatum* (8.334)
and Juno concludes her plea to Juturna with the words 'qua uisa est
Fortuna pati Parcaeque sinebant / cedere res Latio, Turnum et tua
moenia texi. / nunc iuuenem imparibus uideo concurrere fatis / Par-
carumque dies et uis inimica propinquat.' (12.147–50). Even to a deity
the ways of Fate may at times seem whimsical.[46]

Jupiter's reassurance to Venus in 1.257–8 that 'manent immota tuorum / fata tibi' raises the question: how rigid is Fate? Jupiter himself, this time reassuring Juno of his impartiality in a short speech in which *fortuna* and *fata* both occur twice within six lines, declares that 'sua quoique exorsa laborem / fortunamque ferent' (10.111–12). This suggests that an individual's initiative can at least be a contributory to the *nexus naturalium causarum*[47] that constitutes his fate. Not that the initiative is free where the individual's judgement is distorted by divine possession, as with Dido and Turnus, or driven by divine threat and exhortation, as with Aeneas. But *sua exorsa* does seem to introduce an element into the narrative that is not wholly laid down in advance. Moreover, though the broad outline of events is certainly laid down, their detailed course and tempo are not.[48] Thus Vulcan in 8.398–9 can inform Venus that 'nec pater omnipotens Troiam nec fata uetabant / stare decemque alios Priamum superesse per annos'. In fact the interventions of Venus and Juno both have the effect of complicating and delaying the working out of Fate, but they cannot alter its course, as Juno recognizes in 1.21–2 and 10.67. Most of Jupiter's interventions are directed to resolving these complications and speeding these delays.

Sometimes however he intervenes merely to keep Fate on course. Thus at 2.687 ff. Anchises prays for a sign from the god to validate the portent of Iulus's halo. A meteor appears and the old man is at last persuaded, as it seems nothing else could have persuaded him, to flee with his son and grandson from burning Troy. At 7.107 ff. the Trojans, newly landed in Italy, are inspired by the god (*monebat*) to use their wafers as plates, so fulfilling Celaeno's prophecy (3.255–7).[49] In 11.901 'saeua Iouis sic numina poscunt' reveals that the *furor* that is now manifest in 'his inability to organize his campaign rationally'[50] is not only the work of the *saeuae Iunonis numina* unwittingly acting as the agent of Fate but is also approved by Jupiter, whose divine will assents to Fate's decrees.

One intervention in the later books is worth looking at in detail, since unlike most of the other internal motivations exhibited in the poem it is causally redundant.[51] At 10.689 ff. Jupiter inspires the Etruscan Mezentius to enter the battle. The epithet *ardens* that is used of him along with *alacer* and *acer* (cf. 729, 897) suggests that he needed no divine *monita* to urge him on. However Jupiter's attention confers special status on his entry at this point and its sequel. In the preceding two books Mezentius has been the most prominent warrior on the Italian side after Turnus. The contrast between the two is great. Unlike the pious Turnus Mezentius is *contemptor diuom* (7.648; cf. 8.7), and his quick temper and brutal arrogance (8.481–2, 569–71, 10.742) are due not to any divine possession but to natural disposition. This is to be his last appearance on the battlefield; after beholding his son's

corpse he too will die at the hand of Aeneas, unmourned by his own
people (10.904–5). It seems then that Jupiter in summoning him to
battle is despatching him to the executioner who will put an end to
his career of savagery. But all these are minor interventions by Jupiter
compared with his efforts to counteract Venus and Juno.

He sends Mercury to Carthage, first in Book 1 to forestall further
hostile action by Juno, and then again in Book 4 to set Fate on course
after the distractions and delays brought about by the unholy alliance
of the goddesses. At 5.685 ff., when Juno acting through Iris inspires
the women to attack the ships, he sends a rainstorm to quench the
flames in answer to Aeneas's prayer. The good fortune of a sudden
shower is thus converted into an example of *pietas* rewarded and the
rescue of the ships given an appropriately magnified status. Later in
the same book *imperio Iouis* (5.726) Anchises appears to Aeneas in a
dream to urge him on his way, leaving the older members of his party
with Acestes in Sicily. Nautes had already advised just such a course
(704 ff.), but there is no suggestion that without the divine intervention
Aeneas would have heeded his prophetic advice.

At 9.77 ff., after Juno instigates the attack on the Trojan camp,
Jupiter intervenes in response to Cybele's entreaty, to save the ships
once again. The metamorphosis is a sign to both sides that even in
their leader's absence the Trojans can still trust in their destiny, and
Turnus's misconstruction of the portent provides a context for charac-
terizing his defiant qualities of leadership. In Book 10 Jupiter allows
Juno one last intervention on Turnus's behalf (96 ff.).

After the Iliadic weighing of the fates of Aeneas and Turnus Jupiter
extracts Juno's final submission (12.807 ff.). He sends one of the Dirae
in the form of an owl to confront Turnus and his sister. The eerie
apparition alarms Turnus (867–8) in a way that Aeneas completely fails
to do (894–5) and drives Juturna from the battlefield that she has
hitherto stubbornly refused to quit. Turnus is left alone to fight it out
with Aeneas. He had been driven to *furor* first by the Dira Allecto
sent by Juno; now it is a Dira sent by Jupiter that heralds the disastrous
outcome of that *furor*.

From all this we can now infer a particular significance in the
ambiguous uses of *fata* noted earlier (p. 158): the decrees of one deity,
intended to impede the progress of *Fatum*, turn out to be its unwitting
vehicle, the decrees of another, intended to hasten its progress, may turn
out temporarily to delay it. But above all stands Jupiter ready to intervene if *Fatum* is too far off course or schedule.[52]

Now the idea of Fate as a mechanism that needs to be continually
tinkered with is decidedly odd; it is rather as if the 18th century Deists'
clock, having been wound up by the Creator, not only struck its

appointed hours at unpredictable intervals but needed constant adjust-
ment by the divine clock-maker to ensure that it would strike at all.
But such a conception of Fate was unavoidable if there was to be any
place for actions by men or gods that was not just part of the mechanism itself. Logically it would have been far simpler to return to the
more loosely structured Homeric theodicy, with its more rudimen-
tary ideas of $\mu o \hat{\iota} \rho a$ and $\Delta\iota\grave{o}s$ $\beta o \upsilon \lambda \acute{\eta}$, or else like Lucan to have retained
the concept of a constraining and immutable Fate while eliminating
independent interventions by the gods. But Vergil needed both Fate
and the gods in his poem, for artistic as well as ideological reasons.
Fate was needed to bind the sequence of events in the poem, which
began with the flight from Troy, to the long centuries of Roman
history which culminated in the imperial *pax Augusta*. Equally he
needed the gods: not only because the story of his poem, like the
Odyssey, is a sequel to the *Iliad* contemporaneous with the wanderings of Odysseus (cf. the episode of Achaemenides in 3.588 ff.),
but also because the gods of the Homeric Trojan, as of the traditional
Italian, mythological past were still part of contemporary Roman
religion. Jupiter, Venus, and Juno, Faunus and the Penates all had
their own history, which was also the history of the people who
worshipped them.

   Divine intervention in the external world – the raising and quelling
of storms, the sending of portents etc. – is as much a feature of Roman
history as it is of literary mythology. Juno can thus be seen as representing the superhuman forces that seem to be working against the completion of the Trojan journey,[53] Venus the forces that seem to be
assisting it. So far as internal motivation is concerned, psychological
explanation, as we noted earlier (p. 145), had already diminished the
area of divine activity. Nevertheless there are certain crucial decisions
and actions in the lives of men that cannot be accounted for in terms
of what is known of their characters. These lacunae in our under-
standing of internal motivation, which might be put down to $\ddot{a}\delta\eta\lambda o\iota$
$a\grave{\iota}\tau\acute{\iota}a\iota$ $\dot{a}\nu\theta\rho\omega\pi\acute{\iota}\nu\omega$ $\lambda o\gamma\iota\sigma\mu\hat{\omega}$, are in the *Aeneid* attributed to external supernatural forces acting upon the human mind.[54] The gods of traditional
epic have thus found a new role and one that has much in common
with the 'God of the gaps' in modern theology. Dido and Turnus are
both destroyed by the onset of a *furor* that is apparently out of character.
Hence it is assigned to the agency of Venus and Juno operating
respectively through Cupid and Allecto. Modern readers may demythologize these divine interventions into current theories of natural
causation and interpret them as mental breakdowns, pathological conditions and the like, but there is no justification for interpreting as
Vergilian allegory[55] an aetiology that accords both with the traditions

of the literary genre and with conventional piety. However, in their variety, elaboration and complexity the external and internal motivations by gods go far beyond anything that survives from earlier epic.

Aeneas presents an instructive and disquieting contrast to Dido and Turnus. The *furor* with which he reacts to the sight of Helen in Book 2 and to the death of Pallas in Book 10 is entirely spontaneous and in character. In the former instance he is saved from whatever impiety his madness had conceived by the intervention of Venus; in the latter no divine curb is placed upon his vengeful fury, which is most brutally exposed not in the catalogue of slaughter in Book 10 but in the manner of Turnus's death at the end of Book 12. Moreover he has constant need of divine encouragement and exhortation. Hector's commission to him is quite forgotten until Venus's urgent warning (2.619 f.); the Penates rescue him in Crete from a disaster that he shows no resource in overcoming; it is only the arrival of Jupiter's ambassador Mercury that prises him away from Dido and Carthage and only the ghost of Anchises, again sent by Jupiter, that persuades him to complete the last part of the journey from Sicily. Not much of an heroic ideal in all this save in one important respect: it is Aeneas's *pietas* that enables him to respond appropriately to the divine initiatives and to overcome those elements in his character, not all of them violent or ignoble, that stand in the way of duty, and so to emerge as the prototype of a distinctively Roman form of heroism.

One last topic remains to be considered. The lofty seriousness of the theodicy that on the above interpretation underlies the whole divine participation in the narrative is on a number of occasions dangerously undermined by the anthropomorphic realism with which the gods are portrayed.

When Juno sets about raising the storm in Book 1, she bribes Aeolus in typically Homeric (or for that matter Ovidian) fashion by promising him the fairest of the nymphs Deiopea (65 ff.). When the storm finally penetrates the consciousness of Neptune (124 ff.), he reacts just like a Roman magistrate who has been affronted by some intrusion upon his *prouincia*, declaring 'non illi (sc. Aeolo) imperium pelagi saeuomque tridentem / sed mihi sorte datum'. This realistic piece of ἠθοποιία, reinforced by the famous simile of the orator quelling an unruly mob (149 ff.), belittles the dignity of the intervention. Similarly Juno's reaction to Aeneas's welcome by Latinus (7.308–10) has the petulant tone of a patrician lady who, finding herself outwitted by some social inferior and unable to enlist any sympathy from her peers, resorts in desperation to the criminal underworld to find an agent for her spite: 'magna Iouis coniunx . . . uincor ab Aenea . . . flectere si nequeo superos, Acheronta mouebo'.

It might be objected that such a criticism concedes too little to the conventions of the genre. But we can judge Vergil against himself. Venus's request to Neptune (5.779 ff.) for safe conduct of the Trojan ships and his response to her are both free of the overdrawn anthropomorphism that elsewhere impedes our suspension of disbelief. What could have seemed a whimsical intrusion by the deities is presented as an event consistent with divine dignity, with Venus's permanent role in the poem and with Neptune's past behaviour.

The double-dealing between Juno and Venus in 4.90 ff. has often provoked unfavourable comment. It is not just that the goddesses are depicted as if they were two rivals in comedy striving to outwit each other; but the noble Dido is in the process reduced to a pawn in an unnecessarily squalid game. Indeed it says much for Vergil's poetic talent that he is able in spite of this to establish the queen as a great tragic heroine.

The most egregious instance of frivolous anthropomorphism comes much later, in the seduction of Vulcan (8.370–406). The Homeric precedent, Thetis's request for arms from Hephaestus (*Il.* 18.368 ff.), is appropriately emphasized (383–4). Venus's task is of course more delicate; for she is pleading with her husband, on behalf of the son of one of her adulterous escapades. So what we get is a scene more reminiscent of Hera's seduction of Zeus in *Il.* 14.153 ff. or Demodocus's amusing tale of Ares and Aphrodite in *Od.* 8.266 ff. The spectacle of an adulterous beauty-queen calculatingly turning her charms on a long-suffering husband would have delighted Callimacheans – even Ovid could not have done it better – but its mix of domestic comedy and vivid sensuality gravely detracts from the seriousness of the surrounding narrative. Evander has just taken leave of Aeneas with the lofty moral advice: 'aude, hospes, contemnere opes et te quoque dignum / finge deo rebusque ueni non asper egenis' (364–5). Immediately after comes the splendid description of the night shift in Vulcan's workshop and the production of the monumental shield (407 ff.).

Even Jupiter's crucial intervention in Book 4 is strangely motivated. He seems to be careless, if not actually ignorant, of what is going on between Aeneas and Dido until the angry torrent of prayer comes up from Iarbas (198 ff.). Thereupon 'oculos ... ad moenia torsit / regia et oblitos famae melioris amantis' and Fate is swiftly brought back on course. Again we can compare Vergil with himself. In Book 11 no human prayer is needed to prompt Jupiter to act: 'at non haec nullis hominum sator atque deorum / obseruans oculis summo sedet altus Olympo' (725–6). For the epic tradition of course there is nothing untoward in the idea that gods have now and then to be coaxed or chivvied into acting their parts; nor would popular piety in Vergil's day have found anything alien in Iarbas's prayer and its sequel. Nevertheless the notion of a divine superintendent of Fate who is not wholly self-directing but needs on occasion to be activated by human information and entreaty does detract from a serious view of the theodicy of the poem.

In short the gods of the Hellenized literary-religious tradition, immortals of superhuman powers but with all the frailties of character that belong to their human creators, were not capable of bearing the serious burden of causation that Vergil placed upon them. Better to have swept away all the divine personalities and replaced them with more abstract beings, which could represent the mysterious forces operating in the physical and mental world for and against the success of Aeneas's mission, and above these, ultimately setting the limits to their interaction and directing the overall course of events, Fate itself, conceived in something like its Stoic form. This would have been a revolutionary step in a genre where anthropomorphic gods and modes of divine intervention in human affairs were so firmly installed; but it would also have been a reversion to something like the older Latin concepts of deity (see n. 6 below). The revolutionary step was in fact taken by Lucan, and it may not have been just his Stoic convictions or the incongruity of importing divine machinery into recent historical events that led him, while filling his poem with sacrifices, portents, and the sense of super-natural forces constantly pressing on human events, to omit the conventional divine machinery altogether.

NOTES

1. In the proem to the *Iliad* the only explicit reference to divine forces is Διὸς δ' ἐτελείετο βουλή (5), in the *Odyssey* βοῦς Ὑπερίονος Ἠελίοιο (8). At the start of *Argonautica* there is no hint whatever that the human events in Apollonius's narrative are closely and continually linked to divine actions and initiatives and the first reference to a deity, to Athena's role in the building of the Argo (18–19), is almost casual.

2. In the Latin tradition there was ample precedent in Naevius (*BP* 13, 16, 21 Marmorale) and Ennius (*A* 22, 175, 291, 457 Vahlen). See J. Perret, *Virgile* (Paris, 1965), p. 132. That the status-conferring role of the gods was essential even to epic poems on recent historical subjects is clear from Cicero's practice of introducing into his autobiographical epic pieces a *concilium deorum* and a long address by Urania to the poet (*ad Q. fr.* 3.1.24, *Div.* 2.17). Serious doctrine thus lies behind the satiric context of Eumolpus's assertions in Petron. *Sat.* 118: 'non enim res gestae uersibus comprehendendae sunt, quod longe melius historici faciunt, sed per ambages deorumque ministeria et fabulosum sententiarum tormentum praecipitandus est liber spiritus ut potius furentis animi uaticinatio appareat quam religiosae orationis sub testibus fides'.

3. On the divine ingredients in Livy's history see W. Liebeschuetz *JRS* 57 (1967), 45 ff.

4. As in our reaction to the ghost of Hamlet's father or to the statue of the Commendatore in the final act of *Don Giovanni*. There is a clear contrast with the incidental use of divine activity as a metaphor of physical events, e.g. Bibaculus's 'interea Oceani linquens Aurora cubile' and 'Iuppiter hibernas cana niue conspuit Alpes' (Macrob. *Sat.* 6.1.31, Quint. 8.6.17). Both the dramatic effect and the status conferred by such images are independent of belief in the gods.

5. Otherwise the divine machinery merely ensures that the story is kept at a distance from reality, within the region of fantasy. See K. F. Quinn *Virgil's Aeneid: a critical description* (London, 1968), p. 305 for precisely this view of the gods here.

6. After a discussion of the heavenly bodies (54) and the deification of natural products – *Ceres, Liber* (60), functional abstractions – *Fides, Mens* etc. (61), and human benefactors – *Hercules, Castor* etc. (62). The *Fides* group has Greek parallels of course, but it was characteristic of primitive Roman religion to proliferate such deities, defined precisely by their *prouinciae* (a practice ridiculed in Aug. *Civ. Dei* 4.21) but otherwise quite vaguely conceived (cf. Varro *ap.* Serv. *in Georg.* 3.1 on whether *Pales* was male or female). They were therefore unsuited to pictorial or poetic elaboration, unless like *Cupido* or *Fortuna* they were personified in the Greek fashion.

7. Jupiter is the universal father who helps (*iuuat*) all his children; Juno also the 'helper', the atmosphere between earth and heaven; Venus the procreative desire that comes (*uenit*) to all creatures. The Penates dwell in the *penetralia* of the home, their name derived from the food store (*penus*), etc. Etymologies were as important for the Stoics as for Plato and usually just as fanciful.

8. Cf. Lucretius's explicit use of *Bacchus* and *Ceres* (2.655 ff.) and the introduction of Venus into the proem, inspired by Empedocles's use of Ἀφροδίτη for his creative principle φιλότης (Simplic. *Phys.* 158.24), as the personification of the creative process by which *concilia* of atoms are formed.

9. Protests to this effect were as old as Xenophanes (Sext. *Math.* 9.193), whose anti-anthropomorphism (Clem. *Strom.* 5.109.3) was, however, not total (Sext. *ibid.* 144, Simplic. *Phys.* 23.20).

10. Cicero elsewhere says explicitly 'at hoc quidem commune est omnium philosophorum ... numquam nec irasci deum nec nocere' (*Off.* 3.102).

11. 'pietate ac religione atque hac sapientia quod deorum numine omnia regi gubernarique perspeximus omnis gentis nationesque superauimus', Cicero boasted on a public occasion (*Harusp. Resp.* 19); '... nostrae ciuitatis quae numquam profecto sine summa placatione deorum immortalium tanta esse potuisset', declares even the sceptical pontifex maximus Cotta in *N.D.* 3.5.

12. Especially topical for the Augustan reader were the ceremony of the temple gates of Janus (7.601 ff.) and the *ara maxima* of Hercules (8.185 ff.).

13. No doubt a feature of Hellenistic κτίσις epics; cf. Callim. *Aet.* 2.75–83 Pf on the religious legends about the origin of Zancle. For Apollonius see J. U. Powell *Coll. Alex.* 4–8. But the blend of secular and sacred was so fundamental to Roman political institutions that the combination of Homeric divine machinery and Roman cult must have been prominent already in Naevius and Ennius.

14. Cic. *N.D.* 2.6; cf. Liv. 2.20.12.

15. The quasi-scientific rules governing divination, which enabled them to be assimilated to more rationalized theologies like Stoicism, distinguished the two groups very sharply: portents were interpreted by the highly systematized *diuinatio artificiosa*; dreams, which were significantly grouped with *furor uaticinantium* and thus more closely related to the condition of ἐνθουσιασμός, were the subject of *diuinatio naturalis* (Cic. *Div.* 1.11, 34 etc., with A. S. Pease's commentary).

16. Lines 987–8; cf. Nisus's words to Euryalus (*Aen.* 9.184–5): 'dine hunc ardorem mentibus addunt,/Euryale, an sua quoique deus fit dira cupido?', followed a couple of lines later by the forthright 'mens agitat mihi'. This is not a clue to Vergil's concept of the gods' role in events but part of his characterization of Nisus, to be set beside, for instance, the agnostic tone of 'Iuppiter aut quicumque oculis haec aspicit aequis' (ibid. 209).

17. Equated in classical times with Ἑστία and the μεγάλοι θεοί of Aegean religion (see nn. 21, 22), they are more likely to be indigenous cognates than derivatives of these.

18. The incident illustrates the fragile boundary between internal and external phenomena. Hector appears in a dream to Aeneas but the *sacra* that he passes to him belong to the external world and are thereafter carried by the hero wherever he goes. By contrast the theophany of Venus, 'aetherios inter ... nimbos/ dona ferens' (8.608 ff.), though private to Aeneas, is an external event, the visit of a mother to her son. Hence the reality of the arms given to him poses less difficulty; but the incident is correspondingly harder to demythologize than either the Hector-dream or even the appearance of Venus to Aeneas at 1.314 ff.

19. Dido also has her Penates (1.704); so has Evander (8.123), and the early morning sacrifice made jointly by Evander and Aeneas to the local Lar and Penates (8.543) underlines their association with the intimate hospitality to strangers in the home. That their precise function was uncertain is clear from Cicero's brief account of them (*N.D.* 2.68).

20. The difficulty of reconciling *in somnis* (151) with *nec sopor* (173) already troubled ancient

readers, as Servius's note shows. Perhaps it is an indication that Aeneas himself, who is telling the story, was uncertain.

21. That their identification was debated in classical times is clear from Macrobius (*Sat.* 3.4.6–13), who cites (1) Nigidius's opinion that they were Trojan versions of Apollo and Neptune, both of whom appear independently in the Aeneid; (2) Varro's opinion that they were originally from Samothrace and that 'qui diligentius eruunt ueritatem Penates esse dixerunt per quos penitus spiramus, per quos ... rationem animi possidemus'; (3) Hyginus's view that they were θεοὶ πατρῷοι 'gods of our ancestors' or 'of our fatherland' (cf. *patriosque Penatis* at 2.717). In the *aedes deum penatium* on the Velia, which was restored by Augustus (*R.G.* 19, 36), they were depicted as two seated youths in military dress, according to Dionysius of Halicarnassus (*A.R.* 1.68), who like Varro identifies them with the Samothracian μεγάλοι θεοί, i.e. the Καβῖροι. Moreover, there is evidence in coinage of the 1st century B.C. to suggest that this iconography owed something at least to the Dioscuri; see R. B. Lloyd, *AJPh* 77 (1956), 38 ff.

22. The line-ending *magnis dis* is Ennian (*A* 201 V). It is not clear whether the *magni di* are here distinct from the Penates (cf. *magnos ... penatis* at 9.258). Macrobius (loc. cit. n. 21) cites the view of Cassius Hemina that the *di magni* were the Samothracian θεοὶ μεγάλοι and then adds 'eosdemque Romanorum penates proprie dici θεοὺς μεγάλους', citing *Aen.* 3.12, which he presumably understood as 'and with the Penates, the great gods'. It has been conjectured that *dis magnis* was actually inscribed upon the statue of the Penates in the Velia temple. See R. D. Williams *Aeneidos Liber Tertius* (Oxford, 1962), pp. 54–5.

23. The indigenous Neptunus was defined solely by his *prouincia* (cf. n. 5), as was Portunus – 'deus portuum portarumque praeses' (Varro *ap. Schol Ver. Aen.* 5.241; cf. Cic. *N.D.* 2.66) – who is also assigned to a Trojan context (5.241).

24. Nautes owes his skill as a counsellor explicitly to *Tritonia Pallas* (5.704).

25. This Italian cult is, however, carefully linked to the Greek Artemis by the strange tale of Hippolytus's resurrection.

26. Hence her brother Apollo's rejection of the second part of Arruns's vow at 794–8.

27. Cf. Poseidon's hostility to the Greeks during and after the Trojan War, aggravated by Odysseus's treatment of Polyphemus (*Od.* 1.68 ff.).

28. The Olympian action at a distance in both instances is typical, and it is an oversimplification to interpret the two agents Allecto and Iris as 'scarcely more than a personification of Juno's suffering' (Michael C. J. Putnam, *The Poetry of the Aeneid* (Cambridge, Mass., 1965), p. 88).

29. J. Perret, op. cit. p. 131, plausibly suggests that in the traditional version of the story Turnus was indeed motivated by plain jealousy, as the Latins were by resentment towards the alien usurpers.

30. An Italian Achilles, also born of a goddess (6.89–90; cf. 9.742, 10.76), with a distinguished human pedigree (7.56), including an Argive connection (371–2). Subsequently we learn of his outstanding physical prowess (783 ff.) and his piety (9.23–4, 10.620; cf. 7.438–9). Every detail combines towards a re-creation of the Homeric ideal hero, to set against the Vergilian Roman ideal embodied in Aeneas.

31. The line describing the actual intervention, 'Irim de caelo misit Saturnia Iuno' (9.2) echoes – again significantly – the descent of Iris to the Trojan women at 5.606, from a context where the goddess's machinations were frustrated.

32. It would be interesting to apply the external/internal interpretation of divine interventions used in the present study to these and other passages in Homer.

33. Who later provides explicitly the content of the simile describing Aeneas's first glimpse of Dido (498 ff.).

34. There is a precedent in the *Odyssey*, where Telemachus's despondency is abruptly ended by his encounter with the disguised Athena (1.113 ff.) and he assumes a confidence and maturity that amaze even his own mother (360–1) as well as the suitors (381–2).

35. 567–88 contain enough unusual features of style and language to justify the suspicion that they are, as they stand, not Vergilian but rather the work of an early interpolator (presumably prior to Lucan 10.59), one of the many (Suet. *Vita* = Donatus *Praef. Buc.* 41) who were unable to resist the challenge of the *uersus imperfectos* in the poem. However, the content of the passage is surely an astonishing choice for an interpolator to have made, unless he had some evidence of Vergil's intentions. The whole of this section of the poem still awaited its final revision at Vergil's death, as

witness the half-lines at 468, 614, and 623, and it may reasonably be conjectured that Vergil had left enough lines and fragments (there are many phrases that certainly sound authentic scattered through the suspect passage) to leave his intentions clear. The disconcerting picture they gave of the hero would have made Varius grateful to have the excuse of their fragmentary character for excluding them from his edition. The same considerations would explain why the passage as we have it, cobbled together from the poet's *disiecta membra*, was not admitted into the authorized version that is reflected in the manuscript tradition of the poem itself and in the abundant citations of the *Aeneid* in the grammarians, but surfaced only in Servius's preface to his commentary and in the *Servius Auctus* note on 566. For a detailed discussion of the passage and a very different conclusion see G. P. Goold, *HSCP* 74 (1970), 130–68. R. G. Austin's view of the passage, *Aeneidos Liber Secundus* (Oxford, 1964), pp. 217 ff., is close to the one proposed here, though not all Austin's interpretations of detail are acceptable; e.g. *sceleratas* (576) is indeed 'a piece of self-condemnation', the judgement of Aeneas the narrator on Aeneas *furens* (595).

36. *infelix* in 712, as elsewhere, probably has both the senses 'barren' and 'ill-fated'. Dido had borne Sychaeus no children. At 4.327–30 she refers poignantly to the fact that, though she and Aeneas have lived together as husband and wife, she is not pregnant. This is significantly rare, if not unique, in classical myth and legend, where it is normal for even a single act of sexual intercourse to produce offspring.

37. Iulus-Ascanius thus plays a crucial part in both the beginning and the end of the affair.

38. B. Otis, *Virgil: a Study in Civilized Poetry* (Oxford, 1964), p. 226, sees Jupiter's interference as an external parallel to the stirring of Aeneas's conscience; but this reduction of Vergil's divinities to something like their Apollonian role ignores the subtle detail of the Vergilian narrative.

39. Otis op. cit. p. 94 rightly sees *amor* and *furor* as threatening *pietas* and *fatum*, but in imposing this antithesis on Dido and Aeneas respectively he reduces them to Morality *personae* and diminishes the essential tragedy of their relationship.

40. See R. D. Williams, op. cit. p. 134.

41. Prompted by the continuing strife between the goddesses, it is a far cry from the serenity he showed (1.254 ff.) in comforting the despairing Venus. V. Pöschl, *Die Dichtkunst Virgils: Bild und Symbol in der Aeneis* (Innsbruck, 1977³), pp. 16 ff., makes altogether too much of that *serenitas*. For it is only one facet of Jupiter's character, as it is of the Roman ideal that Pöschl seems to regard the god as symbolizing allegorically. Not for nothing did Jupiter wield the least serene of punitive weapons (1.230); on occasion he could exhibit as much *saeuitia* as Juno (cf. 1.4 with 11.901).

42. By contrast in *tuorum fata* (1.257–8) and *fatis contraria nostris* / *fata Phrygum* (7.293–4) the genitives and *nostris* are all 'objective', viz. 'the fate that has been assigned to your people' etc.

43. The construction of the sentence is odd. Helenus can hardly be forbidden by Juno to divulge what he has been barred from knowing. So we must either understand something like *etiam si sciret* with *fari* ('Juno forbids him to speak, even if he did know') or take *-que* twice over, first as coordinating *prohibent* and *uetat* and then *scire* and *fari* ('The Fates prevent Helenus and Juno prohibits him from knowing and speaking the rest.')

44. Cf. the Stoic definition of τύχη as ἄδηλος αἰτία ἀνθρωπίνῳ λογισμῷ (Stob. *Ecl.* 1.7.9). A good illustration is Palinurus's use of *forte* (6.349) in describing his own death, which, he does not know but we do, has been contrived by a god.

45. The classic Stoic posture of resignation; cf. Sen. *Ben.* 2.18.8: 'ducunt uolentem fata, nolentem trahunt'.

46. In fact *Fortuna* represents the impact of Fate, for prosperity or the reverse, upon those who are affected by it but cannot comprehend the broader providential plan.

47. The phrase is from Tac. *Ann.* 6.22, where a view of Fate (probably Stoic) is cited that leaves us with *electionem uitae* but, once our choice is made, commits us to *certum imminentium ordinem*. We may choose our role in the drama but the part is already written and we cannot conjecture much of its content in advance.

48. Cf. the doctrine that *magna di curant, parua negligunt* (Cic. *N.D.* 2.167), where *di* is virtually synonymous with *Fatum*. Unlike the more austere concepts of Fate this doctrine did leave some freedom of action to the individual, provided of course that he was left unmolested by divine forces.

49. It is not clear whether Aeneas's attribution of the prophecy to Anchises (7.122–3) is a mark of the unfinished state of the poem or a subtle indication from the poet that the hero's memory of his early wanderings is still dominated by his father.

50. The phrase again is from R. D. Williams; *The Aeneid of Virgil Books 7–12* (London, 1972), p. 432.

51. More typical is the god's motivation of another Etruscan captain to attack Camilla's forces: 'Tarchonem in proelia saeua / suscitat et stimulis haud mollibus inicit iras' (11.727–8). For here there is no suggestion that if left to himself he would have joined the battle at this moment.

52. The ambiguity is very potent, for instance, in Venus's irate question to Jupiter (10.34–5): 'cur nunc tua quisquam / uertere iussa potest aut cur noua condere fata'?

53. Perret, op. cit. p. 130, follows Boissier in seeing *ira Iunonis* as causing all the important incidents in the poem, but this ignores the love affair at Carthage. Pöschl, op. cit., regards Juno first (p. 14) as the mythological personification of the historical power of Carthage. This could certainly apply to Ennius's Juno (see *A*. 291 V, cited by Servius on 1.281). But it accords ill with Vergil's account of Juno's reconciliation to Rome's illustrious future (12.827), which would leave the other addressees of Dido's famous prayer (4.607–10) with the task of implementing its demands (622–9). Nor does Jupiter's reference to the future wars with Carthage (10.11–15) necessarily imply Juno's involvement. Later (p. 17) Pöschl converts the goddess into a divine symbol of the demonic forces of violence and destruction. But the violence she is responsible for comes from her opposition to Fate and is far from being her monopoly in the poem. For Otis, op. cit., p. 309, Juno is the external stimulus corresponding to and exciting the inner response; this seems once again to reduce the deity to Apollonian redundancy.

54. Likewise Vergil's contemporaries the elegists continued to fill the gap in the aetiology of love with the traditional gods of erotic literature: the lover who acts unpredictably and out of character is afflicted with *dementia, insania*, the result of being vanquished and possessed by Venus or Amor.

55. The view that the gods of the *Aeneid* were allegorical figures of psychological phenomena, symbols that the reader decodes as he goes along, was first and most influentially elaborated by R. Heinze, *Virgils epische Technik* (Stuttgart, 1914³), pp. 291–318.

ADDITIONAL NOTE (1989)

Page 56 line 36
  For '(p. 158)' read '(p. 54)'

Page 57 line 28
  For '(p. 145)' read '(p. 41)'

VIRGIL AND THE CONFISCATIONS

By MICHAEL WINTERBOTTOM

This brief article tries to make sense of the first and ninth *Eclogues* with as little recourse as possible to evidence from outside the poems. In particular, it does without the doubtful aid of Servius, who arguably knew little more than we about the meaning and background. Where I give no references (except for the most familiar historical events) I am conjecturing, or adopting the conjectures of others. I have cut secondary references to a minimum, because the doxography of the *Eclogues* is too vast to be entertaining. Those who are new to the problems can easily find their bearings in the books of H. J. Rose, L. P. Wilkinson, and Gordon Williams.[1] Old hands will know where I am being original: rarely, of course, if ever, for in this field of scholarship more than most it is true that 'nihil iam dictumst quod non dictum sit prius'.

Virgil was born near Mantua in 70 B.C. (Suetonius, *De poetis* ap. Jerome, fr. 1 Hardie). He was not ill disposed to Julius Caesar, who had granted citizenship to his own Cisalpine Gaul; and when Caesar was murdered in 44, the youthful Virgil naturally transferred his allegiance to the Julian heir apparent, the even more youthful Octavian. When a comet coincided with Octavian's games for the dead Caesar (Suet. *Jul.* 88), Virgil wrote the lines we now read at *Ecl.* 9. 46–50: 'Daphni, quid antiquos signorum suspicis ortus? | ecce Dionaei processit Caesaris astrum, | astrum quo segetes gauderent frugibus et quo | duceret apricis in collibus uua colorem. | insere, Daphni, piros: carpent tua poma nepotes.' This is clearly part of an early *Eclogue*, where, as later in *Ecl.* 4, political support is clothed in rural metaphor: the new potentate will bring lasting peace to the countryside.

During the events leading up to Philippi, Virgil was writing other *Eclogues*, including perhaps the fifth. Political references have been suspected there; we cannot be sure of them. But line 40 'spargite humum foliis, inducite fontibus umbras' will be important later. After Philippi, the victors made a division of labour, Antony to set the East in order, Octavian, more invidiously, to settle the discharged veterans on confiscated Italian lands. Virgil's home region was among those affected. He was not himself involved, for he was comfortably off, and had for some time been living in central Italy.[2] But he felt the deepest sympathy for the dispossessed. Nor did he need to imagine their anger; their demonstrations took place in the streets of Rome (App. *B.C.* 5. 12). Whether before or after the Perusine war in 41 (the timing is of no literary importance), he wrote a poem expressing his distress. It was not addressed to Octavian,

though it referred to him in laudatory tones; it called him *iuuenis*, and it
came near to calling him *deus*. We know the poem as *Ecl*. 1.

Tityrus sits beneath his beech, singing. He has visited Rome to buy his
freedom, and, receiving it in return for his *peculium*, has received also
something for which he did not pay—permission from the *iuuenis* to go on
working his small farm. It is no grand estate: big enough for Tityrus, but
all stone, swamp, and reed. This is not the way in which Virgil would have
thanked Octavian for any favour to himself.[3] Tityrus in any case is an old
freedman, no proper counterpart for the young Virgil. Yet in a way
Tityrus *is* Virgil, for Tityrus is personally unscathed by the power politics
of the day. He has enough, and he can court the woodland muse (2)—just
as Virgil is doing in the very act of composing the *Eclogue*. For Tityrus, as
for Virgil, all is well. Misfortune is reserved for others. Meliboeus is
wandering to an unknown exile; it might even have to be Britain. *He*
cannot sing any more (77), because his little farm is now the property of a
soldier, worse, a barbarian (70–1). He is bitter, and his bitterness is shared
by Virgil; for Meliboeus echoes the early lines of hope: 'insere, Daphni,
piros: carpent tua poma nepotes' (9.50). That is not true of Meliboeus:
'insere nunc, Meliboee, piros, pone ordine uitis' (1.73). The fields he has
planted will be reaped by another: 'his nos conseuimus agros!' (72).
Tityrus can do no more than offer him a lodging for the night; tomorrow
he must go on.

The poem balances carefully between eulogy and criticism of Octavian.
It is not stated that the *iuuenis* is responsible for Meliboeus' plight in the
way that he is responsible for Tityrus' happiness. But 'en quo discordia
ciuis | produxit miseros' (71–2), and it takes two to make a *discordia*.[4]
Virgil, far from expressing personal thanks to Octavian, is expressing
personal disquiet, perhaps even an uneasy conscience. *He* may sit in his
study composing bucolic poetry; for others life in the country is less
idyllic. All is well with Tityrus; but what of Meliboeus? .

The first *Eclogue* is not addressed to Octavian, and perhaps it was not
sent directly to him. But it is a political comment, of a kind that rescued
Virgil from being a passive Tityrus; and it would have failed of both its
eulogistic and its critical purpose if Octavian had never read it. But it
produced no effect; the confiscations went forward, and no doubt Virgil
never expected anything else. He addressed, or began to address, a less
veiled poem to Varus.[5] *Ecl*. 9. 27–9 represents some lines from it: Varus
will be praised by the swans of poetry 'superet modo Mantua nobis |
Mantua uae miserae nimium uicina Cremonae'. No bucolic this, perhaps.
But whatever its genre, it too had no effect. *Eclogue* 9 is the expression of
Virgil's disappointment at the failure of his own efforts; it is possible to be
disappointed even where one has never had much hope.

Moeris and Lycidas are on the way to town. Moeris is subordinate to a new landowner; the old has gone,[6] dispossessed by an *aduena*. There has been violence, or threat of it, that might have proved fatal both to Moeris and to *ipse Menalcas*, 'the master Menalcas', maybe, or just 'Menalcas too'. Menalcas has gone. In his absence Moeris and Lycidas can no more compose new songs than could Meliboeus: 'nunc oblita mihi tot carmina' (53). Only when Menalcas returns will their power of song return too: 'carmina tum melius, cum uenerit ipse, canemus' (67). Lycidas had heard a rumour that Menalcas had saved a tract of country (it is carefully left unstated whether it was his own estate, just as we do not know if he is Moeris' old landlord). But the rumour was mistaken: 'carmina tantum │ nostra ualent, Lycida, tela inter Martia quantum │ Chaonias dicunt aquila ueniente columbas' (11–13). Poetry is powerless in civil war. Menalcas had discovered this; so had Virgil.

In this single sense Menalcas *is* Virgil, just as in one single respect Tityrus was Virgil. Both Menalcas and Virgil had protested against dispossessions, using the only weapon they had, poetry; both had been snubbed. This time, however, Virgil gives us more of a clue to the identification than he gave us in *Ecl.* 1. In the absence of Menalcas, asks Lycidas, 'quis caneret Nymphas? quis humum florentibus herbis │ spargeret aut uiridi fontis induceret umbra?' (19–20). The allusion to the fifth *Eclogue* (40) is unmistakable. But that need not mean that Virgil lost a farm; all that the ninth *Eclogue* tells us is that Menalcas could not save a farm, and it does not tell us that it was his own.

What Menalcas and Virgil principally have in common is their trade. And the fragments of Menalcas' poetry[7] with which Moeris and Lycidas beguile their journey are from Virgil's own workshop. Two, the addresses to Varus and Daphnis, are, we have conjectured, from earlier political poems. Two are close adaptations of Theocritus (23–5 = *Id.* 3.3–5; 39–43 = *Id.* 11.42 ff.) of the kind that Virgil might well have produced at the earliest and most imitative phase of his bucolic activity. The escapist world of Theocritus and the world of Roman reality are here consciously juxtaposed. The lines on the *astrum Caesaris* are the climax of the group. Their optimism intrudes as sardonically here as their bitter parody by Meliboeus in the first *Eclogue*.[8]

Menalcas has gone. Virgil, that is, despairs of pastoral poetry. In the first *Eclogue* he displayed his disquiet at the contrast between his own good fortune and the ill fortune of others, disquiet too at the role of pastoral poet in troubled times. In the ninth, the disquiet has reached a crisis. He and his poetry, he now realizes, have no place in the countryside, 'tela inter Martia'. In altered circumstances Virgil regained optimism for a moment; in 40 he wrote the fourth *Eclogue*, with its implication that the countryside had found peace after all. But when he came to assemble his *Eclogue* book, he placed the Tityrus poem first, to proclaim a new committed pastoral, Roman and humane; almost at the end he set the Menalcas poem, with its confession that pastoral is powerless in a ruthless world. Only *Eclogue* 10, where Gallus discovers that pastoral can do nothing in the face of *Amor* ('tela inter media', 45), is allowed to separate *Eclogue* 9 from the end of the roll.[9]

NOTES

1. *The Eclogues of Vergil* (Berkeley and Los Angeles 1942), ch. 3; *The Georgics of Virgil* (Cambridge 1969), ch. 2; *Tradition and Originality in Roman Poetry* (Oxford 1968), 307–28. It is with this last that I share most, though not all.

2. In any case Williams, 308–9, rightly stresses that *Ecl.* 1 is not set in any identifiable part of Italy; nor, despite the allusion to Mantua, is *Ecl.* 9 (ibid. 317).

3. At most, it might be thanks for not having lost a farm, or for some unknown act of protection; even then the emphasis on the worthlessness of the farm seems ungracious. But the crucial point is that Tityrus shows no sympathy for Meliboeus, beyond offering him temporary hospitality; but Virgil can hardly have wished to represent himself as the complacent witness of the sufferings of others. Tityrus is made old and grizzled precisely to prevent us from identifying him with Virgil, and from transferring his complacency to the poet. On the other hand, Virgil *does* show sympathy for Meliboeus, by writing the poem. What Tityrus and Virgil do have in common I state in the text.

4. And to be in a position to save is itself in a way invidious; see Cic. *Sull.* 72: 'quia maius est beneficium quam posse debet ciuis ciui dare, ideo a uobis peto ut quod potuit tempori tribuatis, quod fecit ipsi.' The stress on the protection of Tityrus only makes worse the non-protection of Meliboeus.

5. Virgil seems perfectly happy with Varus in *Ecl.* 6. So perhaps he did not feel that Varus' failure to relieve Mantua was culpable. Or, more radically, the lines may not imply that Varus was in a position to save the city; see K. Büchner, *PW*, Sonderdruck, P. Vergilius Maro, col. 218: 'Ebenso aber ist es denkbar, dass nur bei Rettung Mantuas der Dichter äusserlich und innerlich in der Lage sein, Varus zu preisen.' See also Williams, 322, whose arguments from 9.27–9 can thus be evaded.

6. This seems to be implied by 'ueteres migrate coloni' (4). But the background is not altogether clear (Williams, 313–14).

7. The first two extracts are certainly Menalcas'. If 37 'id quidem ago' means, as the commentators assume, ' 'tis *that* I am busy with', namely trying to recall one of the songs of Menalcas' (Page; but the line is very abrupt on any account after 30–6), 39–43 will be his. 46–50 might be Moeris' ('te', 44), but symmetry would suggest that if three extracts are Menalcas' the fourth should be too. If this is true, Virgil will be emphasizing that even though Lycidas (33–4) and perhaps also Moeris (51–5) are poets in their own right, they can only, in the new circumstances and the absence of Menalcas, sing the poems of another; and even those they are fast forgetting (38, 45, 53).

8. The pessimistic echo is normally used (though see Williams, 327) to prove the priority of the ninth *Eclogue*. But context matters; there is nothing optimistic about the lines addressed to Daphnis in *their present position*. The echo, I have suggested, is of the poem where 9.46–50 were originally placed.

9. I have been much helped by the advice and encouragement of Robin Lane Fox, and by the stimulation of countless pupils, not least Andrew Frost.

AGRICULTURE AND THE *GEORGICS*

By M. S. SPURR

'As writes our Virgil, concerned more with what made the best poetry than with complete accuracy, since his object was to delight his readers rather than to instruct farmers.'[1]

Seneca passed this judgement on the *Georgics* after witnessing certain agricultural practices where he was staying (at Liternum on the north-west coast of Campania), which appeared to disagree with a statement of Virgil's (*G.* 2.58). He then proceeded to mention another Virgilian agricultural error (*G.* 1.215–16), selected from 'all the others' (*alia omnia*) that he says he could have discussed, in order to drive his point home.

While it may be that Petrarch and some other humanists adopted Virgil as their agricultural guide, recent scholarship has accepted Seneca's judgement. Thus two influential modern commentators (whom the English-speaking student is likely to read early in his research on the *Georgics*) describe it as 'pertinent' or 'wise'.[2] They consider the agricultural content to be something of a defective surface, which covers symbolic depths: 'the intellectual didactic material is, at surface level, the subject of the poem; but the real subject is emotional or indeed spiritual.'[3] This means that, as readers of the *Georgics*, we must 'eradicate from our minds any lingering notions that the poem is utilitarian'.[4] Instead the poem can be seen to 'convey the essence of a way of life, hard and sometimes tragic, but regular and often rewarding'. What that life might be is defined more precisely: 'there was a feeling abroad among thinking people, reflected also by Horace, that a simple, Sabine-type, peasant life was happier and morally healthier.'[5] We are reminded that 'the district Virgil knew best, the Po valley and the surroundings of Naples, happened to be the ones where the small holder (*colonus*) still flourished.'[6] And as the student continues to read through the recent and growing literature on the *Georgics*, he or she will also inevitably come across some version of the further view that Virgil, whether or not following some 'official line' was concerned about 'the desecration of the countryside during periods of war', and 'the poem is therefore related to ... the urgent desirability of restoring Italian agriculture'.[7]

In what appears to be a climate of considerable renewed interest in the *Georgics*, it will be worth while to step back a moment from the symbolic depths, which are being explored with ever increasing interpretative skill and imagination,[8] to consider some of the readily accepted generalizations that regard the *superficies*: Virgil's supposed agricultural inaccuracy, his supposed description of the small subsistence farm and the supposed ruin of Italian agriculture. This is not to suggest that the search for a profounder significance is in any way mistaken. But if the poem is to succeed as a unified whole, both surface and depth (even if that distinction does not turn out to be largely illusory), must be accorded due appreciation.

Seneca the Agriculturalist?

In his eighty-sixth moral letter to Lucilius, then, Seneca reports on a demonstration, by the new owner of Scipio Africanus' old estate, of the speedy establishment, or perhaps restoration, of an olive plantation. Two methods to this end are discussed, both of which are apparently new to Seneca. In his view they contradict Virgil's statement (*G.* 2.58) that newly planted trees will grow so slowly that they will provide shade not for the farmer himself but for his grandchildren. To take the second method first (*Ep.* 86.19), on examination it turns out to be nothing other than a crude form of propagation by the planting out of olive cuttings from the parent tree, which is discussed by the three major prose agricultural writers, Cato, Varro, and Columella.[9] Whereas they advise the careful planting of cuttings in a well-tended nursery in preparation for future transplanting into an olive grove, Aegialus, Seneca's host, cuts vigorous young branches from the parent tree and plants them directly in the olive grove.[10] In fact, Columella mentions in passing (and thus with no hint that the technique is new) this cruder method as one way of propagating fruit trees (5.10.6–9) but apparently not olives, which are treated with greater care. From the agricultural point of view, Aegialus' technique would be no quicker, as regards the eventual establishment of the oliveyard, and would certainly be less secure of success.[11]

The first demonstration on which Seneca reports (*Ep.* 86.17–18) is even more agriculturally dubious and is also confusingly described. It appears that Aegialus selected certain mature trees, pruned them with extreme severity, cut off their roots and then replanted them deep in the earth. This seems scarcely credible. Severe pruning is sometimes practised these days in order to rejuvenate an old or damaged tree but the treatment does not include transplanting.[12] In both cases Aegialus carefully stamped down the earth around the freshly transplanted trees or cuttings, an agricultural 'hint' for which Seneca shows his admiration. Had either he or Aegialus read their Cato they would have realized that this technique was at least some two hundred years old, and that, moreover, Cato's reason for doing so contained more agricultural sense than Seneca's own explanation.[13] One further curiosity concerns the season for this transplanting. It would seem that Seneca witnessed it during late June, whereas the agricultural writers (in tune with modern advice) advise transplanting in spring.[14]

Thus rather than passively accept Seneca's criticism of Virgil's agricultural inaccuracy, we should begin to have grave misgivings about his own agricultural knowledge. Moreover, when the context of *Georgics* 2.58 is examined, we might legitimately begin also to doubt his knowledge of Virgil, since he has misleadingly removed the line *tarda venit seris factura nepotibus umbram* from its context. Not only does it refer to arboriculture in general (and not to olives in particular), but it actually belongs to what Virgil is telling us not to do, namely the growing of trees from seed, since that method takes too long. Therefore, Virgil instructs, olives should be propagated from cuttings (*G.* 2.63).[15]

Nor should Seneca's second agricultural example, to prove his point about Virgil's inaccuracy, inspire greater confidence. He reports that in late June near Liternum he saw beans being harvested and millet being sown. Virgil, Seneca reminds us, had included both among spring-sown crops (*G.* 1.215–16). Yet the truth of the matter is that millet can be sown either in the spring or summer. Moreover, from other ancient evidence, it would appear that in fertile parts of Campania (of which Liternum was one) millet was a particularly prized crop, which could be sown in the early summer in order to fit into a three-fold annual rotation pattern.[16] To be complete, Virgil should have said that millet was *either* a spring *or* summer crop, although it is true to say that most commonly, in Italy, it was sown in the spring. Seneca's observation, on the other hand, again reveals more about his, than Virgil's, agricultural ignorance.[17]

Virgil's Selectivity

We must therefore beware against charging Virgil with agricultural inaccuracy.[18] Nevertheless it does seem that Virgil is selective in his treatment. Thus it has been stated that the *Georgics* would be useless as a guide to agriculture for the novice farmer. This argument then proceeds to the conclusion again that, if the didactic material is of no real help, the meaning or significance of the poem must lie elsewhere.[19]

This selectivity is in contrast, it has been argued, with the agricultural prose writers: 'But what strikes one particularly on comparison with Varro, or still more with Columella, is what Virgil

selects to treat, and how much he decides to omit.' As an example of
this, Wilkinson proceeds: 'Book 2 is nearly all devoted to the vine:
there are only a few lines on the equally important olive, and other
trees receive the most cursory treatment.' And in a later work he
remarks (again on the slight treatment of olives): 'Nothing could make
it clearer that the *Georgics* is a poem, not an exhaustive handbook.'[20]
Compare:

[Olives are given so few lines because] 'Virgil wishes to leave behind his series of
precepts about the work which the farmer must do and to give a picture of Nature's
unaided contributions to human welfare. The great theme of the whole work is the
balance between the bounty of Nature and the toil of man . . . .'[21]

Caution is again necessary, since much of this is misdirected. After
treating vines in some 130 lines (*G.* 2.259–419 with a digression at
2.315–345), Virgil does appear to give olives short shrift (*G.* 2.420–
425). But before we assign a deeper significance to this we should
understand the simple agricultural fact that, for the Romans at least,
olives could succeed with very little cultivation. According to
Columella, the olive was the best of all trees precisely because it
produced such goodness with the minimum of care (5.8.1). Whereas
he wrote two and a half books on viticulture (books 3.1–5.7), he
advised on olives in two short sections of one book (5.8–9). Thus one
could almost invert the argument to say that had Virgil in the second
book been describing 'the bounty of Nature' the olive, with all its
essential uses for mankind compared to the little expenditure of effort
necessary for its cultivation, should have received a lengthy encomium.
Instead it is clear that Virgil's treatment of the olive was in proportion
to its perceived agricultural needs.

Further on the general question of selectivity, even a rapid glance
at the pages of Cato's *de agricultura* or Varro's *de re rustica* will reveal
that the prose writers also were highly selective. Cato's treatise appears
to be an incomplete and random assemblage of agricultural precepts
and while Varro's work exhibits a much greater (too much, some
modern commentators complain) logical organization of material, it
could never be described as a comprehensive farming manual.[22] To
concentrate for a moment on Varro will be particularly valid, since
his treatise appeared only a few years before the *Georgics* and certainly
influenced Virgil, perhaps considerably. In book 1, which deals with
agriculture proper, in the middle of a discussion of various soils Varro
includes, illogically, an excursus on different methods of staking and
supporting vines (1.8). Then, later, towards the end of the book where
he discusses harvesting, he mentions briefly with what grapes one
should begin the grape harvest (1.54.1) but then jumps immediately

to the pressing (1.54.2–3); while for olives, he provides some details on the olive picking but says almost nothing about the pressing (1.55).

To account for this selectivity, and for what often seems, according to our present standards at least, to be a lack of logical organization of material, is not easy.[23] One thing, however, is surely clear: these treatises were not written for novice farmers. Instead they presumed that their readers already possessed considerable agricultural knowledge and close acquaintance with the varying climatic and topographical conditions in Italy. On opening his discussion of vines Pliny could say that he took common knowledge for granted and would address himself only to matters which required clarification (*N.H.* 17.8).

Thus criticism that Virgil's didactic material is too selective to be of practical use is out of place. The concept of the 'novice farmer' is a modern one. It should rather be understood that the selectivity of the *Georgics* fits the tradition of the agricultural handbook. Of course it is important to remember that Virgil was also writing in the tradition of didactic poetry and selectivity is apparent in Hesiod, the first extant writer in that genre.[24]

Furthermore, complaints of an unsystematic or illogical organization of material would surely have surprised Virgil's contemporaries. Instead, one could argue, Virgil's division of his subject into four books represented a considerable achievement, if not advance, in rational composition. And all commentators draw attention to the orderly and compact way in which Virgil presents the subject of each of his four books in the opening four lines of the poem.

Finally, for an interesting clue as to how the Roman reader of an agricultural treatise could derive the maximum practical benefit from a superficially disordered work, we can turn to Varro (3.2.13). He describes a certain Seius who made large profits from the specialized breeding (*pastio villatica*) of dormice, thrushes, pigeons, etc. desired by the urban market. Seius' success was ascribed to the fact that he had collected together all the relevant comments, hitherto 'scattered and unsystematic' (*separatim ac dispersim*), in the available agricultural manuals. Absence of systematic treatment, then, was the rule rather than the exception. But that did not necessarily damage the utility of the didactic material.

Given this necessary correction of the orthodox view of Virgil's selectivity, nevertheless it will be true to say that one criterion of this selection process was his desire to keep his readers entertained. There is a clear hint of this in *Georgics* 1.75–6, where Virgil appears to anticipate a certain unwillingness of his audience to listen to 'humdrum tasks' (*tenuisque curas*). He proceeds to describe otherwise possibly dull details on the construction of the threshing floor in a particularly poetic way. However, it is most important to realize that this 'honeying of the cup' does not signify any distortion of the agricultural accuracy.[25] Prose manuals of agriculture (and of other technical subjects) sought also to entertain the reader lest he become bored and not wish to continue, but this does not detract from their informative worth. There can be no doubt that Virgil wished to 'delight his readers', in Seneca's phrase: but to equate that with agricultural inaccuracy could not be more incorrect. By 'delighting', a writer makes his didactic material all the more memorable.

Literary Borrowing

To quantify how much of the agricultural content of the *Georgics* is Virgil's own and how much is derived from other sources is probably impossible. Thus Wilkinson expresses extreme diffidence in attempting to confront the problem.[26] It will bear on the question of Virgil's agricultural reliability if one believes that he borrowed substantially from Greek sources and thus incorporated material incompatable with rural Italy.

Yet is this a real problem? Does it matter that Virgil followed a work by Aratus on weather signs or by Eratosthenes on the zones of heaven? Reactions of animals and birds at the prospect of rain, phases of the moon, and indication of weather from the sun surely fitted both Greece (or Egypt) and Italy?[27] Or if Virgil adheres to Theophrastus' botanical analysis of the vine, we can surely accept that vines in Greece were similar to those in Italy.

But we can go further than this. While it can be shown that Virgil derives details from Theophrastus' highly technical discussion of plant propagation, he clearly seeks to organize what was in his source an abstract account into advice of a practical nature. Thus, as has been seen above, he rejects the propagation of trees by self-sowing from seeds and instead prescribes layering for vines and cuttings for olives (*G.* 2.56 ff.). When he comes to mention the varieties of vines (2.89 ff.), he makes a clear distinction between Italian vines and those from the eastern Mediterranean. Regarding wines, Virgil singles out, at the head of his list, Italian varieties: Falernian and Aminean are included, while, interestingly, the less well-known Rhaetic, from Cisalpine Gaul, is his first choice. This seems to reflect the poet's personal preferences, based on his own experience (2.94–7).[28]

It is this Italian emphasis which is so obvious in the poem and which should dispel any doubts about an imagined distorting dependence on Greek sources. Following his review of wines, Virgil invites the reader 'to cast his eyes abroad' (2.113) and refers in turn to cultivation in Arabia, Egypt, India, China, and Persia (2.113-135). The reason for this excursus is soon made clear: 'none of these places could rival Italy ....'; and thirty lines praising Italy, and mentioning specifically places from the Northern lakes to Campania, bear out his statement. He concludes the passage with: 'I sing the song of Ascra throughout the Roman towns' (2.176). As every student knows, that is an open reference to Hesiod; but Virgil would have been surprised were it to be understood as anything more than homage to the founder of the genre of didactic agricultural poetry. Certainly it should not be taken to signify that Virgil borrowed more than the minimum amount of agricultural detail from Hesiod: Virgil does, after all, sing his poem throughout the *Roman* towns. Again, it can be added, the prose agricultural writers also used Greek sources but with a judicious independence derived from their own knowledge of Italian agriculture.[29] Indicative of their independence is Pliny's comment that the agricultural information of the greatly celebrated Carthaginian agronomist, Mago, was really applicable only to North Africa (*N.H.* 17.128).

An important feature of this reassuringly Italian emphasis is Virgil's characteristic method of involving the reader and himself in the agricultural content of the poem. This does not simply fit well with the generally prescriptive (e.g. in the use of imperatives) tradition of the agricultural prose writers, or just reflect a didactic poetic technique of Lucretius. Rather it provides the effect of direct personal observation. This begins immediately after the invocation at the opening of the first book with the *mihi* of line 45. It is helped by phrases such as *quid dicam* (1.104) and *ecce* (1.108) and is referred to most clearly in *vidi* (1.193, 197), *saepe ego .... vidi* (1.316–318) and *memini me .... vidisse* (4.125–127). This sense of autopsy appears also in the way in which Virgil backs up a general precept with a concrete Italian example, such as Mantua's river meadows (2.198f.), or fertile soil near Capua and between Vesuvius and the sea (2.222f.) It is also apparent in those particular details which bespeak a local agricultural knowledge, such as the choice of Rhaetian wine (see above); of the oak as a supporting tree for vines in an *arbustum* (2.290 ff.), which is much more unusual than the elm (1.2; 2.361), but might have been selected, since, as we know from Pliny (*N.H.* 17.201), it was a tree used for this purpose north of the Po; of the scattering of ash as manure, or dust on ripening grapes, or the sowing of beans in the spring, all of which practices, again, were perhaps common in the Transpadane region of Virgil's boyhood (*N.H.* 17.49;18.120).

Peasant Farm or Villa?

Without notable exception, modern commentators assume that Virgil was describing the work on a small farm. Yet ancient readers of the *Georgics* would have entertained no doubt that Virgil, like Cato and Varro before him, and Columella later, was writing primarily about a rich man's estate. Just a few agricultural considerations will suffice to demonstrate this, perhaps to some, disturbing revelation; and these can even be taken from the first book, which deals with cereal farming, the usual preserve of the subsistence peasant farmer, according to conventional modern views of the agricultural development in Italy during the later Republic and early Empire.[30]

The first agricultural advice, which comes after the invocation to rural deities and Octavian, is to break up the land in early spring with a plough drawn by oxen (1.43 ff.). That the land was to be ploughed in spring means that it has been allowed to lie fallow during the autumn and winter and is to be sown either later in spring or, more likely, in the following autumn. This is clearly a technique adopted on a farm where the cultivator is not constrained to use all his land each year in order to subsist. Moreover, the use of a team of oxen signifies a considerable acreage under pasturage or fodder crops, rather than under crops solely for the human household. While a plough drawn by an ass might be common enough on a small farm, oxen are the mark of a larger estate.[31]

As an alternative to fallowing, Virgil continues (1.71), the farmer should consider a rotation pattern (1.74 f.), and for this, especially in poorer soil, a rich manuring will be necessary (1.80). While some simple rotation of grain and beans was probably practised even on the peasant farm, the variety of rotation crops, which include fodder crops, prescribed by Virgil, and the abundance of manure necessary for success, again belong to the larger estate.[32]

The conclusion that the poet is envisaging a large farm is further borne out by the element of choice, that the farmer is supposed to have, of what to plant where. Thus the 'micro-climates' of the different sectors of the farm are to be carefully considered (1.50–61); and the long excursus on choice of soils refers not only to regions the length and breadth of Italy but also to the varieties of soil to be found on the one (large) property (2.177–258). Once the right soil has been chosen and worked by the plough – which might mean the bringing under cultivation of part of the farm hitherto left as woodland (1.50f.; 2.203ff.: a luxury not open to the subsistence cultivator)–the remaining clods of earth must be pulverized and then the field levelled with a wicker-work harrow (1.95). The harrow was included among the equipment of the villa estate by Varro; and Columella was later to advise its use in careful preparation of a field to be sown as pasture.[33]

A mark of rational agriculture is careful seed selection. The best seeds must be chosen from the previous harvest and stored separately for a later sowing. Varro, and later Columella, emphasized this, and Virgil draws attention to it with *vidi* (1.197). Otherwise the crop will degenerate. Again, however, this element of choice was more characteristic of the large farmer, since the peasant would grow a mixed field of cereals, either as the result of careless seed-selection or from scarcity of the right sort of seed.[33] With all this careful agriculture practised on rich soil, it is not surprising that the crop could run the risk of being too abundant and thus prone to wind-flattening (1.111). One precaution was to allow sheep into the cereal fields while the crop was still in leaf, before the ear had emerged (1.112–3). This practice was explained in greater detail later by Pliny (*N.H.* 18.161), and can probably be understood as another of Virgil's own observations. A possible danger to the crop during its later development is thus avoided and, instead, is transformed into a positive benefit for the animals of the farm, since such special pasture is highly nutritious. Elsewhere Virgil recommends that calves be fattened on it (3.176). All this, which refers to a well-integrated system of cereal and livestock, again is surely more likely on the rich man's farm.[35]

Other, increasingly obvious, considerations will serve to confirm this hypothesis. Although Virgil says very little about harvesting (Varro had treated the matter in depth at 1.50), threshing does receive attention. Construction of the threshing floor (1.178 f.) signifies something more permanent than a patch of hardened ground, which was what at most, it can be assumed, the poor cultivator used for the purpose.[36] The threshing process could then be carried out with sledges and drags (1.164), both of which were part of the equipment of the villa estate (Varro 1.52; 1.22.1), drawn by oxen. It could also be effected by driving horses around the threshing floor (3.133), a technique not mentioned elsewhere in the extant literature before Columella (2.20.4). Since horses were in no way essential to cereal cultivation, their presence can only indicate the largest of Roman arable estates, which had enough land given over to pasture and fodder crops to breed and maintain such status-associated animals.[37] On such a farm will be seen Virgil's oxen drawing wagons filled with grain (2.205–6), and the granaries will burst (1.49; 2.518). The subsistence cultivator, who would have kept his hard-won grain in a heap inside his house (cf. *Moretum* 15-16), is again far from sight.[38]

It should therefore be accepted that Virgil follows the agricultural handbook tradition in this too, and so the agricultural material of the

Georgics concerns principally the villa estate. 'Principally', since Virgil, like the agricultural writers, especially Varro and later Columella, with his Italian-wide purview, clearly does not limit himself to just one ideal farm. Instead he envisages a range of possible villa estates and even, on occasion, the small farm. In this way the reader can come to understand the variety (and complexity) of the agricultural reality of Roman Italy.

To take an example from Columella, while not straying from the immediately foregoing discussion: his advice on threshing clearly refers to arable farms of various sizes. Largest were those where horses were available; next down the scale were those estates which could dispose of enough oxen, but no horses, to trample the grain; then come comparatively smaller estates with only 'a few teams of oxen', *pauca iuga* (but we should remember that a 200-*iugera* arable farm required two *iuga*: Columella 2.12.7; so a farm of some considerable size is still being envisaged), which utilized threshing sledges and drags. Otherwise, if the ears of grain only were harvested, they could be threshed with sticks during the winter when food was required, or could be trodden by *pecudes*. This more general term for 'animals', most probably indicates the ubiquitous ass or mule, rather than oxen or horses, and so the last two alternatives probably refer to small-scale cereal cultivation at subsistence level. Thus in this passage it can be seen how Columella rapidly surveys a wide range of types of arable farming.

This range is noticeable also in Virgil. Firstly by comparison with Columella, we can assume that when he refers to horses threshing the grain (3.133), he envisages a very large estate; while in Book 1, a smaller estate (but of at least 200 *iugera*), which uses oxen and threshing sledges, is in mind. As regards various *modes* of arable farming on the large estate, in Book 1 he appears to describe a specialized cereal farm where burning off of the stubble can be practised (1.84ff.); while elsewhere he refers to an *arbustum* (which signifies mixed cultivation of cereals with orchard trees, olives, or vines supported on trees, in the same field), where burning of the stubble would be clearly impossible.[39]

In a description of death caused by plague, farming without oxen is vividly depicted: 'Thus men break up the earth with mattocks and dig in crops with their own fingernails' (3.534–5). Yet this might not be far from normal agricultural practice for the poor peasant cultivator, as we can glean from passing references in other writers, and so Virgil's description derives its power from reality.[40] Happier, certainly, was the gardener in the vicinity of Tarentum, who had put his plot of land, however small, to profitable use (4.125–46). Flowers were always in demand in towns and so, with the money from their sale, he no doubt purchased, rather than cultivated, his basic foods.[41] It is possible too that the beekeeper elsewhere in Book 4 owned only sufficient land for successful honey production. Varro (3.6.10) had described profitable apiculture carried out by two brothers of his acquaintance on a one-*iugerum* plot. Like the Tarentine gardener (who also kept bees 4.139–141), they were involved in a type of highly specialized farming dependent on a flourishing urban market. Most small cultivators in Roman Italy, however, must have practised mixed farming in an attempt to produce as many of their basic needs as possible themselves. A more typical scene is perhaps alluded to in Book 1. 291–6, where Virgil seems to describe a poor peasant or tenant farmer and his wife.

But elsewhere, it must now be emphasized, Virgil refers to varieties of the villa estate. Thus the well-known line: 'Praise huge estates but cultivate a small one' (*laudato ingentia rura/exiguum colito*, 2.412–3), is not a recommendation of the peasant way of life but refers to relative sizes of the villa estate. 'Huge estates' were those which could not be cultivated in the intensive mode advised throughout the *Georgics*, since the amount of land was too great for the available labour force. Columella significantly cited Virgil's words while referring disparagingly to the *amplissima veterata* (1.3.10) of enormous estates which included a large acreage of unworked land. These were the infamous *latifundia* criticized by Pliny, who also refers for support to Virgil here (*N.H.* 18.35). What all the agricultural prose writers, and Virgil with them, considered to be ideal was the villa estate cultivated well and intensively.

This revelation, that the *Georgics* describe primarily the rich man's farm, while being highly important in itself also rids us of the old conundrum of why, if his audience consisted of the rich and educated class, did Virgil write about peasant cultivators. The various attempted solutions to the puzzle – that Virgil was looking back nostalgically to Rome's peasant origins, or that he looked forward to some supposed Augustan policy of agricultural restoration based on the small cultivator, or even that he participated in a 'feeling of thinking people that a simple peasant life was happier and morally healthier' (see n. 5 above) – will all become redundant. Several symbolic interpretations of the poem will then also necessarily appear misdirected. Virgil was a realist who wrote about the Italy of his own time for his own class. The conventional misconception derives partly from the ancient biographical tradition, which conceived of Virgil as the son of a peasant farmer or poor potter. Cautious scholars no longer accept this, although the tradition is still reflected uncritically in some

modern editions.[42] He was instead more likely to have belonged to a
rich landowning family. One apparent reading of the Life of Virgil
compiled by Probus, that his father's land was of sufficient size to
settle sixty veterans, may not have been far from the truth.[43] As the
son of a wealthy landowner he naturally wrote about the type of
farming he knew best. One objection to all this is that slaves are not
discussed in the *Georgics*. Villa estates were staffed by slaves and thus
omission of this topic is taken to confirm the view that Virgil's subject
is the subsistence cultivator.

> Most of Italy consisted of rough upland pasture exploited for absentee landlords of
> huge estates by slaves under a bailiff, not by those to whom the poem is addressed:
> farmers working a smallholding with their own hands. . . . . nevertheless the deliberate
> exclusion of slavery from the *Georgics* can only be seen as highly significant: the
> contrast with the contemporary assumptions of Varro, a large landowner, is striking.[44]

This article has instead shown that there is no contrast with Varro's
assumptions. Virgil's lack of any direct discussion of slavery can only
be seen as an example of his selectivity. There was nothing inherently
poetic about agricultural slavery and thus it was an obvious choice
for suppression. By convention also, slaves did not appear in serious
literature. If Virgil's own *Eclogues* are an important exception to this,
that is because they belong not to reality but to the 'imaginary world
of ideas'.[45] Moreover, it is most important to observe that Varro, and
later Columella, once they had discussed that section of the farm's
instrumentum, 'equipment' (as Varro defined slaves), make very little
direct mention of them thereafter. Their presence is instead tacitly
assumed and the landowner-reader is addressed and advised throughout in the second person singular. That is to say, were the 'slavery
sections' omitted from the works of the prose writers, the agricultural
instructions could conceivably (but of course mistakenly) be understood as directed at a peasant cultivator.

Thus we should rather take it for granted that the workforce of the
Georgics included slaves as the farm's core of staff, although, again as
the agricultural prose writers make clear, a villa estate would also
employ free men as hired labourers, on a regular basis, or as extra
help at harvest time and for other heavy tasks, and as well might lease
out part of its land to tenant farmers. It is probable that the
considerable workforce several times alluded to in the *Georgics* was
also drawn from all these sources of labour.[46]

Desecration of the Italian Countryside and the Ruin of Agriculture

> [The poem] contains passages in praise of Octavian (the future Emperor Augustus)
> which indicate poignantly the longing of the Romans for an end to the civil wars

and the return of peace. For Virgil this longing was focused on the desecration of the countryside during periods of war, and the poem is therefore related to the political and social needs of the time, to the urgent desirability of restoring Italian agriculture.

Thus Williams voices a traditional, and traditionally vague, view of the *Georgics*.[47] Yet it is difficult to comprehend how the recent civil wars could have desecrated the Italian countryside in any significant way. In 49 B.C. Caesar crossed the Rubicon and sped down the Adriatic coast, careful not to alienate people *en route*. At the time landowners were only worried about the safety of their farms, as Cicero complains, and were not preoccupied with politics. The fact that the tide of feeling throughout Italy turned rapidly in Caesar's favour shows that he did not interfere with agriculture apart from requisitioning local grain on taking up his siege position at Corfinium. Pompey conscribed some slave shepherds in Apulia. Neither act could have had much effect on Italian agriculture.[48]

Indeed, were one to think back over Roman history, no war on Italian soil could have been more deleterious to Italian agriculture than the Second Punic War, when Hannibal ravaged the countryside for some sixteen years. At least one important modern historical work has considered that period to be a major turning point in the development (and decline) of traditional Italian agriculture.[49] Yet a careful examination of the sources demonstrates that destruction was limited to certain areas only and, in any case, an occupying army has to eat and so must beware wholesale desecration.[50] Moreover, it was not easy permanently to ruin the countryside. Pliny recounts a story (*N.H.* 18.182), which shows how difficult it was to destroy an emergent cereal crop. Olives, as was noted earlier, are very hardy; and to ensure the end of a vineyard, complete eradication followed by burning is necessary, as Columella's instructions for the clearing out of an old vineyard demonstrate (3.11.4).

Nor should the resourcefulness of the Italian peasant be underestimated. Cereal yields, with or without war, fluctuated enormously from year to year. Peasants would have been inured to hardship and a precarious existence. To supplement or even replace cultivated crops in times of shortage, recourse could be had to many wild plants, even acorns, and hunting. These alternative sources of sustenance have to be emphasized, because modern historians rarely take them into consideration.[51]

Again, to argue or assume (as is sometimes done) that, with her husband on military campaign and with children to support, the Italian peasant woman was unable to cope with the family farm, is a generalization of little worth. Varro, with a certain admiration, describes how he had seen Illyrian woman 'carrying logs of firewood and children at the breast at the same time', and continues, 'this shows that *our* women who, after giving birth, lie for days under mosquito nets are worthless and contemptible' (2.10.8). The personal pronoun *nostrae* surely refers only to women of the upper, and urbanized, classes. It is clear, too, from occasional remarks by the agricultural prose writers, that children could be usefully employed in farming.[52]

There can, however, be no glossing over the effects of warfare on the individual or local scale. Farms and villages could be abandoned and burned, and people killed. And women and children would not be able permanently to replace male labour. Yet to generalize about the wholesale decline of Italian agriculture, or about profound changes to the rural economy as the result of warfare, shows little awareness of the agricultural reality and underestimates the tenacity of the peasant. A further important point is that the permanent workforce on the villa estate was made up of slaves, who were not, under normal circumstances, enrolled in the army. Thus conscription for military campaigns would not seriously interrupt work on the large farm.

With such general considerations in mind, some further events of the civil war period can be briefly examined before turning once more to the text of the *Georgics*. Such scene painting as Lucan's deserted Italian towns, crumbling houses and abandoned and overgrown fields, as a direct result of the war between Caesar and Pompey must be, then, attributed to poetic licence (*B.C.* 1.24 ff.). Yet our main historical sources are also prone to exaggeration. Famine began to oppress Rome, because grain importation by sea was blocked by Sextus Pompey and because Italian agriculture was ruined by the 'wars' (Appian, *B.C.* 5.18). Now the extent of inland Italy which fed Rome was very limited. It was a fact about the ancient world that, since land transport was so costly, a town's productive agricultural territory was necessarily confined. Each area had to be self-sufficient, unless it enjoyed easy access to the sea (as did Rome), where transport was much less expensive. Thus if it is true that because of war Rome was unable to procure supplies from its hinterland, this cannot be taken to show that Italian agriculture as a whole had been interrupted. Moreover, since Sextus Pompey's blockade continued for the best part of six years (42–36 B.C.), and Rome did not starve, it is probably a considerable exaggeration even that agriculture within the city's *territorium* had failed.

But, in any case, what were the 'wars' to which Appian referred? His previous account concentrates on Antony's siege of Mutina in Cisalpine Gaul (*B.C.* 3.49 ff.). Yet this campaign was clearly very localized. Then he describes the proscriptions by the newly-formed second triumvirate (42 B.C.). Many rich enemies of Antony, Lepidus, and Octavian were killed, or fled to join Sextus Pompey, and their properties were seized (ibid. 4.5 ff.). Yet new owners took over their estates and agriculture continued productively, as we can deduce from the report that the beneficiaries from the proscriptions were alarmed for their new lands when a truce was made with Sextus Pompey in 39 B.C. (ibid. 5.74).

Otherwise that treaty was greeted with rejoicing in Rome and Italy, since, according to Appian, it heralded the end of a variety of ills, including the desertion of slaves, the cessation of agriculture, and, especially, famine. But Sextus Pompey's blockade of grain supplies could only have affected Rome and perhaps one or two coastal cities unable to be fed completely from their territories, not the whole of Italy. Appian states that Sextus also made raids on the coasts of Italy; but raids are by definition localized and temporary affairs and were also resisted by Octavian.[53]

Perhaps the desertion of slaves was more pertinent. This would affect the villa estate, Virgil's central subject. Yet it cannot be determined whether the 30,000 slaves who crewed Pompey's fleet and were captured by Octavian in 36 B.C., were agricultural slaves.[54] From Appian's account they would seem to have been a mixture of both urban and rural, mainly from the eighteen most flourishing towns of Italy, whose land had been promised to the triumvirs' veterans (*B.C.* 4.85) A number also came from Sicily (ibid. 5.13). Again, therefore, it cannot be right to generalize from this about Italy's agriculture.

It was when the news came out that the land of the eighteen finest Italian towns was under threat of confiscation that Lucius Antonius, the trumvir's brother, began to make political capital out of the discontent against Octavian. Those destined to lose land were joined by others who feared similar treatment. 'Thus almost the whole of Italy rose up', in Appian's words, against Octavian (ibid. 5.27). But that again is certain exaggeration, which perhaps stemmed originally from Lucius' anti-Octavian propaganda. From Appian's account we hear that Octavian's enemies were soon confined mainly to one town, Perusia, and dealt with rapidly and effectively in the winter of 41/40 B.C. (ibid. 5.33 ff.). 'So ended the war which had promised to be long drawn our and most harsh to Italy' (ibid. 5.49). But as it was, its effects could not have been far reaching.

Those rich landowners, anxious about their properties, who joined Lucius, did not, we must assume, destroy their own vines, olives, and livestock. In the autumn of 41 B.C., when the crisis was reaching a head, it is possible that, in the uncertainty many of them did not sow

cereals, especially if they had sufficient supplies in their granaries
from previous years. But a year's fallow in some areas could not have
had a lasting deleterious effect on Italian agriculture. Indeed, of those
originally threatened with confiscation, senators certainly were later
excused (Dio, 48.8.5), and many other influential men succeeded in
retaining their lands. If in the end small holders suffered from
confiscation as much as, if not more than the rich, the allotment of
their land to veterans meant only the replacing of one set of small
cultivators with another – and not the destruction of agriculture.[55]

After distribution to veterans, there is no evidence of a diminution
in prosperity of the areas concerned. It used to be thought that the
newly settled veteran was likely to fail as a farmer and that the land
he took over declined rapidly in productivity; but recent studies have
done much to dispel such preconceptions, which were based mainly
on the understandable laments of the dispossessed shepherds in the
Eclogues.[56] In the *Res Gestae* Augustus, looking back over his reign
with historical perspective, could state that his various veteran
settlement programmes had been a success (28; cf.15.3;16.1). Despite
the tone of self-glorification, there is no substantial evidence to counter
or disprove his statement. Italian agriculture, especially as practised
by the rich, continued to flourish.

It has been necessary to explore in some detail these events of the
confused period of the civil wars in order to demonstrate the fragile
basis of traditional generalizations about the effects of war on the
Italian countryside and agriculture. Virgil, it has been argued above,
described the contemporary Italian scene in the *Georgics*, with special
emphasis on the villa estate. Thus we should expect to find by and
large a portrayal of flourishing agriculture. And we do.

Nothing could be clearer than the *laus Italiae* in Book 2 (136–176).
Especially worthy of a note is the praise of Italian cities (2.155–7),
which is corrective of Lucan's bleak view, or of any exaggerations
that might be based on the distribution to veterans of lands belonging
to Italy's finest *oppida*. Varro also had spoken in such glowing terms
in his treatise on agriculture published in the mid-thirties B.C.: 'You
who have travelled through many lands; have you ever seen any land
more fully cultivated than Italy? .... What useful product is there
which does not only grow but also flourish in Italy? What emmer
wheat shall I compare to that of Campania, what bread wheat to that
of Apulia, what wine to Falernian, what oil to Venafran?' (1.2.3,6).
Of course, Varro, like Virgil, wrote from the standpoint of the rich
echelons of society and he described principally the continued success
of the villa estates. But there can now be no doubt that his eulogistic

appreciation found recognizable reflection in the contemporary agricultural situation.[57]

Virgil's encomium of Italy (2.136–176) throws into high relief in a sustained fashion what is always latent, and often obvious, throughout the *Georgics*. In fact the flimsy case for desecration of the Italian countryside rests ultimately on one short passage, which occurs at the end of Book 1 among the catalogue of troubles which followed from the assassination of Julius Caesar:

> . . . . . to the plough
> no due honour is given, fields are unkempt since the farmers have been taken away
> and curved sickles are transformed into straight hard swords.
>
> (1.506–508)

In particular he lays emphasis on the wretched state of Italian farming, contrasting the miserable conditions of the battle-ravaged countryside (506–8) with the potential beauty and glory of ordered agriculture, the theme with which so much of this book has been concerned.[58]

But the context of Virgil's emotive words is the whole world, not Italy. As a result of Caesar's death, according to the poetic hyperbole, wars rage throughout the world from East (the Euphrates) to the West (Germany).

Williams is right to call these references to wars indefinite,[59] but he is wrong to specify Italy as the country where agriculture was ruined. When Virgil writes 'the whole world is in arms, neighbouring cities everywhere fight with each other, nowhere is due respect given to the plough', that is a generalized and highly emotional statement and every element of it indefinite. It comes as a climax of a poetic 'heaping-up' of laments, which had included among other wonders a list of portents (469–88). It cannot be taken as a realisitic picture of the state of Italy's, or any other nation's, agriculture. Clearly indicative, however, of the conventional and inverted interpretation of this passage is Williams's reference to the other agricultural description of Book 1, apart from this short passage, as 'potential' rather than real.

Restoration of Italian Agriculture

It used to be thought that Octavian/Augustus was interested in the restoration of Italian agriculture and thus that Virgil was following some official directive in writing the *Georgics*. Such a policy might then be hinted at in Virgil's reference to Maecenas' 'commands' (3.41). However, it has since been pointed out by historians that Augustus did very little to help Italian agriculture.[60] Thus interpreta-

tion has changed, Maecenas' *iussa* are toned down, and the writing
of the *Georgics* has less to do with agriculture than with restoration
of Roman morality:

The attunement of the *Georgics* to future Augustan policy was more moral than
agricultural. Nor need we press the words 'your behest, no easy one, Maecenas'
(3.41): whatever encouragement may have come from the statesman, its inspiration
is clearly literary and personal ....[61]

This is a clear case, it would seem, of a historical argument's effect
on literary interpretation. Yet then how can we account for Horace's
attribution of the prosperity of Italian agriculture to Augustus in the
last poem of Book 4 of the *Odes*? Was it merely an indication of
imperial propaganda, which some critics discern more clearly in Book
4 than in the previous three books, akin perhaps to the partisan
historical account of Velleius Paterculus; or was it even a verbal
anticipation of the *Ara Pacis*?[62]

. The truth, however, is less extreme. Firstly, Italian agriculture did
not, as has been argued, require restoration. Thus Augustus did not
need to put into effect an agricultural 'policy' in the same explicit
way as he introduced moral reform. Yet it is wrong, on the other
hand, to deny completely that he fostered the continuation and growth
of Italian agricultural prosperity already in existence.

During his reign Augustus established, or re-established, some 40
veteran colonies and settled other veterans in many *municipia* in Italy.
Imperial money flowed into these towns to construct public buildings,
theatres, and such important utilitarian structures as aqueducts.
Augustus understood the key to a successful Italian rural economy:
prosperous towns that stimulated the agricultural productivity of their
territoria. He also repaved roads, built and repaired bridges. Transport
of produce was thus facilitated, no doubt helped also by the campaign
against brigandage.[63] In these ways Augustus was concerned to
increase the well-being of rural Italy; but they were the sort of
methods which could only succeed in an already flourishing situation.
Agriculture was already in full swing in Italy and Augustus did not
have to intervene in any direct way as, for example, he did in Egypt,
where he set soldiers to clean out irrigation canals.[64] Thus Horace's
or Velleius Paterculus' attribution of agricultural prosperity to
Augustus can be seen as pardonable exaggeration with a core of truth.
Had Virgil lived longer and written the *Georgics* later, his *laudes
Italiae* would have glowed with even greater enthusiasm.

Conclusion

Virgil ensured that his agricultural information was correct. Accuracy
of detail contributes largely to the realistic picture of the Italian

countryside as a whole. Thus can be understood the otherwise perplexing fact that the later agricultural prose writers, Pliny and Columella, cite Virgil, even more often than Cato or Varro, as a source of agricultural knowledge. No doubt Columella hoped to make his long work more entertaining and literary by the inclusion of excerpts from the *Georgics*, but that cannot explain the seriousness with which Virgil's authority is adduced; and Pliny cites Virgil without quoting the relevant verses, and thus does not seem so interested in literary adornment. Columella once points out (4.11.1), from his own considerable experience, that Virgil was mistaken, but is careful to show that the error was shared by earlier prose writers as well. Then again, as noted above, Virgil provides valuable new information, and his originality in these cases seems reinforced by Columella's observation (3.10.20) that some sound Virgilian advice occurs in no other written source. We must assume that estate owners who read the prose treatises also considered Virgil a reliable source of agricultural information.

But practicality apart, there are other important reasons to accept and attend seriously to the precise agricultural content of the *Georgics*. Only thus, as has been pointed out, can be kept in check some of the more fanciful and generalized overall interpretations of the poem. Dismissal of the agriculture liberates a dangerously wide-ranging hunt for symbolic meaning. Instead 'surface' and 'depth' must work (and be considered) together, if the poem is to succeed as a unified whole.

Virgil certainly explored, in no necessarily consistent way, the varied symbolic associations which the countryside evoked in the poetry of the time. These associations are given more credibility and vitality in the *Georgics* than in other Augustan poems, since they depend on, and grow out of a realistic, rather than idealized, view of the countryside and agricultural activities. Moreover, several of these topics such as the historical-moralizing tradition of praising the past, when Rome was supposedly self-sufficient, not reliant on imported foodstuffs, when urban avarice, sloth, and luxury did not exist, and when ancestral moral and religious values were focused in the countryside belong also to the tradition of the agricultural prose writers, as always an important key to the correct understanding of the *Georgics*.[65]

Then, too, another cogent reason for closer attention to the agricultural detail of the poem lies in the proper appreciation of how Virgil succeeds in bringing to life very precise agricultural terms. In other words, it is the very ability to incorporate technical terms and turn them into poetry, which makes the poem so astonishing. This appears constantly but is rarely recognized. In lines 97–8 of Book 1,

for example, *proscindere* is the technical term for the first ploughing
(see Varro, 1.29.2), and *in obliquum* refers knowledgeably to the tilting
of the plough (Columella, 2.2.25; Pliny, *N.H.* 18.178). These two
terms are interwoven with words which personify the earth, *suscitat*
and *terga*; while the whole hard job of breaking the compact soil is
emphasized by 's', 'c' and 't' sounds. It is the startling poetry at this
immediate level, which is often neglected during the search for deeper
meanings.

In conclusion we can return to reconsider and recast Seneca's
judgement of the *Georgics*. Virgil did not sacrifice accuracy to audience
delectation. Instead it is that very agricultural accuracy which gives
life and strength to the poem *and* (therefore) delight to its readers.

NOTES

1. Seneca *Ep.* 86.15 'ut ait Vergilius noster, qui non quid verissime, sed quid decentissime
diceretur aspexit, nec agricolas docere voluit, sed legentes delectare.'

2. 'Pertinent': L.P. Wilkinson, 'The Georgics' in *The Cambridge History of Classical
Literature II: Latin Literature*, E. J. Kenney, W. V. Clausen (eds.) (Cambridge, 1982), p. 322.
This article, which contains Wilkinson's latest thoughts on the *Georgics* (others are to be found
in his recent translation of the poem for Penguin Classics), is by no means a mere summary of
his earlier book *The Georgics of Virgil, A Critical Survey*, (Cambridge, 1969). There (p. 15) he
referred to Seneca's comment as 'obvious'. 'Wise': R. D. Williams, *Virgil, The Eclogues and
Georgics*² (New York, 1983), introduction, p.x. (This is the most recent English edition of the
Georgics.) For Petrarch's use of the *Georgics* as a practical handbook: Wilkinson, op. cit. (1969),
p. 290 f.

3. Williams, op.cit., introduction, p.x. (It is not clear why he chooses to describe the didactic
material as 'intellectual'.)

4. M. J. Putnam, *Virgil's Poem of the Earth: Studies in the Georgics* (Princeton, 1979), p. 7.

5. Wilkinson, op. cit. (1982), p. 323 and p. 320.

6. Ibid., p. 320., cf. idem, op. cit., (1969), p. 54. See also K. Quinn, *Texts and Contexts,
The Roman Writers and Their Audience* (London, 1979), p. 134, who assumes that Virgil is
describing the world of the small subsistence farmer.

7. Williams, op. cit., introduction, pp. x–xi.

8. See for example the review of recent studies of the *Georgics* by K. W. Gransden in *JRS*
72 (1982), 207–209 and especially J. Griffin, 'Haec Super Arvorum Culta', *CR* 31 (1981), 23–
37. For the development of the now orthodox literary approach to the *Georgics*: Brooks Otis,
Virgil, A Study in Civilized Poetry, (Oxford, 1964), p. 145: 'It is only very recently that some
critics – I think especially of Burck, Klingner and Büchner – have refused to treat Virgil with
such naïveté (*sc.* reading the *Georgics* as a poem about agriculture) and have tried to penetrate
the deeper meaning of the poem....' He provides bibliographical details on the history of
interpretation of the *Georgics* in Appendix 6, p. 407. See also Wilkinson (1969), p. 71 ff. and p.
314 f. Readers of *Greece & Rome* have been well served with articles on the *Georgics*: cf. the
contributions of L. A. S. Jermyn in *G & R.* 18 (1949), 49–69; 20 (1951), 26–37 and 49–59; an
early article by Wilkinson, 19 (1950), 19–28; and more recently J. Griffin, 26 (1979), 61–80.

9. The only very approximate dates that we have of the publication of the three agricultural
treatises are: first half of the 2nd century B.C. (Cato), second half of the first century B.C.
(Varro), and middle of the 1st century A.D. (Columella). Columella (3.3.3) mentions Seneca as
the owner of exceptionally productive vineyards near Nomentum. Seneca may have been one
of Columella's patrons, although that need not mean that Seneca ever read his or any other
available agricultural manual. See: M. T. Griffin, *Seneca, A Philosopher in Politics* (Oxford,
1976), pp. 290f.

10. We know, that Aegialus, a freedman, gained a considerable reputation for successful farming near Liternum (Pliny, *N.H.* 14.49).

11. Cf. Food and Agriculture Organization of the United Nations (FAO), *Modern Olive Growing* (Rome, 1973), pp. 27f.

12. Yet it is quite possible that Virgil himself refers to this supposedly new method at *Georgics* 2.30–1 (and see note ad loc. in Conington's edition). The poet expresses his astonishment that such a replanting system could work – *mirabile dictu*. One further difficulty in comprehending Seneca is caused by textual corruption (*Ep.* 86.14), where he is describing what sort of olives are treated in this way. The usual reading of editors appears to mean that the olives are healthy and productive. It would seem senseless then to prune so radically and then transplant.

13. Seneca speaks of keeping the cold and wind from the roots. Cato advises the firming of the soil around the roots at 28.2; 49.1. A serious danger is that otherwise the roots will become waterlogged when it rains: ibid. 61.2.

14. Ancient agricultural advice: Cato 40.1: Varro 1.30; Columella 5.9.6–7. Modern advice: FAO, op. cit., pp. 27f. Modern, yet traditional, practice is also to transplant cuttings (usually into a nursery) immediately after the winter pruning. Virgil perhaps alludes to this by his stress on *putator* 'pruner' (*G.* 2.28).

15. Varro had clearly stated that in the case of slow-growing trees, such as the olive, it takes too long to grow them from seed and thus advises propagation from cuttings (1.41.6). Virgil makes exactly the same point, but Seneca misunderstands.

16. Cf. M. S. Spurr, 'The Cultivation of Millet in Roman Italy', *PBSR* 51 (1983), 1–15.

17. It would seem also that Seneca is disputing Virgil's statement that beans were a spring crop. Yet, where winters were severe (inland hill and mountain zones and the Po valley), they had to be spring-sown. In warmer areas there was a choice, although it was generally acknowledged that spring-sown yielded less than autumn-sown beans (Columella 2.10.9). Pliny the Elder considered, rightly perhaps, that Virgil was thinking particularly of the Po valley (*N.H.* 18.120)

18. There are, in fact, only very few real agricultural 'mistakes' in the *Georgics*: he is incorrect to state that repeated ploughing of poor soils causes loss of moisture, as Williams points out in his note on 1.70, following K. D. White, 'Virgil's Knowledge of Arable Farming' *Proceedings of the Virgil Society* 7 (1967–68), 11–22. But it is not usually explained that this was what was generally believed at the time (Columella 2.4.11; Pliny, *N.H.* 18.242), and thus the error can hardly be ascribed just to Virgil. Other mistakes: pear trees can not bear apples, nor plum trees cornels, after grafting (2.33–4; but again a shared error: cf. Varro 1.40.5). He recounts wondrously how mares in Asia Minor are impregnated by wind (3.269–75) but even Columella was prepared to credit similar stories (6.27.7). In Book 4 the queen bee is a *rex*, and Virgil advocates *Bugonia* as an effective method of reproducing bees. Yet, again, both were common, if not universal, ancient misconceptions. The female sex of the queen bee was only decisively proved in the mid-18th century: K. Thomas, *Man and the Natural World* (London, 1983), p. 62 n.

19. See for example, G. Kramer, 'The Didactic Tradition in Virgil's Georgics', in A. J. Boyle (ed.), *Virgil's Ascraean Song. Ramus Essays on the Georgics* (Melbourne, 1979), pp. 7–21. (This is one of the new works reviewed by Griffin [n. 8 above], who incidentally approves of Seneca's judgement on Virgil.) See also Brooks Otis, op. cit., p. 148.

20. Wilkinson, op. cit. (1969), pp. 67f. and *Virgil, The Georgics* (Harmondsworth, 1982), p. 95.

21. Williams, op. cit., p. 172.

22. See E. Rawson, 'The Introduction of Logical Organization in Roman Prose Literature,' *PBSR* 46 (1978), p. 14f. For a review of previous judgements on the worth of Varro's treatment, whether from the agricultural or compositional point of view: J. E. Skydsgaard, *Varro the Scholar, Studies in the First Book of Varro's de re rustica* (Copenhagen, 1968), pp. 89 ff.

23. Rawson, op. cit., argues that Latin prose composition on a systematic basis, of the sort now taken for granted, was a gradual development, certainly not complete by Varro's time, although he contributed significantly to its progress. Thus to judge work of that period by later ideals is unjustified.

24. See M. L. West (ed.), *Hesiod, Works and Days* (Oxford, 1978), pp. 53ff.; 252f.

25. Thus, too, when Lucretius says (1.926–950) that he uses poetry to enliven and make

palatable the dry reasoning of philosophy, as doctors honey the cup that contains medicine, he does not mean that he will thereby sacrifice the serious didactic content to poetic imagination. Poetic digressions and 'purple passages' enhance the directly informative sections and make them more effective.

26. Wilkinson, op. cit. (1969), pp. 223–5 and (1982), p. 31f.

27. For a detailed account of Virgil's adaption of the works of Aratus, Eratosthenes, and Theophrastus: Wilkinson (1969), pp. 234 ff., 242 ff. Some have worried that the rooks which Virgil describes (following Aratus) were uncommon in Italy but see T. F. Royds, *The Beasts, Birds and Bees of Virgil* (Oxford, 1918), pp. 40f.

28. Wilkinson, op. cit. (1969), p. 245: 'But there is no known predecessor to Virgil's selective and discriminating list, and it may of course represent his own taste. At any rate he has diverged here from Theophrastus. . . .' The fullest ancient account of Italian wines is given by Pliny the Elder (*N.H.* 14.20–76). Varro's comment on Theophrastus is noteworthy: 'His books are more suited to philosophy students than farmers' (1.5.2).

29. For their use of sources: H. Gummerus, *Der römische Gutsbetreib als wirtschaftlicher Organismus nach den Werken des Cato, Varro und Columella*, Klio Beiheft 5 (Leipzig, 1906, reprint edn. Aalen, 1979). For Varro in particular: Skydsgaard, op. cit., K. D. White, 'Roman Agricultural Writers I: Varro and his Predecessors', in *Aufstieg und Niedergang der römischen Welt 1.4*, ed. H. Temporini (Berlin, 1973), pp. 439–97.

30. The conventional view is that, as a consequence of the growth of slave-staffed villa estates and the eradication of the peasantry in the second century B.C. onwards, cereal cultivation was replaced by the cultivation of vines and olives. See for example: A. J. Toynbee, *Hannibal's Legacy*, 2 Vols. (London, 1965), 247 ff., 286 ff., and *passim*.

31. Pliny the Elder said that one of the main functions of asses was ploughing (*N.H.* 8.167). Economical to feed (Columella 7.1.2), the ass would have been inexpensive and its forage not difficult to find even on the least prosperous peasant farm.

32. Cato and Varro both concern themselves with rotation patterns but do not treat all the possibilities envisaged by Virgil. This could indicate Virgil's own experience. Pliny noted Virgil's advice on fallowing but remarked that this was possible only on a large enough farm. Otherwise a rudimentary rotation system should be adopted (*N.H.* 18.187). No doubt many small holders continued to grow grain year after year on the same land, with resulting low yields.

33. Varro 1.23.5 refers to the making of such a harrow (a 'drag' would be a better term, since it is mentioned by Virgil and Columella [2.17.4] as an implement only for levelling ploughed fields), without describing its use. See K. D. White, *Agricultural Implements of the Roman World*, (Cambridge, 1967), p. 147. Virgil's reference to its function may again be the result of personal knowledge.

34. Spurr, op. cit., 9.

35. Various other references to fencing sown fields (e.g. 1:270–1; 2.436) show that Virgil was considering a farm with a combination of cereal cultivation and livestock farming. The livestock provides manure for various crop rotations (1.80) and in return will need forage crops and pasture. Fences will have to be constructed as part of the livestock management – to keep the animals in, or out of, fields at different times.

36. Pliny, *N.H.* 18.295 and Columella 2.19.2.

37. A convenient summary of the reasons for horse breeding is found in Varro 2.7.15: cavalry, carriages, racing, and breeding. Cf. Virgil 3.72–208. They were not employed for ploughing until the Middle Ages: C. Parain, 'The Evolution of Agricultural Technique', in *The Cambridge Economic History of Europe*, M. M. Postan (ed.), i. 142 ff. Virgil's long passage on horses in Book 3 is probably the most obvious proof that his work concerns the agriculture of the upper classes.

38. It has recently been argued that the originator of the agricultural didactic poem, Hesiod, was a wealthy peasant: P. Millet, 'Hesiod and his World', *PPhS* 30 (1984), 84–107, but comparison will show that Virgil's farming was carried out on a much larger scale.

39. E.g. 2.416.

40. E.g. Strabo 5.2.1; Pliny, *N.H.* 18.178; Horace, *Odes* 3.6.38–9.

41. Flowers: Cato 8.2; Varro 1.16.3; Columella 10.308; It is clear that the *dapibus inemptis*

(4.133) of Virgil's gardener refer only to fruits and vegetables. He must have purchased grain and wine, for which we are told his land was unsuited.

42. E.g. Williams, op. cit., introduction, p. vii.

43. P. A. Brunt, *Italian Manpower 225 B.C. - A.D. 14* (Oxford, 1970), p. 329; C. G. Hardie, 'Virgil', *OCD*² (Oxford, 1970), p. 1123. If the reading *sexaginta veterani* is credited, and if the veterans received an average of 35 iugera apiece (L. Keppie, *Colonisation and Veteran Settlement in Italy 47 –14 B.C.*, British School at Rome (London, 1983), p. 90), then Virgil's father was a rich man. Not all the 2,000-odd *iugera* would have been included in one farm. Instead the pattern of landholding was to own several estates, of, perhaps, *ca.* 200 *iugera* (Varro 1.19.1), often in the same area. An example often cited is Sextus Roscius of Ameria in Umbria, who owned thirteen farms in the Tiber Valley in the vicinity of his home town: Cic. *S. Rosc.* 15;20. A poem sometimes ascribed to Virgil, *Catalepton* 8, speaks of his father missing Mantua and Cremona after his expropriation. Perhaps his estates were located in the territories of both towns.

44. Wilkinson, op. cit. (1982), p. 22f. It can be noted here that Wilkinson's attempt to back up the conventional notions with the statement that in the Po valley and the Naples area the small holder still flourished (n. 6 above) is, as it stands, misleading. Archaeological surveys over the last fifteen years have shown it is likely that small farms remained numerous throughout many areas of Italy. And we know too from archaeology that there were plenty of agricultural villas in the Po valley and Campania. The point of departure for such evidence remains the important article: M. W. Frederiksen, 'The Contribution of Archaeology to the Agrarian Problem in the Gracchan Period', *Dialoghi di Archeologia* 4–5 (1970–1), 330–357.

45. G. Williams, *Tradition and Originality in Roman Poetry* (Oxford, 1968), pp. 294f., 303 ff.

46. Varro 1.17 for slaves, hired labourers, and (probably) tenant farmers. Cf. Columella 1.7. References in the *Georgics* to labour include: 1.210 *exercete viri* which will refer to ploughmen, either slave or hired; 1.259 ff. the sort of tasks that can be done by the various members of the workforce (cf. *alii*, 1.264), which resemble the prose writers' admonitions to keep the labourers always at work, even if the weather is too bad to go out: e.g. Cato, 2.3; 39.2. Work can be done after dark (Cato 37.3, Columella 11.2.90) and before light (Varro 1.36) in winter. Besides not working, another danger was that the agricultural slave might run away, even from the most vigilant owner's estate (Cato 2.2) and this is referred to by Virgil at 1.287. 1.291 f. perhaps refer to a tenant couple (and the Hesiodic *nudus ara, sere nudus*, 1.299, suits such a picture), whereas the reapers of 1.316 were probably a mixture of slaves and hired labourers (cf. Varro 1.17.3). Slave girls to carry out the spinning (1.390) came under the supervision of the slave bailiff's female partner, as Columella later made clear (12.3.6). The planting of vines was (and is) a very hard job, because the earth must be dug to a depth of up to four feet, depending on the nature of the terrain (Columella 3.13.8). It was probably usual to hire labourers for this operation, since Columella refers to a *conductor*, a 'contractor' (ibid. 3.13.12). Thus Virgil's reference to the establishment of a vineyard with 'much expense' (*multa mercede*, 2.62) should be taken literally. Yet the 'digger' referred to at 2.264 is probably a slave, as is the *vinitor* (2.417). A vinedresser was a skilled and valued slave, but a *fossor* also could be skilled (thus the formula *optimus fossor*, Columella 11.1.12). The division of labour on a slave-staffed villa estate was quite marked (see especially Columella ibid.).

47. Williams, op. cit., introduction, pp. x–xi.

48. Caesar, *B.C.* 1.18.4;1.24.2.

49. Toynbee, op. cit., *passim*.

50. Brunt, op. cit., pp. 269–77.

51. On alternative sources of food see the chapter 'Wild and Cultivated Plants' in J. M. Frayn, *Subsistence Farming in Roman Italy* (London, 1979), pp. 57–72. Virgil mentions hunting: 1.271, 307–9; and refers to collection of berries, and sometimes acorns, as food: 1.305–6; 1.148; 1.159.

52. Children's work could include: vine trimming, cutting back ferns, hen keeping (Columella 11.2.44; 2.2. 13; 8.2.7) and shepherding (Varro 2.10.1)

53. Appian, *B.C.* 5.19;56 (raids in the south of Italy). After Octavian recovered Sardinia he 'strengthened the coast of Italy with many garrisons', ibid. 5.80. Even if, as Cicero said in

another context, merely the threat of hostile attack caused men to flee their fields (*De Imp. Pomp.* 16), that would mean only a very temporary setback for agriculture.

54. The figures comes from *Res Gestae* (25.1) and may well be exaggerated, since Augustus represents the war against Sextus Pompey as a war entirely against slaves and pirates.

55. Brunt, op. cit., pp. 330–343f. Brunt believes that the Perusine War was more widespread than is argued here (cf. p. 290.f.). But the only other hard evidence is the sacking of Sentinum and the capitulation of Nursia, small towns in comparison with Perusia (Dio, 48.13).

56. For a typical comment about the failure of veterans as farmers: Wilkinson, op. cit. (1982), p. 320. On contemporary laments see, for example, Williams, op. cit., p. 95 on *Eclogue* 1.70–2; Keppie, op. cit., p. 101.

57. To explain Varro's enthusiasm some commentators consider that his praise of Italy belongs to a much earlier draft of the work, since they believe in an agricultural crisis in the thirties B.C. See J. Heurgon, *Varron, Economie Rurale: Livre Premier* (Paris, 1978), p. 105. Editors of Virgil will point out that the *laus Italiae* was a well-established traditional literary feature which had nothing to do with reality. A recent acute study shows, perhaps rightly, that the passage contains some pessimistic elements in the form of moral admonition against violence and the pursuit of luxury: R. F. Thomas, *Landscapes and People in Roman Poetry. The Ethnographical Tradition, PCPhS* Supp. Vol. 7 (1982), pp. 39 ff. But such moralizing is also part of the agricultural manual tradition (see n. 65 below).

58. Williams, op. cit., p. 156. Cf. the long-standing unchallenged words of T.E. Page, *Virgil, Bucolics and Georgics*, (Leicester, 1974; first edition 1898), p. 242, ... 'The words admirably connect the whole lament for the ruin of Italy with the subject of the *Georgics*'.

59. Williams, op. cit., p. 156 (on line 1.509).

60. E.g. A. H. M. Jones, *Augustus* (London, 1977), p. 142 f.

61. Wilkinson, op. cit. (1982), p. 320.

62. Horace, *Odes* 4.15.5: *fruges et agris rettulit uberes*; cf. Vell. Pat., 2.89.4. The *Ara Pacis* was dedicated in 13 B.C. (the year in which it is quite conceivable that Horace wrote 4.15), although not 'opened' until 9 B.C. For an interpretation of the monument as a piece of Augustan propaganda: S. Weinstock, 'Pax Augusta and the Ara Pacis', *JRS* 50 (1960), 44–58;cf. J. M. C. Toynbee, 'The Ara Pacis Reconsidered' *JRS* 51 (1961), 153–6. For Horace as propagandist: C. O. Brink, *Horace on Poetry, Epistles Book II. The Letters to Augustus and Florus*, (Cambridge, 1982), pp. 523 ff.

63. On Augustus' settlement of veterans see: Brunt (1971), pp. 326 ff. and Keppie, op. cit., pp. 115 ff., for works of public utility, including roads. The campaign against brigandage: Suet. *Aug.* 32.1.

64. Suet. *Aug* 18.2. After continual difficulties with the grain supply to Rome, Augustus reached a settlement which suited grain merchants, the Roman poor, and arable farmers (*aratores*). In the context, the 'farmers' were surely Italian and local to Rome, and it could have been that the cultivation of cereals in the environs of the city was declining because of growing imports. Although the precise details are unclear, it does seem that, in this local and particular case only, Augustus intervened directly in Italian agriculture: Suet. *Aug.* 42.

65. Cato, *praef.*: farming is better than all other pursuits, as our ancestors rightly judged. Varro, 1.13.6–7: modestly-sized agricultural villas are better (as our ancestors thought) than luxurious and parasitic suburban villas; 1.69.3: violence is endemic in the city of Rome; 2 *praef*: luxury and idleness in towns; Rome relies on imports; farmers have left their land for the easy life at Rome; 3.1.1–5: the country is sacred to the gods and country life more noble and traditional. All these moral topics are dealt with also by Pliny, *N.H.* 1.1–22, and in the long preface of Columella.

I should like to thank Malcolm Davies and Elizabeth Rawson for their valuable criticism of an earlier draft of this article.

ADDITIONAL NOTE (1989)

Page 73 line 40
For '1.75–6' read '1.176–7'

Page 74 line 31
For '2.56 ff.' read '2.63 f.'

Page 74 line 37
  For '2.94–7' read '2.95–7'

Page 74 line 41
  For '2.113' read '2.114'

Page 75 line 1
  For '2.113–135' read '2.115–135'

Page 75 line 3
  For 'praising Italy, and mentioning' read 'praising Italy, mentioning'

Page 75 line 32
  For '2.222 f.' read '2.224 f.'

Page 76 line 40
  For '2.203 ff.' read '2.207 ff.'

Page 79 line 4
  For '3.6.10' read '3.16.10'

Page 83 line 25
  For '5.13' read '5.131'

Page 83 line 38
  For 'our' read 'out'

Page 85 line 24
  For 'due respect' read 'due honour'

Page 88 lines 22–3
  For '(This is the most recent English edition of the Georgics.)' read '(R. F. Thomas, *Virgil*, *Georgics*, 2 vols. (Cambridge, 1988), has appeared since the original publication of this article. Thomas attends closely to the Roman prose agricultural authors, essential for the proper understanding of the *Georgics*.)'

Page 89 line 12
  For '49.1' read '49.2'

Page 91 line 32
  For '1.287. 1.291 f.' read '1.286. 1.291 ff.'

Page 92 line 2
  For '16' read '15'

Page 92 line 41
  For '42' read '42.3'

THE FOURTH *GEORGIC*, VIRGIL, AND ROME

By JASPER GRIFFIN

> The last word has not yet been spoken on the relation of the
> second half to the first half, and to the Georgics as a whole.
> (F. Klingner, *Virgils Georgica* (Zürich, 1963), p. 161 = *Virgil*
> (Zürich, 1967), p. 298)

Never were more prophetic words penned than these of Friedrich
Klingner. Many and various have been the interpretations put forth since
then, and some of them have been very strange indeed. The reader who
has duly confronted Coleman, Otis, Segal, Bradley, Wender, Wilkinson,
Wankenne, Coleiro, Hardie, Joudoux, Wormell, Otis again, Parry, Putnam, Cova, Chomarat, and Stehle,[1] feels dismay; perhaps despair. For
some, the point of the Aristaeus and Orpheus episodes is political
propaganda (so Coleiro: Gallus could have survived had he humbled
himself like Aristaeus, the moral being the duty of subordination to the
Princeps; so, rather differently, Joudoux: the poem is propaganda for the
supremacy of Octavian, in terms of the threefold Indo-European structure
of Dumézil). For others, it is moral (so, for instance, Wender: Orpheus
turned away from the hard and morally ambiguous farmer's life, as lived
by Aristaeus; Aristaeus gets bugonia as his reward, while Orpheus is
dismembered and scattered in order to fertilize the earth); or religious (so
Chomarat: the experience of Aristaeus is presented under the schema of
initiation into a mystery religion);[2] or political and moral (so Wormell and
Otis: Aristaeus 'stands for the sinful self-destruction, atonement and
revival of the Roman people'; life emerges from death, 'in political terms,
the Augustan restoration from the anarchy of civil war'; 'Aristaeus, it is to
be presumed [*sic*], was induced to heed the lesson').

Some find very general solutions indeed; perhaps Virgil 'posits existence as made up of this strange mixture of tragic and comic, human and
divine, of death and birth ... serving as complements and inextricably
intertwined' (Putnam); Castiglioni[3] and Klingner give accounts not dis-
similar. For others, the answer is more specific, one might almost say more
specifically modern. Thus for Bradley, 'the myth of Orpheus provides an
alternative view of culture'; while Aristaeus stands for 'the work culture',[4]
the control of Orpheus is exerted through play, not work, 'not productivity but creativity', and so the work culture inevitably destroys Orpheus
because his existence is an intolerable affront to it; he is doomed 'at the
hands of a repressive civilization'—represented, rather to our surprise, by
the Maenads of Thrace. Others have taken the episode as being primarily

concerned with poetry. The eloquent paper of Adam Parry shows us Orpheus' grief for Eurydice becoming eternal song, and 'the song in turn becomes the condition for the recreation of life': the cruel and dark sides of nature, revealed in the rest of the *Georgics*, can be faced and comprehended only in song, in art. In a more specific way, Hardie sees the poem as about Virgil's own quest for the inspiration and poetic power to write epic. Having killed Orpheus within himself, Virgil as Aristaeus goes down to consult his own *anima*, makes the sacrifice of his excess of ambition, and regains the honey of poetic inspiration. Nor, finally, are those lacking who argue that the episode may be virtually, or entirely, unconnected with the rest of the *Georgics*,[5] added either as a lament for Gallus (Coleman), or simply following the fashion for epyllia (Richter). The last word of this whirlwind doxography[6] shall be the magisterial *non liquet* of Wilkinson:

To sum up, I believe that Virgil would have thought an *aition* for 'Bugonia' a suitable ending for a book on bees, Aristaeus a suitable hero for this *aition*, and epyllion a suitable form for it. He would have looked for a contrasting story to insert in his epyllion. Why he chose Orpheus for this is more a matter of speculation, and also to what extent either the Orpheus passage or (more plausibly) the Aristaeus epyllion has a symbolic meaning for the interpretation of the *Georgics* as a whole.[7]

We have been warned: 'parcite, oves, nimium procedere; non bene ripae | creditur.' 'And yet the attempt is worth making. After all, this is one of the most beautiful things in ancient poetry, and here as strongly as anywhere in Virgil's work we must feel that more is meant than meets the ear.[8] He will not lightly have put at the end of a long poem a strikingly melodious and pathetic conclusion, whose connection with what precedes, and whose position in his work as a whole, he has made merely mysterious. We are entitled to expect that the poet did not end his poem with so complex and unexpected an episode, and one whose interpretation has proved so difficult, if he had not had something complex to say; but also something to which he attached importance. 'Itur', therefore, 'in antiquam silvam.'

Virgil treats his bees, in the fourth *Georgic*, as if they formed a sort of human society.[9] They have *domus, lar, statio, tectum; fores, limina, portae; aula, oppidum, patria, penates, sedes augusta, urbs*. They have divine reason and practise high-minded communism. Their patriotism is absolute. They will work themselves to death (204) or give their lives in battle (218). Their devotion to their ruler is incomparable (210). They are thrifty (156, 177), orderly (158), indefatigable (185); they all move and rest as one (184, 'omnibus una quies operum, labor omnibus unus'). At 201 Virgil calls them Romans, *Quirites*, and scholars have pointed out that the characteristic Roman virtues of *labor* and *fortitudo* ('das sind römische Tugenden κατ' ἐξοχήν', Dahlmann, p. 11), and also *concordia*, are their leading qualities.[10]

There are clear resemblances with the praise of the Italian countryman and his virtuous life at the end of the second *Georgic* (work, justice, concord, and defence of home, children, and *penates*). All this is clear enough, but disagreement begins when we come to interpret these facts.

At one extreme, especially in Germany, some have felt confident that Virgil means his bees to represent an absolute model for human society. Dahlmann goes so far as to say that this separates Virgil from other ancient writers: 'We are dealing with a framework which is simply and absolutely paradigmatic, which corresponds to the absolutely valid, rational, and right.'[11] Schadewaldt speaks of 'a charming model of a charmingly ordered natural ideal state'.[12] In English, Wormell implies a similar view, ending his account of the bees' nature by saying that 'this description constitutes a challenge to contemporary human standards and attitudes'.[13] Reservations of several sorts arise, if we try to imagine Virgil recommending to his contemporaries as an absolute model a society like this: impersonal, collective, Stakhanovite, without art. Did the author of the sixth *Eclogue* and the fourth *Aeneid* really think that is what the ideal society would be like—a place with no comprehension or sympathy for Corydon, for Nisus and Euryalus, for Virgil himself?[14]

Fortunately we are not left with no other counter-argument than this general one. Virgil deals with his bees in a tone which does not exclude irony. The epic battle of bees ('ingentes animos angusto in pectore versant') ends with these two lines:

> hi motus animorum atque haec certamina tanta
> pulveris exigui iactu compressa quiescent. (86–7)

With consummate skill, Virgil combines a grave humour (the warriors are after all only tiny insects), with a deep and poignant under-tone: human battles, too, end with a handful of dust.[15] Such a phrase as that he uses of the aftermath—'melior vacua sine regnet in aula' (90)—has a similar irony; so has, for instance, 106,

> nec magnus prohibere labor: tu regibus alas
> eripe . . .

Nor can the choice of Cyclopes (170 ff.) as a comparison for bees be without its humour.[16] One could labour the point; but it is clear that Virgil presents the bees and their community in a way which combines admiration ('ingentes animos') with a cool sense of proportion ('angusto in pectore'). Adam Parry was right to pick out this complexity,[17] which surely rules out any straightforward paradigmatic purpose on Virgil's part. From another point of view, it seems to me incredible that the poet could have expected, or even hoped, that his audience (in 29 B.C.!) would accept as their own ideal future a society in which the king is treated with more than Oriental devotion:

praeterea regem non sic Aegyptus et ingens
Lydia nec populi Parthorum aut Medus Hydaspes
observant ...   (210–12)

What, then, did he mean by his treatment of the bees? A clue is given by
a remarkable omission. Bees and honey in antiquity were constantly
associated with poetry and poets. The connection is indeed so familiar that
I relegate to a footnote[18] an anthology of evidence, stressing merely that
even Varro, a source of Virgil and by no means an excessively poetical
writer, in his treatment of apiculture, says of the bees: 'Cum causa
Musarum esse dicuntur volucres' (*R.R.* 3.16.7). But Virgil does not make
any such connection, and by choosing to suppress it he makes us realize
that the society represented by the bees is one from which the arts are
consciously excluded. Instead of singing, his bees make mere noise—'fit
sonitus, mussantque oras et limina circum' (188), or in time of war they
'imitate the trumpet' (72).[19] Their honey is never brought by Virgil into
connection with poetry or the Muses, although it is 'aërii mellis caelestia
dona' (1), and although in the second half of the poem he will be dealing
with the song of Orpheus, son of a Muse. When is it permitted to argue
from silence? This silence, it seems to me, is striking enough for us to feel
that it has a significance. I venture on to speculative ground in trying to
say what it signified.

Virgil did not want to connect his bees, inspired though they are, with
poetry or song. They exhibit many great virtues, but they are not poetical,
and they are free from the bitter-sweet pains and pleasures of love (*Buc.* 3.
110; *G.* 4. 198 ff.). In both they contrast clearly with Orpheus, the
fabulous singer who dies for love (and who in this poem is never shown as
doing any work or having any other function than song).[20] The virtues
they exhibit are indeed the virtues of the old Roman people; but so are
their deficiencies. Rome, great in *mores antiqui*, was not a home of the arts,
in the view of the Augustans, until

> Graecia capta ferum victorem cepit et artes
> intulit agresti Latio.[21]

At *Ars Poetica* 323 ff., in a famous passage, Horace laments that the
traditional Roman education unfitted the Roman for the arts. It is from
this point of view that we must, I think, handle the problem. When Virgil
was still at work on the *Georgics*, he had already in mind the Roman epic
which he hoped to be able to produce. The prologue to the third *Georgic*
shows him grappling with it, and already keenly aware of the difficulties
which such a poem would offer. At that time he apparently was thinking,
or wished to give the impression that he was thinking, in terms of a poem
on Octavian, with glances back to Troy—the reverse of the *Aeneid* (a poem
on Aeneas with glances forward to Augustus).[22] Difficulties of style (was

Octavian to be handled like a Homeric hero? What of the gods?),
difficulties of material (Horace, *Odes* 2.1 warns Pollio of the risks involved
in writing of recent history), the immense difficulty of making recent
politics in any way poetic: all these, and others, must have been weighing
on Virgil's mind. But not least of his problems, I think was the nature of
imperialism itself, and of Virgil's attitude to Rome.

It is not my intention to depict Virgil as 'anti-Augustan';[23] the term is a
crudity. But justified revulsion against its excesses must not conceal the
central fact about the *Aeneid*; that it is a poem of loss, defeat, and pathos,
as much as it is of triumphant destiny.[24] Aeneas loses his country, his wife,
Dido, Pallas; he must kill Lausus and meet among the dead the mistress
who killed herself when he left her. To console him he has the vast
impersonal gifts of destiny. But not only Aeneas must sacrifice all the
wishes of his heart in the service of his fate; the imperial people, too, must
pay a high price for its imperial calling. Nowhere does that emerge more
poignantly than in the famous passage, *Aen.* 6.847–53:

> excudent alii spirantia mollius aera
> (credo equidem), vivos ducent de marmore vultus,
> orabunt causas melius, caelique meatus
> describent radio et surgentia sidera dicent:
> tu regere imperio populos, Romane, memento
> (hae tibi erunt artes), pacique imponere morem,[25]
> parcere subiectis et debellare superbos.

This unrivalled speech is at once a boast and a lament, a proud claim by a
conqueror and a sigh of regret for the cost. Virgil, poet, philosopher, and
aesthete, in the middle of his great poem, in which the Latin language and
the Roman destiny alike were carried to a beauty which must have seemed
impossible, yet must surrender to the Greeks (*alii*—he cannot bring
himself to name them) the arts and the sciences. The traditional claim of
the Roman patriot, that native morals outshone Greek accomplishments
('ut virtutis a nostris sic doctrinae ab illis ⟨sc. Graecis⟩ exempla petenda
sunt', Cic. *de Or.* 3. 137), is given a pregnancy and a pathos which
transform it. 'Hae tibi erunt artes': these are your arts, man of Rome—not
the seductive beauties of Greece, which meant so much to Virgil as a man,
and without which his poems could not have come into existence, but the
hard and self-denying 'arts' of conquest and dominion. It is the price of
empire that the Roman must abandon for this imperial destiny, splendid
and yet bitter, so many forms of beauty.

Virgil embodies this cruel cost again in an episode of his own invention,
much criticized in antiquity, from Probus onwards:[26] the shooting of the
stag of Silvia in the seventh book. The beautiful tame creature ('forma
praestanti', 483) is shot by Ascanius, without malicious intention on his
part. 'Ascanius does not mean any harm: he yields to a young man's

keenness to excel in sport, "eximiae laudis suscensus amore", and thus, by wounding poor Silvia's pet, becomes a tool in the hands of Allecto.'[27] The Italian rustics flock up with improvised weapons, 506:

> improvisi adsunt, hic torre armatus obusto,
> stipitis hic gravidi nodis; quod cuique repertum
> rimanti telum ira facit.

Then the Trojans come rushing from their stronghold (521), and the fighting becomes a regular battle in full armour (523 ff.).

Such a beginning to the great war, the *maius opus* of the second half of the *Aeneid*, has not unnaturally distressed or perplexed some scholarly readers.[28] As a *casus belli*, says Macrobius, all this is 'leve nimisque puerile'. Why did Virgil put such an unexpected scene in so important a position? R. Heinze suggested that he was concerned to make the responsibility of the Trojans for the war as venial and as slight as possible; a mere accident while hunting.[29] Klingner drew the distressingly flat moral[30] that 'if one looks more closely, it is not the death of the tame stag which creates the danger, but the presence of a population of shepherds, half civilized and easily aroused by a triviality'—almost as if he were making an official report to King Latinus on a regrettable incident in a country district. Wimmel sees here a device for making the war 'pastoral' and 'unheroic', one of Virgil's many 'anti-epic procedures'.[31] None of these suggestions seems to do justice to the emotional weight and force of the passage. The stag is tame and beautiful: shot by the incomers, it flees home to its loving mistress, like a human creature:

> successitque gemens stabulis, questuque cruentus
> atque imploranti similis tectum omne replebat.

One surely need invoke no hypothetical lost poem to explain the grief it causes. It remains true that Ascanius did not know what he was doing; he meant no harm—but the harm is done. Aeneas has no wish to fight the Italians, and he does all he can to avoid war, but he must fight and kill his future allies. He tries hard to avoid killing Lausus (10.809 ff.), but he must kill him. He does not even want to kill Turnus (12.938) ... Above all, he had no desire to cause the death of Dido, and yet she, who would have been 'all too happy, if only the Trojan ships had never touched my shores' (4.657), who was so splendid, attractive, and noble when they arrived, is driven to disgrace and suicide when the destiny of Aeneas takes him to Carthage. And Dido, in the first frenzy of her love, is compared to a deer, shot by a shepherd, who does not know that he has hit her:

> uritur infelix Dido totaque vagatur
> urbe furens, qualis coniecta cerva sagitta
> quam procul incautam nemora inter Cresia fixit

> pastor agens telis liquitque volatile ferrum
> nescius: illa fuga silvas saltusque peragrat
> Dictaeos; haeret lateri letalis harundo   (4.68–73)

The recurrence of the image deserves more attention than it receives.[32]
The climax of the three stages in which Juno and Allecto stir up the war is
given a form that recalls the suffering of Dido; she too was beautiful,
destroyed by the Trojans not by their will ('liquitque volatile ferrum
nescius'—'invitus, regina, tuo de litore cessi'). Like the archer in the
simile, Aeneas does not know what he has done: 'nec credere quivi | hunc
tantum tibi me discessu ferre dolorem' (6.463). But that is the effect of the
Trojan destiny; to cause suffering without willing it, to cause the destruction of so many beautiful things from Silvia's stag to the singer Cretheus,
slain by Turnus:

> ... et Clytium Aeoliden et amicum Crethea Musis,
> Crethea Musarum comitem, cui carmina semper
> et citharae cordi numerosque intendere nervis,
> semper equos atque arma virum pugnasque canebat,   (9.774–7)

the singer Cretheus, to whom Virgil gives so moving a farewell. And with
the poet go the lovers—Dido, and Nisus and Euryalus, and Cydon, lover
of boys:

> tu quoque, flaventem prima lanugine malas
> dum sequeris Clytium infelix, nova gaudia, Cydon,
> Dardania stratus dextra, securus amorum
> qui iuvenum tibi semper erant ...   (10.324–7)

At the end of the *Aeneid* Aeneas is left only a bride he has never met.

In the *Aeneid* Virgil has succeeded in devising ways of bringing out this
complex of ideas, central to his vision of Rome and of history: of Roman
destiny as an austere and self-denying one, restraining *furor* and *superbia*,
and imposing peace and civilization on the world; at the cost of turning
away, with tears but with unshakable resolution, from the life of pleasure,
of art, and of love. 'Mens immota manet, lacrimae volvuntur inanes.' In
the *Georgics* he was already confronting the same problem,[33] and not
finding it easy.[34] The bees presented him with a powerful image for the
traditional Roman state, in its impersonal and collective character. To
avoid cluttering the argument, and to enable those who need no evidence
for this description of Roman society to proceed more lightly, I have put
into Appendix I some support for it.

No wider contrast can be imagined than that between the exquisite and
sensuous beauty of the evocation of Pasiphae in the sixth *Eclogue*, or the
self-indulgent and lyrical passion of Gallus in the tenth, or the love-lorn
singer Orpheus, living and dying entirely for art and love, and, on the

other side, the old Roman, 'non sibi sed patriae natus', whose subordination of his own emotions to the state goes so far that for patriotic reasons he will put his own sons to death.[35] Virgil does show us how, in his own style and ethos, he can deal with this traditional Roman figure; Anchises points out to Aeneas the unborn shade of L. Brutus, first consul, who killed his sons for conspiring with the Tarquins:

> vis et Tarquinios reges animamque superbam
> ultoris Bruti, fascisque videre receptos?
> consulis imperium hic primus saevasque securis
> accipiet, natosque pater nova bella moventis
> ad poenam pulchra pro libertate vocabit,
> infelix, utcumque ferent ea facta minores:
> vincet amor patriae laudumque immensa cupido.   (6.817–23)

I cannot do better than repeat the judgement of Eduard Norden (ad vs. 822): 'The lines are a noble monument for the poet who succeeded in combining without disharmony his tender sensibility with his admiration for the rigid grandeur of the old "fortia facta".'[36] In such passages of his epic Virgil has succeeded in bringing together two attitudes and doing full justice to them both. The axes of Republican authority are cruel, and Brutus must be an unhappy man; and yet political liberty is a thing of beauty, and his motive was glorious. Unhappy, he is also proud—with all the moral complexity of that word and that quality. Anchises, legendary founder, both extols and grieves for the work of his people. His history of Rome begins as a glorification: 'nunc age, Dardaniam prolem quae deinde sequatur | gloria . . . expediam dictis . . .'. It ends with the pathetic lament for Marcellus: 'o nate, ingentem luctum ne quaere tuorum . . . heu miserande puer . . .'. Not only in detail but also as a whole, the utterance of Anchises juxtaposes the two aspects and leaves them unresolved. In the *Georgics* Virgil has not yet mastered this tremendous technique of compression. The bees and Orpheus do not approach each other in so small a compass, and Virgil indulges himself with a long episode in the plangent and exquisite style which he has learned and improved from Catullus and the νεώτεροι. It is a style which in most of his writing he denied himself.

The bees, then, with their collective virtues and their lack of individuality and art, serve as a counter-part to the old Roman character. Their patriotism and self-denial (and devotion to their 'king' is only devotion to the state and to authority, not an encouragement to emperor-worship) are admirable. If Rome had only retained more of such qualities, then the tragedies and disasters of the Civil Wars, and of the end of the first *Georgic*, would never have occurred. Hence a real, not a feigned or insincere, admiration and nostalgia for them—and for their human form, the old Italian way of life:

> hanc olim veteres vitam coluere Sabini,
> hanc Remus et frater.

In the *Aeneid* this strand of thought and feeling will be fully repres-
ented; the austere life of Euander (especially 8.364 f.), the speech of
Numanus Remulus (9.598 ff.), the tempering of Trojan luxury with
Italian toughness ('sit Romana potens Itala virtute propago', 12.827).[37]

But as the *Aeneid* does justice also to the sacrifice demanded of the
Imperial people, so too in the *Georgics* we see the human incompleteness
of such a collective state.

In the first *Georgic* Virgil depicted with passion the disasters which lack
of order has brought on the world: 'fas versum atque nefas, tot bella per
orbem | tam multae scelerum facies.' Only Caesar can rescue a world
turned upside down, and Virgil prays desperately for his success. The
reconstruction longed for in the first *Georgic* is, we may feel, under way by
the fourth; order is being restored, and the poet becomes aware of the
cost—a society efficient and admirable, but impersonal and dispassionate.

The deficiency hinted at in the actual account of the bees emerges with
great emotional force when they are juxtaposed with Orpheus and
Eurydice. The bee-master Aristaeus has inadvertently caused the death of
the beautiful Eurydice—we are reminded of the archer in the simile in
Aeneid 4, and of Ascanius in *Aeneid* 7. Like Aeneas, he does not even know
what he has done. Like Aeneas, too, he has a divine mother who helps and
advises; like him, he is a founder. He has bequeathed us an *ars* ('quis deus
hanc, Musae, quis nobis extudit artem? . . . pastor Aristaeus', *G.* 4.315–
17), but the practical one of regaining lost *parvos Quirites*, not the art of
song.[38] It is, in fact, an *ars* like that promised to the Roman by Anchises—
'hae tibi erunt artes'. And it is a harsh one, whose cruel side is not glossed
over: 'huic geminae nares et spiritus oris | multa reluctanti obstruitur' (300
f.): 'sacrum iugulis demitte cruorem' (542).

The bees, patriotic, rational, and impersonal, are brought back from
death by the device of bugonia. In the fullest sense, 'genus immortale
manet' (*G.* 4.208):

> . . . multosque per annos
> stat fortuna domus, et avi numerantur avorum.

So too will Rome stand for ever: 'his ego nec metas rerum nec tempora
pono', says Jupiter (*Aen.* 1.278). As Rome is upheld by his will, the bees
too derive their nature from him (*G.* 4.149). But what of the singer and his
love? And how is the poem as a whole to be understood?[39]

The sweet singer Orpheus, robbed of his love through Aristaeus' fault,
is shown in poignant endless lamentation. The emotional style and the
verbal beauty of Proteus' account of his suffering and song make it a unity,

and it is here that the emotional emphasis surely falls, not on the episode of
Aristaeus:

> te, dulcis coniunx, te solo in litore secum
> te veniente die, te decedente canebat . . .

The narrative is given a 'neoteric' structure; the scene in which the gods of
the dead give back Eurydice and impose the prohibition on looking at her
is compressed to nothing (487, a mere parenthesis—'namque hanc dederat
Proserpina legem'), as in the *Ciris* ('si parva licet componere magnis') the
decisive actions of the wicked heroine, her crime, her appeal to Minos, and
her rejection, are compressed into five lines (386–90). But what was a
mannerism in such a poem, or even in Catullus 64, is here put to emotional
use: after Orpheus' long lament (464 ff.) and the pathetic description of the
dead (471 ff.), no explicit passage of hope and optimism is allowed to break
the mood; already at 488, 'subita incautum dementia cepit amantem'. The
whole is plangent, mellifluous, pathetic.[40] No work of art, no human love,
can prevail over the power of death; Eurydice is gone for ever, and
Orpheus, still singing, has been sent by the cruel maenads to join her.

The account of the first bugonia, 528–58, forms in style a remarkable
contrast. A dry and matter-of-fact tone succeeds to the languorous beauty
of Orpheus and Eurydice, emphasized by the exact repetition of lines (538,
540, 544, with 550–62, as if to say: This is what he was told, and this is
what he did). The bees are reborn. Some readers are content to regard this
as a happy ending: 'Catastrophe reigns over the conclusion of the Third
Book, confident elevation is restored at the end of the Fourth';[41] 'Books 1
and 3 are gloomy or pessimistic; 2 and 4 are cheerful and optimistic.'[42] For
my part I cannot feel that the restoration of bees outweighs the suffering
and death of Orpheus and Eurydice, especially in view of the way Virgil
has handled the story. An exquisite ambivalence surely prevails. Life goes
on, and the virtuous bees will for ever practise their virtuous collectivity;
but the artist and his love must die, leaving nothing but the song. For love
and art go hand in hand with *furor* and *dementia*, with subordinating
reason and interest to emotion. We think of Corydon, who accuses himself
of *dementia*, and neglects his work to sing (*Buc.* 2.69–72), of the erotic
myths of which Silenus sang all day (*Buc.* 6), of the ingenuous Meliboeus,
who neglects his work to listen to singing, and confesses, 'posthabui tamen
illorum mea seria ludo' (*Buc.* 7.17), of the suicidal passion of Nysa's lover
(*Buc.* 8), of Gallus abandoning himself to love and song and idleness (*Buc.*
10), of the ravages of passion in the third *Georgic*. And yet the song
outlasts the singer: still in death Orpheus' voice proclaims his love, and his
song fills the air—

> Eurydicen toto referebant flumine ripae.

It would be an optimistic writer who should hope for universal assent, at this time of day, to an unprovable account of the fourth *Georgic*. The theory here proposed, that this poem bears upon Rome and poetry, upon imperialism and individual sensibility, perhaps finds some support in the poem's very last words:

> haec super arvorum cultu pecorumque canebam
> et super arboribus, Caesar dum magnus ad altum
> fulminat Euphraten bello victorque volentis
> per populos dat iura viamque adfectat Olympo.
> illo Vergilium me tempore dulcis alebat
> Parthenope studiis florentem ignobilis oti,
> carmina qui lusi pastorum audaxque iuventa,
> Tityre, te patulae cecini sub tegmine fagi.   (559–66)

These eight lines divide naturally into two juxtaposed halves; while Caesar is thundering on the Euphrates, civilizing a welcoming world, and winning immortality, Virgil for his part, the frivolous (*lusi*) author of the *Eclogues*, has been writing the *Georgics* at Naples, flourishing in the studies of inglorious ease. The urbanity of this exquisite signature, a Virgilian combination of pride and humility, is easily missed.[43] The *Eclogues* were not serious and the *Georgics* are not glorious, he says; he has been taking it easy in a cultured resort with a Greek name. Caesar, on the other hand, has been working wonders ... And yet of course we remember that the poem is 'tua, Maecenas, haud mollia iussa', and that 'in tenui labor, at tenuis non gloria'. These two memorable lines alone, casting as they do so ironical a light on *otium* and *ignobile*, suffice to indicate the complexity of the tone. By good old Roman standards, Caesar's actions are glorious, Virgil's are not; Virgil bows gravely to those standards. But the shape of the period puts the poet, not the ruler, in the climactic position, and Virgil overshadows Octavian. Here too Virgil is concerned with the relationship of poetry and the traditional Roman values, as, on the view here put forward, he has been all through the poem. Is poetry less glorious than imperialism? In the *sphragis* to the *Georgics* Virgil has found a way of agreeing that it is, which at the same time, with equal force, implies that it is not. To generalize that *tour de force* through a whole epic—an impossible task! And yet the story of the bees and of Orpheus showed, perhaps, a way in which it might be done.

In this poem, then, the poet is saying something which will be said on a greater scale and with great mastery in the *Aeneid*. Here the link between the suffering of Orpheus and Eurydice, and the rebirth of the civically virtuous bees, is not as convincing as Virgil makes the link between the triumph of Roman *fata* and the suffering of Dido, of Pallas, and of Aeneas himself. In the *Aeneid* the establishment of empire, which will be the justification and the lasting meaning of history, inevitably involves defeat and sacrifice. In the *Georgic* the role of Aristaeus has something of the arbitrariness of purely Hellenistic mythological combination, the same man appearing both as εὑρετής and as seducer, a combination by no means inevitable. In the same way, the balance which Virgil keeps so beautifully in his epic is here less certain; the separate elements have not been fused as completely as they might have been, and the pathos of Orpheus is in grave danger of running away completely from the rest. The 'neoteric' use of mythology reminds us of links like those in Callimachus' *Hecale*, or in Catullus 64; the fullness of passionate lamentation and pathos recalls Catullus' Ariadne or Attis, or the Zmyrna of Cinna. In the *Aeneid* Virgil has out-grown and mastered for his own style these youthful models; the fourth *Georgic*, in addition to its own beauties, shows us a vital stage in that development.

Appendix I: Rome as a Collective State

The *locus classicus* on the collective nature of early Rome is the sixth book of Polybius, who at 2.41.9 contrasts the ὁμόνοια of Romans with the διαφορὰ καὶ καχεξία of Greeks. The refusal of Cato to name individual Roman generals in the last four books of his *Origines*, because he regarded their achievements as *populi Romani gesta* (fr. 1 Peter), appeals to the same sentiment; cf. D. Kienast, *Cato der Zensor* (Heidelberg, 1954), pp. 109 f. Cicero cites him (*de Rep.* 2.2.3) as saying that the Roman constitution was better than any Greek one because it was not the work of a single legislator but created *multorum ingenio*.

  Concordia, ὁμόνοια, these are the positive names for this quality: see E. Skard, *Concordia* in *Römische Wertbegriffe* (Wege der Forschung 34, 1967, ed. H. Oppermann), pp. 177 ff. In the old days there was *concordia maxima* among Romans, says Sallust, *Bell. Cat.* 9; his meaning is illuminated by *Bell. Cat.* 52.23, the opposite: 'ubi vos separatim sibi quisque consilium capitis . . .'.

Ancient Roman society may perhaps fitly be compared to life in one of the monastic orders in the middle ages. Both systems display the same methodical combination of example and precept, of mutual vigilance and unremitting discipline. Both show a community in which the individual is entirely at the mercy of the feelings and opinions of his fellows, and where it is impossible for him to become emancipated from the tyranny of the group. (G. Ferrero, *The Greatness and Decline of Rome* (London, 1907), 1.5)

As far back as we can trace the beginnings of Roman life into the darkness of the remote past, we find the citizen no individualist. He is already living in a well organized community, in which the exercise of personal rights is rigorously subordinated to public opinion and to public jurisdiction . . . (E. T. Merrill, *CP* 2 (1907), 374)

[In early Rome] ein ungewöhnlich hoher Grad von Einformigkeit des Denkens und Strebens ist damit ohne weiteres gegeben, in striktem Gegensatz etwa zu Athen ... (R. Heinze, *Von den Ursachen der Grösse Roms* (Leipzig, 1921), p. 9 = *Vom Geist des Römertums*³, p. 12)

Rome ne s'affranchira jamais tout à fait de l'idéal collectif qui consacre l'individu à l'État; elle ne consentira jamais à y renoncer ... la vieille éducation romaine. La notion fondamentale sur laquelle elle repose est le respect de la coutume ancestrale, mos maiorum. La révéler à la jeunesse, la lui faire respecter comme un idéal indiscuté, la norme de toute action et de toute pensée, telle est la tâche essentielle de l'éducateur ... (H. I. Marrou, *Histoire de l'éducation dans l'antiquité*⁶ (Paris, 1965), pp. 339, 342)

Until the third century no one even had a memorial tombstone. Cumulative pride in the family and in the community were the rewards of life. And even down to the beginning of the second century the Romans are of interest to us for what they were collectively, indeed for the degree to which they succeeded in repressing individuality. (Wilkinson, *The Roman Experience* (London, 1975), p. 26)

C. Nicolet, *Le Métier de citoyen dans la Rome républicaine* (Paris, 1976), p. 521, summarizes Polybius 6: 'Rome toute entière est baignée dans une "discipline" collective, mais librement acceptée, qui renforce considérablement la cohésion sociale; cette discipline n'est pas seulement répressive; elle combine heureusement l'incitation et la prévention, les récompenses et les punitions. D'où le dévouement et le patriotisme des Romains en général.' Cf. also pp. 27 (on *consensus*), 514–16.

The expression 'non sibi sed patriae natus', which of course has just this meaning, is a favourite one of Cicero's (*pro Murena* 83, *pro Sestio* 138, *Philipp.* 14.32, *de Fin.* 2.45).

I have not found anything on Rome as penetrating as the essay by Hermann Strasburger, 'Der Einzelne und die Gemeinschaft im Denken der Griechen', *HZ* 177 (1954), 227–48. By contrast, it sheds much light on Rome.

Appendix II: The Alleged Change to the End of the Fourth Georgic

One of the most celebrated statements of Servius (in *Buc.* 10.1, and in *G.* 4.1) is to the effect that originally the fourth Book of the *Georgics*, 'from the middle right down to the end', contained the praises of Cornelius Gallus, 'which afterwards at the bidding of Augustus he changed to the story of Aristaeus'. Mr. Wilkinson deals judiciously with the story in his excellent book on the *Georgics*, pp. 108 ff., concluding, with Norden[44] and W. B. Anderson,[45] that it is untrue, deriving originally perhaps from a confusion between 'the end of the *Bucolics*' and 'the end of the *Georgics*'.

I am sure that this verdict is correct, and my purpose is to add another argument to those pressed by others, of artistic coherence[46] and of personal tact (how would Octavian have enjoyed a long recital in praise of a subordinate?).[47] Chronological grounds, it seems to me, rule out the story. Virgil at the end of the fourth *Georgic* says he wrote the poem 'while mighty Caesar was thundering on the Euphrates' (560), which doubtless means before Octavian's return to Rome from the East in August 29 B.C. In a circumstantial story which there is no reason to doubt,[48] coming to us from Suetonius through Donatus, we are told that 'when Augustus was on his way home after his victory at Actium and was staying at Atella to get over a relaxed throat, Virgil read the *Georgics* to him for four days on end, Maecenas taking over whenever his voice failed and he had to stop'. Now, Gallus came to grief in Egypt and felt himself driven to suicide either in 27 B.C. (Jerome) or 26 B.C. (Dio).[49] For at least two years, then, a version of the *Georgics* must have been in circulation containing a different ending, which was then replaced 'at the bidding of Augustus'; and replaced so effectively that not a word of it was preserved.

Now this sequence of events is, surely, inconceivable. Rome in the early twenties was not like Stalin's Russia, with an efficient and ubiquitous police which could have enforced such a decree throughout the private houses of readers of poetry, even if Augustus had wanted to do so. Even under the grimmer and more frankly autocratic rule of his successors, attempts to suppress books were a failure. We need only recall Tacitus' comment on the affair of Cremutius Cordus, under Tiberius (*Annals* 4.35):

His books, so the Senate decreed, were to be burnt by the aediles; but they remained in existence, concealed and afterwards published. And so one is all the more inclined to laugh at the stupidity of men who suppose that the despotism of the present can actually efface the remembrances of the next generation. On the contrary, the persecution of talented writers fosters their influence . . .

We know that soon after Virgil's death there was a hunger for more Virgilian poetry, which was fed with so mediocre a composition as the *Culex*;[50] in such an atmosphere, could somebody have failed to unearth a copy of such a gem as a suppressed version of a great poem?

I have no doubt that we can name one man, at least, who would have kept a copy—Asinius Pollio, a patron of poets, including Virgil at the time of the *Eclogues*, a friend of Gallus,[51] and a man who under the Principate 'defended his ideals in the only fashion he could, by freedom of speech. Too eminent to be muzzled without scandal, too recalcitrant to be won by flattery, Pollio had acquired for himself a privileged position.'[52] An episode with Timagenes, about which we happen to be informed, gives the flavour of his relationship with Augustus.[53]

The waspish historian Timagenes, who had won the friendship of Augustus, could not refrain from offensive jokes at the expense of the Princeps and his family; in the end, Augustus forbade him the palace.

After this, Timagenes lived to old age in the house of Asinius Pollio and was lionized by the whole city. Although the Emperor had banned him from the palace, no other door was closed to him. He gave public readings of the histories which he had written after the incident, and he burnt the books dealing with the achievements of Augustus Caesar. He conducted a feud with the Emperor, and nobody was afraid to be his friend . . . The Emperor made no complaint to the man who was maintaining his enemy. All he said to Asinius Pollio was, 'Are you keeping a zoo?' Then, when Pollio began to excuse himself, he cut him short, saying 'Make the most of him, Pollio, make the most of him!' 'If you tell me to, Caesar, I shall bar my house to him at once,' said Pollio. The Emperor replied, 'Do you think I would? Why, it was I who made you friends again.' The fact was that Pollio had at one time been at enmity with Timagenes, and his only reason for ceasing was that the Emperor had begun . . .

This story is highly instructive. We see how urbanely, how moderately, Augustus saw fit to treat a writer who personally angered him; and we see how provocative was the attitude of Pollio. Augustus, we are told, publicly lamented the death of Gallus.[54] It is hard to reconcile all this with the Princeps ordering the universal suppression of a poem praising him; it is perhaps even harder to imagine Pollio failing to seize the opportunity to keep a copy of a poem by a former protégé of his own, praising one of his friends, and suppressed in circumstances discreditable to Augustus. The compromise favoured by some scholars,[55] of supposing that Virgil wrote and suppressed not half the poem but a few lines only, seems to me to founder on the same considerations.[56]

NOTES

1. R. Coleman, *AJP* 83 (1962), 55–71; Brooks Otis, *Virgil: A Study in Civilized Poetry* (Oxford, 1963); C. Segal, *AJP* 87 (1966), 307–25; A. Bradley, *Arion* 8 (1969), 347–58; D. S. Wender, *AJP* 90 (1969), 424–36; L. P. Wilkinson, *The Georgics of Virgil* (Cambridge, 1969); A. Wankenne, S.J., *LEC* 38 (1970), 18–29; E Coleiro in *Vergiliana*, ed. Bardon and Verdière (Leiden, 1971), pp. 113–23; Colin Hardie, *The Georgics: A Transitional Poem* (3rd Jackson Knight Memorial Lecture, 1971); R. Joudoux, *Bull. Ass. G. Budé* 1971, 67–82; D. E. W. Wormell in *Vergiliana* (1971), pp. 429–35; Brooks Otis, *Phoenix* 26 (1972), 40–62; Adam Parry, *Arethusa* 5 (1972), 35–52; M. C. J. Putnam, ib. 53–70; P. V. Cova, *Bull. Stud. Lat.* 3 (1973), 281–303; J. Chomarat, *REL* 52 (1974), 185–207; E. M. Stehle, *TAPA* 104 (1974), 347–69.

2. See already P. Scazzoso, *Paideia* 11 (1956), 25–8.

3. L. Castiglioni, *Lezioni intorno alle Georgiche* (Milan, 1947), p. 185.

4. So for S. P. Bovie, *AJP* 77 (1956), 355, Aristaeus is 'a silhouette of the Roman practical man'—whose characteristic utterance, it seems is in the plangent tones of 321 ff.: 'mater, Cyrene mater . . .'.

5. This old view still has its supporters. W. Y. Sellar, *Virgil*[3], p. 251: 'It must be difficult for anyone who is penetrated by the prevailing sentiment of the *Georgics* to reach this point in the poem (sc. 4.315) without a strong feeling of regret that the jealousy of Augustus had interfered with its original conclusion.' R. S. Conway, *Proc. Class. Ass.* 25 (1928), 31: 'Yet no one who approaches the Fourth Book of the *Georgics* with an open mind, after reading the others, can possibly doubt that there must be some reason for the startling break in the middle of that Book.' Magdalena Schmidt, *Die Komposition von Vergils Georgica* (Paderborn, 1930), pp. 173–7: 'So störend für den Genuss der künstlerischen Einheit und Feinheit der Georgica ist . . . die Eindichtung eines diesem Epyllion wie den Georgica überhaupt wesensfremdes Trauergedichtes

... Wie kommt Vergil aber zu dieser Geschmacklosigkeit der Komposition?' Not many scholars now would actually deplore the insertion of this uniquely beautiful piece of poetry; but Coleiro (see note 1) apologizes for its feebleness with the argument that Virgil naturally found it distasteful to have to suppress his *laudes Galli* and replace them with an apologia for his disgrace and death.

6. A fuller one: Cova, pp. 290 ff.

7. Wilkinson, p. 120.

8. A couple of passages which seem to me to succeed in the difficult attempt to describe Virgil's technique: 'eine neue Art dichterischer Darstellung, bei der in einem beschrankten, unmittelbar dargestellten Gegenstande ein grösserer, der jenen umgreift, mit gegenwärtig wird und dem kleinen Bedeutsamkeit gibt'—Klingner, *Römische Geisteswelt*[4], p. 287; see also p. 303. 'Das Ganze gerät ins Schwanken, und in den wallenden Nebeln, die der Dichter über seine Bilder breitet, taucht in schattenhaften Umrissen eine zweite Welt auf, die näher zu dem Leben des Dichters gehört—K. Latte, *Antike und Abendland* 4 (1954), 157; cf. 161 (= *Kleine Schriften*, pp. 860, 864). 'Die Eigenart der vergilischen Poesie, ... hinter Bildern und Gleichnissen das den Dichter eigentlich Berührende zu verstecken oder es durch diese auszudrücken'—H. Dahlmann, *Abh. Ak. Mainz* 1954, 10, 4.

9. See Dahlmann, 6 (but Klingner was right to reject Dahlmann's idea that the bees are expounded in the regular form of an ethnographical ἔκφρασις: *Virgil*, p. 310 n. 1); W. S. Maguinness, *Bull. Ass. G. Budé* (1962), 443; Servius in *G.* 4.219; *RE* s.v. Biene, 446.19 ff. The general point is an obvious one, and I have not laboured it. 'Haec ut hominum civitates, quod hic est et rex et imperium et societas', Varro, *R.R.* 3.16.5.

10. See H. Oppermann, *Wege zu Vergil* (Darmstadt, 1963), p. 123: 'Im Bienenstaat kehrt die römische *res publica* wieder.'

11. 'Es handelt sich um ein Gefüge schlechthinniger, absoluter Vorbildlichkeit, das dem absolut Gültigen, Vernünftigen, Richtigen entspricht' (p. 13).

12. '... Das zierliche Musterbild eines zierlich geordneten natürlichen Idealstaats', *Hellas und Hesperien*[2] (Zürich, 1974), p. 716.

13. In *Vergiliana*, p. 429.

14. 'L'aspiration à une societé de règle et de travail sous un chef bien-aimé, conclusion virgilienne d'un labeur de dix ans', J. Bayet, *RPh* 4 (1930), 247 = *Mélanges de littérature latine* (Rome, 1967), p. 241.

15. The technical writers know of this dust as only one of a number of ways of settling bees: Varro *R.R.* 3.16.30, Pliny *N.H.* 11.58. Virgil's phrasing is designedly pregnant; compare Lucan on the impromptu burial of Pompey, 8.867:

> pulveris exigui sparget non longa vetustas
> congeriem, bustumque cadet ...

16. Klingner, *Virgil*, p. 314: 'Zugleich kommt der Übermut des glückseligen Spielens ...'.

17. *Arethusa* 5 (1972), 43. See also Otis, *Phoenix* 26 (1972), 58: 'The co-operative state is of course one aspect of reality—Roman and human as well as animal and natural reality—but it is not the whole.'

18. 'Musaeo melle', Lucr. 4.22; 'ego apis Matinae more modoque ...', Hor. *C.* 4.2.27; 'poetica mella', Hor. *Epp.* 1.19.44; Plato, *Ion* 534b; *RE* s.v. Biene, 447.40, 'Daher wurden auch Dichter, Redner, Philosophen, u.s.w., mit den Bienen in Beziehung gebracht'; A. B. Cook, *JHS* 15 (1895), 7, and *Zeus* (Cambridge, i.1914), 443; ἐσήμαινε γὰρ τὸ μέλι τὴν εὐέπειαν τῆς σοφίας, Artemidorus, *Oneir.* 5.83; πλῆρές τοι μέλιτος τὸ καλὸν στόμα, Θύρσι, γένοιτο, Theocr. 1.146, and Gow ad loc.; H. Usener, *RM* 57 (1902) 177 ff. = *Kleine Schriften* (Leipzig and Berlin, 1912), 4, pp. 398 ff., esp. 400 f.

19. Contrast the beautiful line, admired by G. K. Chesterton, in the description of bees in *King Henry V* 1.2:

> Others like soldiers, armed in their stings,
> Make boot upon the summer's velvet buds;
> Which pillage they with merry march bring home
> To the tent-royal of their emperor:
> Who, busied in his majesty, surveys
> *The singing masons building roofs of gold* ...

Dover Wilson, in his note ad loc., suggests that Shakespeare drew this touch from the commentary on the fourth *Georgic* by Willichius (Venice 1543), who adds to Virgil's list of functions: 'Aliae σειρῆνες sunt.' The addition, and the way Shakespeare seizes on it, show what a noticeable gap Virgil left.

20. Those who, like Wankenne, *LEC* 38 (1970), 25 f., talk of Aristaeus and Orpheus as 'two shepherds', are on the wrong track.

21. This view is already implicit in Porcius Licinus, fr. 1 Morel, *Poenico bello secundo* . . . Cf. now H. Funke, *RM* 120 (1977), 168.

22. See E. Norden, *Kleine Schriften*, pp. 400 ff., and, e.g., U. Fleischer, *Hermes* 88 (1960), 327, Wilkinson, p. 172.

23. Some salubrious reservations on this word are expressed by G. Karl Galinsky, *Ovid's Metamorphoses* (Oxford, 1975), pp. 210–17. Also W. M. Clarke in *CJ* 72 (1977), 322: 'One of the most amazing trends in recent literary criticism of ancient literature—the attempt to describe Vergil and Ovid as anti-Augustan, anti-establishment radicals, ideologically opposed to a proto-fascist dictator . . . there is virtually no hard evidence to support it . . .'.

24. See the masterly article by Wendell Clausen, *HSCP* 68 (1964), 139–47, reprinted in *Virgil: A Collection of Critical Essays*, ed. S. Commager (Englewood Cliffs, N.J., 1966). Suggestive but more vulnerable is Adam Parry's 'The Two Voices of Virgil's Aeneid', reprinted in the same volume from *Arion* 2 (1963); see also, in the same book, R. A. Brooks, 'Discolor Aura', from *AJP* 74 (1953), 260–80.

25. The discussion of the passage by Otis, pp. 313 ff., is flawed by his adoption of the bad reading *pacisque*, 'the habit of peace'. See Eduard Fraenkel, *Mus. Helv.* 19 (1962), 133 = *Kleine Beiträge* (Rome, 1964), 2, p. 143.

26. Macrob. *Sat.* 5.17.1–2: 'Quid Vergilio contulerit Homerus hinc maxime liquet quod, ubi rerum necessitas exegit a Marone dispositionem inchoandi belli, quam non habuit Homerus . . . laboravit ad rei novae partum. Cervum fortuito saucium fecit causam tumultus. Sed ubi vidit hoc leve nimisque puerile, dolorem auxit agrestium . . .'. Probus as the likely source: Norden, *Ennius und Vergilius* (Leipzig and Berlin, 1915), pp. 4 ff. With Macrobius' 'cervum fortuito saucium', compare J. D. Denniston and D. Page, *Aeschylus, Agamemnon* (Oxford, 1957), p. xxv on the portent at Aulis: 'the poet tells us in plain language [*sic*] that Artemis was enraged *because eagles, sent by Zeus to be an encouraging portent, happened* [*sic*] *to devour a hare together with its unborn young* . . .'. The ways of poets do not change. Nor do those of commentators . . .

27. Fraenkel, *JRS* 35 (1945), 5 = *Kleine Beiträge* 2, p. 153.

28. Klingner, *Virgil*, p. 511. Heyne was gravely dissatisfied with Virgil here ('Nolo defendere poetam'), as were many earlier scholars. Conington gives a strikingly tepid defence: 'Some have objected to the incident of the stag as too trivial, as if there were anything unnatural in a small spark causing a large train to explode, or as if the contrast itself were not an element of greatness.' The first point—a mere naturalistic defence of plausibility—is flat; the second, I confess, I can make nothing of.

29. *Virgils epische Technik*³ (Leipzig, 1914), p. 190. Heinze was sufficiently in the grip of the hostile tradition about the episode to say that Silvia's distress over the death of her stag can only be understood in the light of an hypothetical Hellenistic poem about Cuparissus—surely a severe criticism of Virgil. But his main point, that nobody is to blame, is, of course, an important one.

30. *Virgil*, p. 513.

31. W. Wimmel, *Hirtenkrieg und arkadisches Rom* (Munich, 1973), pp 48 and 118 ff.: 'ein bukolischer Kriegsanfang.'

32. 'Some personal experience must lie behind both this passage and VII.483 ff.', is Austin's not very helpful comment. Viktor Pöschl surprisingly does not mention the stag of Silvia in his treatment of 4.68 ff. (*Die Dichtkunst Virgils* (Wiesbaden, 1950), pp. 131 ff. = *The Art of Vergil* (Michigan, 1962), pp. 80 ff.). The discussion in H. Raabe, *Plurima Mortis Imago*, Zetemata 59 (Munich, 1974), p. 56, ignores this question.

33. It is a commonplace of Virgilian criticism to say that he was working his way towards the solutions eventually found in his epic. See, e.g., Dahlmann, 13, Hardie, pp. 27 ff., Segal, 321: 'In the Fourth *Georgic* Virgil is already dealing with some of the issues of the Aeneid.' The end of Segal's article (I am unable to agree with most of it) seems to me to be nearer the truth than most recent work which I have read.

34. The well-known problem of the apparently contradictory attitudes expressed at the end of the second *Georgic* towards the greatness of Rome and rustic life (contrast the philosophical

ἀταραξία of 490-9 with the patriotism of 535-5), is surely connected with this uncertainty. See most recently J. S. Clay, *Philologus* 120 (1976), 232 ff.

35. Polybius was impressed by this extremely Roman habit, 6.65.5: καὶ μὴν ἀρχὰς ἔχοντες ἔνιοι τοὺς ἰδίους υἱοὺς παρὰ πᾶν ἔθος ἤ νόμον ἀπέκτειναν, πλείονος ποιούμενοι τὸ τῆς πατρίδος συμφέρον τῆς κατὰ φύσιν οἰκειότητος πρὸς τοὺς ἀναγκαιοτάτους. πολλὰ μὲν οὖν τοιαῦτα καὶ περὶ πολλῶν ἱστορεῖται παρὰ Ῥωμαίοις ... Polybius accepts this as part of the σπουδὴ τοῦ πολιτεύματος of the Roman citizen; no hint of moral ambiguity.

36. 'So verstanden sind die Verse ein schönes Monument für den Dichter, der sein weiches Empfinden mit der Bewunderung für die starre Grossartigkeit der alten "fortia facta" harmonisch zu vereinigen wusste.'

37. In the *Aeneid*, bees appear as the subject-matter of two similes. At 1.430-6 Aeneas sees the Carthaginians hard at work on the construction of their new city, like bees busy with the care of their home and their young—a poignant contrast with the homeless Trojans and their enforced idleness. At 6.707-9 he sees the unborn souls of all nations, 'like bees in a flowery meadow on a fine summer day, busy with their pursuits and humming cheerfully' (Austin ad loc.); he marvels that they can wish to be born into the human world of pain—'quae lucis miseris tam dira cupido?' In both passages Virgil finds it natural to compare bees with men, and his picture of them as industrious, and also as oblivious of the sorrows of human life, certainly does not conflict with my interpretation of them in the fourth *Georgic*.

38. Cf. V. Buchheit, *Vergil über die Sendung Roms* (Heidelberg, 1963), pp. 151 ff., G. K. Galinsky, *Aeneas, Sicily and Rome* (Princeton, 1969), p. 98 n. 4.

39. Adam Parry was therefore misleading to say that 'the song becomes the condition for the recreation of life' (p. 52). Not Orpheus but Aristaeus recreates the bees; song does not set free the half-regained Eurydice. This central fact seems to me to rule out his interpretation of the poem, seductive and powerful as it is.

40. 'Der ganze Abschnitt ist auf tragisches Ethos gestimmt; Zartheit des Gefühls und seelenvolle Ergriffenheit: συμπάσχει ὁ ποιητὴς τοῖς προσώποις. Die Worttonsprache, das Malerische und die Schwermut der Rhythmen lässt sich nicht beschreiben . . .', Norden, *Kleine Schriften*, p. 509.

41. S. P. Bovie, *AJP* 77 (1956), 347.

42. Otis, *Phoenix* 26 (1972), 45.

43. I think it is much underestimated by V. Buchheit, *Der Anspruch des Dichters* (Darmstadt, 1972), pp. 174 ff., who takes it that the poet is making a serious claim for the importance of *Geist*: 'Somit versteht Vergil sein Werk als Beitrag zur Verwirklichung der *aetas aurea Augusti* und sieht die gemeinsame Aufgabe nun erfüll. Daraus resultiert der Anspruch des Dichters' (p. 181). The actual wording of the lines, it seems to me, is incompatible with so straightforward an interpretation.

44. Norden in *SB Berlin* (1934) = *Kleine Schriften*, pp. 468-532.

45. *CQ* 27 (1933), 36-45.

46. Otis, *Virgil: A Study in Civilized Poetry*, pp. 408 ff.

47. 'The over-riding objection', according to Anderson and Wilkinson.

48. Wilkinson, p. 69.

49. R. Syme, *The Roman Revolution* (Oxford, 1939), p. 309 n. 2.

50. Fraenkel, *JRS* 42 (1952), 7 = *Kleine Beiträge* 2, p. 193.

51. Pollio to Cicero, *ad fam.* 10.32.5: 'Gallum Cornelium, familiarem meum . . .'.

52. Quoted from Syme, op. cit., p. 482; cf. ibid., p. 320, 'Pollio . . . was preserved as a kind of privileged nuisance'.

53. Seneca, *de Ira* 3.23.4-8 = 88 *FGH* T3.

54. Suet. *Aug.* 66.2.

55. Otis, op. cit., pp. 412 f.; Wilkinson, *Georgics*, pp. 111 f.

56. I am grateful to Professor E. J. Kenney and Mr. R. O. A. M. Lyne for their helpful criticisms of this paper.

LAOCOÖN AND SINON:
VIRGIL, *AENEID* 2. 40–198

By JOHN P. LYNCH

Excudent *alii* spirantia mollius aera
(credo equidem), vivos ducent de marmore vultus,
orabunt causas melius, caelique meatus
describent radio et surgentia sidera dicent:
tu regere imperio populos, Romane, memento
(hae tibi erunt artes), pacisque imponere morem,
parcere subiectis et debellare superbos.

(Virgil, *Aeneid* 6. 847–53)

Aeneid 2 is for the most part a book of action, telling the whole story of the rapid series of events that led to Troy's final destruction. Aeneas' narrative of these events is fast-paced, almost breathless; it has the flavour and emotional intensity of an eye-witness account rather than a retelling of a past experience.[1] But it is noteworthy that Aeneas begins the story very slowly, by recounting in detail an exchange of speeches between Laocoön and Sinon (40–198). A quick summary of Trojan reactions to the horse might have sufficed for Aeneas' purposes. Virgil's model, Demodokos' song in Homer's *Odyssey*, treats the debate over the Trojan horse by simply summarizing the three positions taken (*Od.* 8. 499–513). When Odysseus asked the bard Demodokos to sing the story of the wooden horse (487 ff.), there is no suggestion, either in the wording of Odysseus' request or in the summary of Demodokos' response, of a pivotal debate between Laocoön and Sinon; in Homer's version of the story the major debate was internal to the Trojans and took place *after* the wooden horse was brought into the city. Why did Virgil have Aeneas linger over the exact words of Laocoön and Sinon? What, beyond a report of causes and events, is suggested by the speeches of Laocoön and Sinon? It would seem that the personalities and oratorical styles of these two men, not just their viewpoints in debate or their roles in the story, are important for the reader to understand. An analysis of the speeches and of the men who make them will perhaps suggest something about Aeneas' interpretation of events at Troy; it may also help to explain why Virgil chose to develop this scene as he does.

The Trojan priest Laocoön is very deftly characterized. His personality shows through clearly in his immediate and vigorous response to the dilemma over the Trojan horse: he is a man of surpassing energy (*Primus ... ante omnes ... decurrit*, 40–1) and of powerful strength (*validis viribus*,

50); he is hot-tempered (*ardens*, 41) and so impatient that he begins his speech on the run (*et procul*, 42). Moreover, Laocoön's words and deeds are one. No sooner does he declare his position than he acts confidently and courageously in accordance with what he has said (50–2).

Laocoön's style of oratory is exactly what might be expected from a man with his emotional and physical qualities. It is vigorous, decisive, spontaneous; in its deliberate artlessness it is reminiscent of the oratory of early Republican Rome. This would seem in fact to be just the association which Virgil intended. Laocoön himself is very much an old Republican figure, a paradigm of virtue and commitment, recalling specifically the prototype of the old Roman, Cato the Elder.[2] So also Laocoön's energetic, blunt, and inelegant style of speaking is reminiscent of the oratory of Cato—that vigorous speaker whose Golden Rule was *rem tene, verba sequentur.*

Consistent with the Catonian ruggedness and vigour of Laocoön's words is the quality of his diction. Several features of archaic Roman oratory[3] are exhibited: the alliteration in verses 44, 46, 47, and 49; the jingling assonance in *inspect*URA ... *vent*URA*que* ... URbi (47), in urBI ... Teucri (47–8), and *qui*ID*quid* ID (49); the anaphoric use of *aut ... aut ... aut*. It has often been noted that such predilection for assonance of all kinds was a characteristic feature of ancient latinity, one 'endemic in Italy';[4] it was the achievement of archaic Roman orators, and pre-eminently Cato, to raise this predilection to the level of art—an art which paradoxically claimed artlessness for itself by incorporating the rugged and eschewing the fastidious.

Laocoön's speech may be compared to a fragment of Cato's *De Falsis Pugnis* (fr. 58, M.),[5] which L. R. Palmer uses to illustrate the 'pathos and power' to which archaic Roman oratory could rise.[6] Apart from assonances of the kind noted above, a notable feature of Cato's oratory can be seen in his short, elliptical, and unconnected rhetorical questions: 'eane fieri bonis, bono genere gnatis, boni consultis? ubi societas? ubi fides maiorum?' In like manner Laocoön's speech begins (42–4) with a series of rhetorical questions that achieve the same jolting effect. There are numerous other similarities as well. The syntactical structure of both speeches is simple; parataxis is preferred to hypotaxis; the subjects of sentences are shifted at will; and connecting relatives or particles are lacking between sentences.[7] The over-all effect achieved in the Cato fragment and in Laocoön's speech is one of spontaneity. Moreover, Laocoön's hysteron-proteron, 'inspectura domos venturaque desuper urbi' (47), conveys the idea of spontaneous speech—of Laocoön's speaking his thoughts as they come into his head. This device, again a kind of deliberate negligence, can also be paralleled in the fragments of Cato's speeches: e.g., 'decem funera facis, decem capita libera interficis' (fr. 59,

M.). For the same effect, Laocoön's most memorable line, 'quidquid id est, timeo Danaos et dona ferentis', is added paratactically to an already complet unit, an afterthought characteristic of colloquial speech and of archaic Roman oratory that valued the impression of spontaneity.[8]

Laocoön's speech neatly fits the description that Cicero gives of Cato's oratorical style (*Brutus* 65–9). Like Cato (*Brutus* 69), Laocoön speaks with striking brevity and in a simple, though unpolished, style. Cato's censorious tone (*Brutus* 65) has its parallel in the raging righteous indignation of Laocoön's words. As Cicero also notes (*Brutus* 65), Cato was famous for his aphorisms;[9] accordingly Laocoön's pointed conclusion, 'timeo Danaos et dona ferentis', is a *sententia* worthy to be included in the collection of aphorisms that was made in antiquity from Cato's writings.[10] The content of Laocoön's aphorism is no less reminiscent of Cato: Laocoön's sweeping condemnation of the Greeks provides a most striking parallel to Cato's well-known anti-Hellenic sentiments.

Cicero goes on to comment on the archaic diction exhibited in Cato's oratory ('antiquior est huius sermo', *Brutus* 68). In Laocoön's speech, the features of style that are reminiscent of archaic Roman poetry are noticed by R. G. Austin in his commentary on these verses. The use of *insania* (42) has an archaic flavour as does *ne* with the imperative (48); *machina muros* (45) may be an echo of Ennius' 'machina multa minax minitatur maxima muris'. The Lucretian element in Laocoön's speech adds to the archaism: Laocoön gives a series of alternative explanations, characteristic of Lucretius, and suddenly breaks off with *quidquid id est*, a Lucretian formula.[11]

That Laocoön's speech is built on the model of archaic Roman oratory therefore seems very likely. The diction of the speech exhibits the same 'curious amalgam' of elements which Palmer has characterized as typical of archaic Roman prose.[12] Within a very narrow compass of verses, Laocoön, by his words and his actions, shows himself to be a rude, old-world figure, outspoken, energetic, stubborn, confident, ruggedly individualistic, and (to be slightly anachronistic) anti-Hellenic. His short, abrupt, and emphatic sentences with their explosive staccato and censorious rage mark him as a man of shrewd common sense, one who is not to be tricked. If he is not Cato himself, he is surely Cato's *vir bonus dicendi peritus*, the prototype of the early Roman. Virgil's characterization of Laocoön therefore carries with it an ethical context of early Republicanism which—as will be suggested later—colours Aeneas' interpretation of events at Troy in significant ways.

Sinon is an equally vivid character, though obviously very different from Laocoön in both personality and style of oratory. Unlike Laocoön, Sinon is a man of words alone, not a man of words coupled with action. The difference between the two as orators might be summed up in the contrast between Roman and Greek as Cato himself saw it: 'The words of the Greeks stem from their lips, whereas those of the Romans stem from their hearts' (Plutarch, *Cato Maior* 12. 5). A modern commentator has ventured a suggestive remark on Sinon's speech: 'Cicero would have enjoyed reading it, and would have recognized its quality.'[13] Clearly if Sinon's speech were to be dated in the history of Roman oratory, it would have to be placed some time after Greek rhetorical rules were enthusiastically studied and consciously applied; that is, Sinon's speech would most probably fall some time within Cicero's span of life. The speech has a definite structure: it falls into three sections (77–104, 108–44, 154–94), each being slightly longer than the preceding. His very first words to the Trojans (69–73) constitute a carefully contrived tricolon of increasing magnitude. Unlike Laocoön, Sinon begins his speech slowly so as to give his audience time to focus their attention: *Cuncta equidem tibi* (77), like Cicero's *Quo usque tandem*, allures the listener by postponing the burden of meaning in the crucial opening statement. Where Laocoön boldly plunged into his speech, Sinon pays strict attention to the rules for proper delivery (*actio*): he stands silent and surveys his audience with his eyes (68); as he speaks he is *pavitans* (107). The first clause of Sinon's speech is bracketed by *cuncta . . . vera* (76–7), the key word *vera* being run over on to the next line for emphasis. In general, Sinon secures his emphasis by careful and artful positioning of words, not by jolting his audience as Laocoön had done. In contrast to the directness of Laocoön's words, Sinon's sentences are filled with subtleties, qualifications, nuances, and circumlocutions. It is clear even from these miscellaneous observations that Sinon is meant to represent a style of oratory far different from Laocoön's Catonian rhetoric: unlike the deliberate negligence of Laocoön's art, Sinon's speech is an example of artistic oratory in which the rules for elegant style are carefully and consciously applied.

This can perhaps best be seen by a general comparison of the constituent parts of Sinon's speech with the rhetorical rules as found in the standard Roman handbooks on the subject.

The first section of the speech (77–104) constitutes an *exordium* or formal introduction. Of the two species of *exordium* defined in Cicero's *De Inventione* (1. 20), Sinon uses *insinuatio*, the kind recommended for the speaker whose listeners are violently hostile. This oblique way of beginning, according to Cicero, gives just enough information to break down the audience's hostility by appealing to their curiosity. The textbook describes Sinon's situation and methods exactly. Especially effective in this connection is Sinon's use of anacoluthon at verse 100, where he tantalizes his audience with the beginning of a sentence and then breaks off with a rhetorical question: 'Nec requievit enim, donec Calchante ministro— |sed quid ego haec autem nequiquam ingrata revolvo | quidve moror?' (100–2). Sinon then hands himself over to the mercy of his hearers

(102–3), a trope known as *permissio* in rhetorical handbooks (cf. *Rhetorica ad Herennium* 4. 39). In Sinon's introduction several *loci* ('common-places') are used to secure *confirmatio* (cf. *De Invent*. 1. 34–77); that is, he works in small details which help lend credence to the account. Examples of *confirmatio* are numerous: Sinon admits the obvious ('neque me Argolica de gente negabo', 78); he introduces his own real name (79); he hints at what sort of person he is ('miserum | nec . . . mendacem', 79–80); he tells of the condition and the accidents of his life (86–7), including his 'pauper pater': and so on, just as is recommended in the most systematic rhetorical handbooks.

Verses 108–36 of Sinon's speech give the *narratio* proper (cf. *De Invent*. 1. 27–30). Sinon's use of *insinuatio* has broken down the audience's hostility so that the Trojans are 'burning to know and to seek the causes' (105). Now the audience is in the proper frame of mind to listen at greater length to the complexities of Sinon's story. Following the rule for a good *narratio* (*De Invent*. 1. 27), Sinon does not just relate the events but introduces the allegedly actual words of a protagonist (116–19). The narration breaks off at verse 136, and Sinon ends with a carefully contrived, climactic peroration (cf. *De Invent*. 1. 98–109). In concluding his personal appeal, he again uses well-known *loci*, this time to secure *conquestio* or *commiseratio*, as such perorations are variously termed in rhetorical handbooks. Sinon calls to mind his fatherland, his children, his father; he swears by the gods and begs his hearers for pity (137–44). His peroration is emotionally charged and brief, as is prescribed by the rules of Greek rhetoric (*De Invent*. 1. 109).

In the third and longest section of Sinon's speech (154–94), the orator now has the upper hand over his audience. The first two sections constitute a plea on his own behalf and carefully avoid giving any specific information about what the Trojans are most eager to hear: the meaning of the Trojan horse. Having been pardoned, Sinon has the audience's full attention; they are now more willing to listen to the most complex part of Sinon's story.

Perhaps the most significant feature of Sinon's speech as a whole is its constant appeal to the psychology of the audience—a requisite feature of all good oratory according to Cicero (e.g., *De Oratore* 1. 17; 1. 53–4). In verses 137–40 Sinon appealed to his Trojan (i.e. proto-Roman) audience's sense of family; in verses 155–9 he pays due regard to his audience's religious scruple and sense of law. In addition to the feeling he shows for the audience's psychology, Sinon exploits the possibilities of delivery (*actio*) to the fullest: he shed tears during his speech (*lacrimis coactis*, 196) and stirred tears in his audience as a result ('Hic lacrimis vitam damus et miserescimus ultro', 145).

In keeping with the *loci* and the artistic structure of Sinon's speech,

many features of the elegant style are exhibited. Sinon's sentence structure
is subtle and complex, an effect which Virgil achieves in verse by frequent
enjambment (e.g. 79–87). Through the use of relatives, adverbs, and
particles connection between sentences is logically tight. The style is
predominantly hypotactic, with many complex periods (e.g. 163–70).
Tricola of increasing magnitude, both with and without anaphora, are
used with conscious artistry (97–9; 172–5). An effective use of litotes is
found at verse 91: *haud ignota loquor*. Although it would be only labouring
the point, it would be interesting to see how many of the stock figures of
diction listed in the *Rhetorica ad Herennium* (4. 18–69) can be paralleled in
Sinon's speech. Even without an exhaustive catalogue there is no doubt
that the speech is striking for both the number and the variety of conscious
rhetorical devices.

It seems unlikely, however, that Sinon's speech is meant to be an
example of good Ciceronian oratory. Though Cicero would have recognized many meritorious features in the speech, doubtless he would have
read it as Virgil intended it to be read: Sinon's style is over-artful and too
elegant—an example of art that calls attention to itself.[14] It is only because
the naïve Trojans are being characterized as totally unfamiliar with Greek
loci that Sinon's speech succeeds. In its over-all construction the speech
adheres more closely to rhetorical precepts than Cicero's more mature
theory and practice would permit. In other words, Sinon's speech is much
more in keeping with the precepts of Cicero's *De Inventione*, an early
handbook, itself heavily indebted to Greek models; the speech would be
viewed more critically from the perspective of the *Orator* and *De Oratore*,
later works in which Cicero was attempting to go beyond the schemata of
Greek rhetorical handbooks.[15] Moreover, if one were to judge according to
the precepts of Cicero's later theory, Sinon's sentence structure is too
involved to be appropriate in the plea; it is a style more suited to history or
to epideictic oratory (cf. Cicero, *Orator* 207). Cicero, who preached and
usually practised restraint in forensic oratory, recommended in his later
theory that, when pleading a case, a speaker should not use periods more
than four hexameters in length (*Orator* 221–2). Yet Sinon's speech
contains no less than three examples of periods that considerably exceed
Cicero's rule-of-thumb: vv. 81–7 (seven hexameters), 153–9 (six hexameters), and 163–70 (eight hexameters). According to Cicero's later
theory, a long and involved periodic style such as Sinon's produces the
impression of insincerity when used in the courts (*Orator* 209). To cite
Cicero's words in another place: '. . . suspicionem artificii apud eos, qui res
iudicent, oratori adversariam esse arbitror, imminuit enim et oratoris
auctoritatem et orationis fidem' (*De Oratore* 2. 156). This Cicero—the
Cicero of the *Orator* and the *De Oratore*—is not likely to have had such a
high opinion of Sinon's speech. The difference between Laocoön's and

Sinon's styles of speaking is in fact something more then the difference between Cato's oratory and that of Cicero: Sinon's speech is meant to suggest the excesses to which rhetorical study could lead—excesses of the very sort which Cicero's later rhetorical theory sought to eliminate from forensic oratory.[16]

However ambiguous Virgil may have been about his task, as the poet of Roman *imperium* he doubtless was expected, and felt obliged to pay homage to early Republican virtue. The most celebrated passage explicitly raising this theme is Anchises' prophecy in Book 6, where Cato himself, the epitome of the early Republican age, is singled out for due honour (*magne Cato*, 6. 841). In beginning the story of Troy's downfall with the contrast between Laocoön and Sinon, Virgil is pointing up the same theme in a more subtle way. In the confrontation of oratorical styles Laocoön and the early Republican qualities which he exhibits are shown to have much more ethical integrity than things Greek. The reminiscence of Cato gives a moral dimension to the conflict between oratorical styles, linking Laocoön to a pristine form of Romanness and Sinon to a decadent form of Greekness. The effect of these associations is to make the Trojan character more sympathetic and palatable to a Roman audience—despite such uncomfortable facts as that the Trojans were Asiatics, that they were defeated militarily by the Greeks, and that the gods were acting against Laocoön and Troy.

What does it mean for Aeneas to introduce the story of Troy's fall with a full account of the speeches of Laocoön and Sinon? In reporting the event within this framework, Aeneas is focusing on the secular and human side of the reasons for Troy's fall. There is very little recourse in his account to religious explanation beyond a wistful statement which evenhandedly distributes responsibility to the *fata divum* and mental error: 'if the fates of the gods, if our minds had not been unfavourably disposed (*laeva*)', Aeneas laments, Laocoön would have prevailed and Troy would still be standing (2. 54–6).[17] Only later in the story is divine agency stressed, and that is done by Venus, who has to illustrate graphically for Aeneas the *divum inclementia, divum,* . . . (2. 602 ff.). In Aeneas' report it is not the walls of Troy which are 'perjured', as they are in Jupiter's eyes (*Aen.* 5. 811); it is Sinon who is 'perjured' through his art. As Aeneas interprets the story at this stage in the poem, the Trojans were not beaten militarily, they were cheated by false rhetoric:

> Talibus insidiis periuurique arte Sinonis
> credita res, captique dolis lacrimisque coactis
> quos neque Tydides nec Larisaeus Achilles,
> non anni domuere decem, non mille carinae.   (2. 195–8)

By introducing and reporting the story of Troy's fall on the level of human interaction, Aeneas is able to claim a military stand-off and moral superiority while admitting defeat. From Aeneas' anthropocentric perspective Troy fell because of the good qualities of her people: their innocence, their honesty, their sympathy, their sincerity—in short, their artlessness. But the *Aeneid* as a whole will show the anthropocentric perspective to be unfortunately, even tragically, limited in its explanatory powers. Aeneas' experiences in the poem will enlarge his perspective as he comes to appreciate more fully the importance of *fata divum* in the workings of human history. More immediately, following right upon the speeches of Laocoön and Sinon, his own graphic account of the terrible slaughter and destruction reveals, as does the *Aeneid* as a whole, how pyrrhic moral victories can be.[18]

NOTES

1. Cf. the use of *ecce* in Aeneas' narrative: vv. 57, 203, 318, 402, 526, 673, 682. The interjection occurs twice as many times in *Aeneid* 2 as in any other book; *Aeneid* 6, for all its amazing elements, has *ecce* only four times.

2. Cato was as much the prototype of the old Roman in Virgil's time as he is now. For Cato's well-known energy, see Nepos, *Cato* 3 ('In omnibus rebus singulari fuit industria') and Plutarch, *Cato Maior* 1. 3. For Cato's bodily strength and vigour, see Plutarch, op. cit., 24. 1. Plutarch appears to be one of the first to note that for Cato *le style est l'homme même* (7. 1). The same maxim may be applied equally well to Laocoön. On the legend of Laocoön there is a wealth of background information in H. Kleinknecht, 'Laokoön', *Hermes* 79 (1944), 66–111.

3. For features of archaic Roman oratory I have used L. R. Palmer, *The Latin Language* (London, 1954), ch. 5; Eduard Norden, *Die Antike Kunstprosa* (Leipzig, 1898) i, pp. 159–293; M. L. Clarke, *Rhetoric at Rome* (London, 1953); A. D. Leeman, *Orationis Ratio*, 2 vols. (Amsterdam, 1963). On Cato's oratorical style in particular, there is some good information in Aulus Gellius, who discusses Tiro's criticisms of some speeches of Cato (*Noctes Atticae* 6. 3). Norden's rhetorical analyses of speeches in Book 6 are very suggestive (*P. Vergilius Maro, Aeneis Buch* VI (2nd edn., Leipzig, 1915)); there are also some useful observations, statistics, and bibliography in Gilbert Highet's *The Speeches in Virgil's Aeneid* (Princeton, 1972), though Laocoön's speech is not analysed.

4. Palmer (above, n. 3), pp. 122, 86.

5. M = H. Malcovati, *Oratorum Romanorum Fragmenta* (2nd edn., Turin, 1955).

6. Palmer (above, n. 3), p. 123.

7. Cf. many of these same features in the opening of Cato's *Pro Rhodiensibus* (fr. 163, M) and see the comments on this fragment by Norden (above, n. 3), p. 167.

8. On the colloquial basis of Cato's language, see Palmer (above, n. 3), pp. 121–2; on the afterthought in archaic Roman writing, ibid., pp. 79–80; cf. also Highet (above, n. 3), p. 132 and n. 69. For the use of *aut* introducing questions as a feature of colloquial style and early comedy, see the commentary of R. G. Austin, *Aeneidos Liber Secundus* (Oxford, 1963), p. 46 (on verse 43 of Laocoön's speech, 'aut illa putatis|dona carere dolis Danaum?').

9. Cf. Plutarch, *Cato Maior* 7. 1: in his speeches Cato was *apophthegmatikos kai agonistikos*. A good example of Cato's censorious rage is fr. 169, M.

10. The remains of Cato's famous *sententiae* are collected in H. Jordan, *M. Catonis praeter librum de re rustica quae exstant* (Stuttgart, 1976), pp. 97 ff.; Plutarch, *Cato Maior* 8–9, gives a large sample. For Cato's anti-Hellenic sentiments, see Pliny, *N.H.* 29. 14.

11. Austin (above, n. 8), pp. 46–7 cites these features of Laocoön's speech that are reminiscent of archaic Roman poetry, but does not generalize on the nature of Laocoön's language. Cf. the remarks of Palmer on Cato's speeches (above, n. 3), pp. 122–3.

12. Palmer (above, n. 3), p. 123.

13. Austin (above, n. 8), p. 93 (on v. 194).

14. Highet (above, n. 3), pp. 282–90 concludes his study with some suggestive remarks about the suspicion of oratory in the *Aeneid* as opposed to the high place given to speaking well in the Homeric epics. He also observes some further qualities in Sinon's speech that emphasize its Greekness and serve to make his words suspect, namely the associations of Sinon's language with Greek tragedy and with the character of Odysseus (pp. 16–17 and 247–8).

15. See Leeman (above, n. 3) i. 120–1, a discussion which nicely reveals the degree of kinship between Sinon's speech and the *De Inventione* rather than the *De Oratore*.

16. The episode about Achaemenides, the Greek castaway left behind after Ulysses' encounter with the Cyclops, has long been recognized to contain numerous similarities to the story of Sinon (*Aen.* 3. 588–654). One commentator suggests that this may be due to the unfinished state of the *Aeneid*: 'when Virgil was writing the second book he used this passage as a quarry, intending to recast or remove it later on' (R. D. Williams, *Aeneidos Liber Tertius* (Oxford, 1962), p. 181). It is equally possible, however, that the reminiscences in *Aeneid* 3 are deliberate and thematic. Virgil may be echoing the Sinon story to pick up the theme of the Troja's *naïveté* of oratory: even with the paradigm of Sinon fresh in their minds, the guileless Trojans are still not suspicious of Achaemenides. For other views of the significance of this episode see Highet (above, n. 3), pp. 28–9, n. 20.

17. Some commentators have taken *deum* in v. 54 with *mens* as well as with *fata*, but as Servius (ad loc.) suggests, such a conjunction is difficult to uphold in view of the way in which *deum* is separated from *mens*; cf. the discussion in R. G. Austin's commentary (above, n. 8) ad loc., p. 50. According to the interpretation put forward in this essay, *mens* would be connected with the Trojan's *naïveté* of rhetoric and would constitute an *ex post facto* comment hinting at the sentiment in vv. 195–8 (quoted in the text below).

18. I would like to thank my friends and colleagues at the University of California at Santa Cruz who read a draft of this essay and offered useful criticism: Harry Berger, Jr., Norman O. Brown, Gary Miles, and Mary-Kay Orlandi. Special thanks are also due to Professor Bernard Knox, Director of the Center for Hellenic Studies in Washington, D.C., whose encouragement led me to work up these ideas for publication.

THE FALL OF TROY[1]

By K. W. GRANSDEN

Fragments and summaries are all that survive of the two primary epics which originally covered the fall of Troy: the *Little Iliad* of Lesches and the *Iliou Persis* of Arktinos.[2] I shall also be referring to the late *Post-Homerica* of Quintus Smyrnaeus. Certain details in Virgil's narrative imply that he and Quintus knew the same source material, though for my purpose here Quintus is chiefly used to indicate another possible mode of narrative treatment, particularly of the relation between the Sinon and Laocoon stories.[3]

We know that the *Little Iliad* included the 'marriage' of Helen to Deiphobus after the death of Paris (Deiphobus' subsequent fate came into the *Iliou Persis*). Then there was the construction of the wooden horse; the stealing of the Palladion by Odysseus and Diomede; the taking in of the horse by the Trojans, who broke down their own wall to get it through, an important detail Virgil retains, as he needs it to help to 'carry' Sinon's story; the character of Sinon himself, in his role of guileful persuader; the nocturnal feasting of the Trojans (just admitted in *Aeneid* 2); and the striking passage in which Menelaus drew his sword to kill Helen but was overcome by her beauty and spared her.[4]

The *Iliou Persis* included the council summoned to consider what to do with the horse; the two snakes which come from the sea and kill Laocoon; the pre-arranged fire signal which brought back the Greek fleet and coincided with the exit of the warriors from the horse was given by Sinon, and this seems to have been his main role in Arktinos' text. In Quintus he has a much larger part to play. There he is a spy planted by the Greeks, and he is the first to speak in the debate about the horse, where he puts forward the *adikos logos*. In Virgil the debate is already under way, with Thymoetes and Capys representing the two opinions, before Sinon appears, and it is to this ongoing debate that Laocoon makes his dramatic and fateful contribution.[5]

Other ingredients of the *Iliou Persis* relevant to *Aeneid* 2 are: the story of Coroebus, who came to Troy to woo Cassandra and died trying to defend her; the killing of Priam by Pyrrhus at the altar of Zeus Herkeios; the killing of Deiphobus by Menelaus and Odysseus – the grim and graphic account of his manifestation to Aeneas in *Aeneid* 6 attests a powerful tradition and recalls also the Hector episode in book 2; in both cases the heroes' mutilation is stressed. And the *Iliou Persis* told how Aeneas and his followers escaped to Mount Ida before the final destruction of the city, indeed after the death of Laocoon, a course earnestly counselled to Aeneas by Hector in the dream-sequence in *Aeneid* 2: *heu fuge, nate dea, teque his, ait, eripe flammis,* 289, advice the hero could not be allowed by the implied author to follow, since it would not have sufficiently demonstrated to the implied Roman reader (nor by Aeneas himself to Dido) the full measure of heroic courage to be properly postulated for the founder of the Roman nation.

Clearly Virgil faced an *embarras de richnesse*. No story, probably, in the ancient world had been more extensively and variously treated. The unfinished state of *Aeneid* 2, attested by the exceptional number of hemistichs (if it really was one of the books he read to Augustus, as tradition tells us, then he must surely have presented it as work in progress), strongly suggests that he had not finally decided on the shape of the narrative and the relation of the various episodes he wanted to include. Moreover, the role of Aeneas needed to be presented with the greatest tact and skill. He must want to stay in Troy and fight on, but fate calls him away. He must not be seen, must not present himself nor be presented, as running away, but as responding to the call of a higher duty. This motif, so strong in the *Aeneid*, is also prominent in Quintus, who stresses how hard Aeneas fought, and how in saving his family, he carried out his destiny to found by the Tiber 'a city glorious and holy for men of the future', as well as showing his familial piety. How prophetically Dido ought to have understood, and in retrospect interpreted, the events of book 2. How brilliantly Virgil, the author behind the voice of the heroic narrator, presented the book as a structural paradigm of book 4. Early in 2, Aeneas says to Dido – it is at a significant moment, when Laocoon thrusts his spear into the horse – 'If fate had not been against us, if our minds had not been deluded, he had surely there and then made us handsel with blood that Greek hiding place, and then, ah, Troy would still be standing; Priam's citadel, thou wouldst still be there.'

Dido is to hear that heartfelt sentiment from Aeneas' lips once more, before he leaves her; he says in 4: 'If fate had let me do it my way, I'd have rebuilt Troy, and Priam's citadel would still be there.' Throughout Aeneas' narrative there is a double hindsight: Aeneas' own, and the implied author's. In retrospect, some kind of sense must be made of what must in the light of history appear to have been the most sensational failure of judgement ever perpetrated. The tradition that the Trojans were silly, strongly felt and entirely appropriate in Greek tradition, presented the Roman poet, and the Roman hero-narrator, with a difficult challenge. The solution Virgil found was an extremely subtle one: the Trojans must be deceived not so much by *Urdummheit* as by wishful thinking. This wishful thinking is first given expression in the passage, very early in 2, in which Aeneas tells Dido with what joy the Trojans wandered freely across the beach-head, for the first time for a decade, with the Greeks gone, apparently for good; and with what a sense of amazement (*stupet, mirantur*, 31–2) they gazed upon the extraordinary object which had so mysteriously materialized outside the city walls. Now in Quintus (who also records the joy and wonder of the Trojans, which we may reasonably suppose to have been a likely ingredient of the cyclic narrative) Laocoon does not intervene in the debate until after Sinon's story, which is there presented as the first contribution to the debate. This is much less convincing and interesting as narrative. That no one should have made any contribution to the debate, or offered any reaction to the phenomenon, until the planted spy had had his say, does indeed present the Trojans as foolish. Moreover in Quintus, the Trojans torture and mutilate Sinon, cutting off his nose and ears (cf. the fate of Virgil's Deiphobus in *Aeneid* 6), so that he is presented as a Greek hero, prepared, like Odysseus, to endure hardship and suffering. Quintus develops this passage with grotesque and gratuitous lack of narrative propriety. Virgil, through the one-off characters of Thymoetes and Capys, neatly dramatizes the traditional debate of the epic cycle – should the horse be destroyed or preserved, is it bad or good medicine – and this works well as narrative, especially when Laocoon makes his intervention. To burn or destroy the horse – or to set it up as a cult object (for the Trojans were superstitious as well as foolish, or to put a better light on their behaviour, religious as well as optimistic) – these were the traditional alternatives, though in the *Odyssey* throwing it down from a hill top replaces burning. Virgil's object in developing the Sinon episode is to make the 'Trojan solution' seem both plausible and right.

Laocoon's intervention, in support of Capys, actually articulates the *melior sententia* and 'prophesies' the truth: *aut hoc inclusi ligno occultantur Achiui*, 45. His opening cry of *quae tanta insania, ciues?* (42) has a Cassandra-like ring, and indeed there are parallels between the two characters, both priestly, both possessed of ignored insights. Aeneas, in telling Dido this story, must tell it with the fullest ironic hindsight, which is as much his as the implied author's. Dido knows, like everyone else, the outcome of the most famous night in history, itself already the subject of some reliefs in one of her own temples. She knows what happened, but not how or why. The reader must not only, like Dido, be attentive to the voice of Aeneas, but to that of the author, and decode the text simultaneously on two levels, 'this is how I reacted' and 'this is how he reacted'. Thus for one nostalgic and incredible moment Aeneas and the narrator dwell on the unthinkable hypothesis 'if we had listened to Laocoon Troy might never have fallen'. But his voice, like Cassandra's, is unheeded. At this moment, as if on cue, as indeed he is, Sinon enters. He is introduced by the signal word *ecce* (57), which is particularly common in book 2. It is the story-teller's signifier for 'And what do you think happened then?'[6]

Sinon's story is in *oratio recta* which adds another voice to this complex narrative. The structure now is: Virgil – Aeneas – Sinon. It is as if Aeneas acts out the role of Sinon. We might almost imagine him putting on a different accent. A possible analogy to Sinon's rhetorical strategy might be found in *Othello* III.i, in which Iago succeeds in making Othello believe things which, though possible, are false. This scene starts when Cassio leaves the stage and Othello asks Iago 'Was not that Cassio parted from my wife?' Iago replies that it could not have been, he would never have sneaked away like that on seeing you coming: the suppressed ellipse is 'unless, of course, he were guilty'. Desdemona, having nothing to hide, confirms that it was indeed Cassio. Othello's 'Went he hence now?' confirms Iago in a lie, but a lie meant to be seen through, meant to discredit Cassio (a guilty sneak) and to establish Iago's credibility with Othello (an honest fellow reluctant to sneak on one officer to another). Once Iago has established credibility on this crucial point – it *was* Cassio, he *was* talking to Desdemona, he *did* sneak away – it is easy for him to convince Othello not merely that Cassio is untrustworthy but (a seeming impossibility) that Desdemona is. ('She did deceive her father, marrying you.') Othello's rather pathetic observation 'Men should be what they seem' might serve as a text for the Trojan reaction to Sinon's story. It is worth adding that while Othello emerges as gullible almost to the point of stupidity, he still retains for the audience heroic dignity and heroic credibility, as Aeneas and the Trojans must contrive to do also.

Sinon begins with a truth, or at least with a story which is more than half true. Like Quintus, Virgil follows a tradition that Sinon was a victim of Odysseus. 'I wonder,' he begins, 'if you have heard the story of Palamedes.' Now this story is a famous one: every one would have known it; it is his initial bid for credibility. Palamedes caught Odysseus out in an attempt to dodge the draft by feigning insanity. Odysseus subsequently put him to death, and Sinon, being, or so he claims, a kinsman, had sided with him. *haud ignota loquor* (91), says Sinon, having got everyone interested and said nothing that was not well-known (the story was in the now lost primary epic *Cypria* which had been composed to cover the events leading up to the *Iliad*). His cleverest card was Odysseus. He was popularly supposed to have master-minded the whole plot of the wooden horse. His villainy is a *donnée* of the *Aeneid*. The words used of him in book 2, the Ithacan, *pellax, dirus, scelerum inuentor*, are in the voice of Aeneas and also of the implied author. Sinon, by presenting himself to the Trojans (falsely) as the victim of Ulysses, gains not only credibility but also sympathy. Having won these from his hearers, he 'does an Iago' and says that he does not expect either sympathy or credibility, for he is, after all, and does not make any secret of being, a Greek. *sed ... autem* (101), he says, and breaks off; 'but what's the use? To you Trojans all Greeks are the same. Why don't you kill me? How that would please the Ithacan.' Shakespeare's Iago too breaks off in an analogous way at just the point at which Othello's curiosity is aroused. There is the same pretended aposiopesis.

Pressed to continue (like Iago), Sinon goes to his next point. Again it is plausible, indeed probably true, that the Greeks sometimes wanted to abandon the siege: the second book of the *Iliad* bears witness to this. But Sinon passes now from the plausible and possible to the entirely fabricated: the oracle of Apollo, he says, consulted by the Greeks in frustration at the adverse weather conditions which prevented their sailing away, warns that an old curse, the sacrifice of Iphigeneia, must be assuaged by another victim. That victim, says Sinon, already earmarked by 'the Ithacan', was himself. Virgil here presents the same story as Quintus. Of course there is no victim, was no oracle. By linking himself to the well-known victim Palamedes through an invented kinship, Sinon presents himself as yet another victim of the crafty Ulysses. The listener makes the connections between disparate elements in the narrative. The technique is one of dialectical reading. Sinon's case would not stand up to cross-examination in a court of law. The listener himself does Sinon's work for him, organizing a series of assertions, some true, some invented, into a coherent and plausible narrative sequence.[7] But all this time, the monstrous effigy stands there, inexplicable, unexplained. If Sinon is a Greek, he ought to know what it is; so far, he has studiously avoided mentioning it. In the story he now presents, a total fabrication, he again wins sympathy and credibility by starting with a truth. Just as he had referred to one well-known story involving Ulysses, the story of Palamedes, so now he refers to another, also involving Ulysses, the theft of the Palladium, a notorious act, even if accounts varied as to whether it was the genuine Palladium that was taken, or whether there were two Palladia, one of which Aeneas himself took to Italy as part of the *sacra*. The very mention of the holy talisman would be enough to send an irrational shudder through the audience. There is in fact no connection between the Palladium and the wooden horse. But that is easily invented. Again the Trojans put together pieces of narrative, true and false, and make their own credible synthesis. That they do this successfully is largely the result of wishful thinking, confirmed (or so it appears) strikingly and dramatically by the fate of Laocoon. But before we come to that, another significant plausibility remains to be noted. It may seem highly probable that the theft of the Palladium turned Pallas against the Greeks, whose champion, in the *Iliad*, she had been. But this divine displeasure, says Sinon, does not mean the end of Greek hostility. And here he utters a resounding and ironic truth: *improuisi aderunt* (182), he says, they will be back when you least expect them. This is a double bluff by Sinon, the irony being directed by the author to the implied reader. But they cannot come back, he continues, until Pallas has been propitiated; Calchas made them construct this horse as an act of expiation.[8] It has been made deliberately too large for you to take it inside your walls, for if you did, you would be protected and will eventually mount an expedition against Greece herself.

Now in Quintus, the Trojans simply open the gates and take the horse in; there is no mention of its being too big. Virgil here follows the *Iliou Persis* in having the Trojans actually breach their own walls to let the monstrous object in. Virgil effectively links this decision to Sinon's story, without which the unthinkable act would surely not have been carried out: the Trojans begin to destroy their own walls, anticipating what the Greeks and the gods together will soon finish. A powerful narrative irony operates through this crucial detail. This is the stupidest thing the Trojans ever did or could have done, yet it must be presented as the supreme challenge to their *pietas*, a challenge to which they rose without hesitation. Moreover, the fate of Laocoon seemed wholly to confirm the rightness as well as the morality of what they did. Virgil links the Sinon and Laocoon episodes into an a–b–a structure: Laocoon–Sinon–Laocoon. Sinon's contention that the horse must be venerated as a cult-object even if the Greek attempt to foil its entry by making it too big can be countered only by an act of auto-destruction, seems to be confirmed when, with another signal of *ecce*

ecce autem gemini a Tenedo tranquilla per alta   (203)

the snakes come from the sea and kill Laocoon and his children. In Quintus they kill only the children, and this occurs inside Troy after the horse has been taken in; Laocoon himself is struck blind after Sinon's story, when he suggests that the horse be burned. This is much less effective as narrative. In Virgil's treatment, the false linking of events into a chain of causality (Laocoon wanted the horse destroyed, look how he has been punished for his blasphemy) is made easy, indeed virtually inescapable for the reader by the a–b–a structure, for which it seems to have been expressly designed. As a result, in the words of Aeneas as the narrator, the Trojans, whom neither Diomede nor

Achilles nor ten years of siege could crush, were finally defeated by a
trick. It was a foregone conclusion at the moment when Laocoon died.
There was his wicked spear, still stuck in the side of the sacred object.
The horse continues to be called sacred until it is inside the city. Then
it is called *monstrum infelix* (245), *fatalis machina* (237). It becomes,
by being correctly named, what it really is, and indeed always was, as
in hindsight the narrator, Dido, and the reader knew all along. It is
as if everyone knows how the play will end except the actors.

Laocoon was a priest and it was while exercising his priestly function
that he is killed. Virgil tells us that he was elected as priest of Neptune;
in an earlier tradition mentioned by Servius he was a priest of Apollo,
the role taken in *Aeneid* 2 by Panthus. Apollo and Neptune were joint
builders of the walls of Troy. It is they who destroy them. Neptune is
specifically singled out in the theophany later in the book:

> Neptunus muros magnoque emota tridenti
> fundamenta quatit. (610–11)

Whether the snakes were sent by Pallas, as Austin assumes, or by
Neptune, is unspecified. But it is a gratuitous death. The only possible
parallel might be Palinurus, another victim of Neptune, also struck
down suddenly and without warning, though the reader is there prepared for *a* victim as the price exacted by the god for the Trojans'
safe landfall in Latium. Palinurus becomes a figure of the unburied
dead and is appropriately assimilated into book 6. The death of
Laocoon, a priest at his own altar (he is sacrificing a bull when he is
struck down, and is compared to a bull inefficiently struck down at
the altar who runs off in pain, a peculiarly horrific simile), has another
significance in book 2.

Having dragged the horse inside the city through their breached
walls, the Trojans deck their temples in a holiday spirit, and fall asleep.
Virgil touches on the tradition, preserved at greater length by Quintus,
that they spent the night on a kind of V-day binge: Aeneas admits
that when Sinon released the warriors from the horse the city was
'sunk in sleep and wine'. During this fatal night Aeneas dreams that
he sees Hector. His mutilated figure symbolizes and portends the
disaster which is even now about to fall upon the city of which he was
for so long a bulwark – a disaster foretold not only by Laocoon but
also by another priestly figure, Cassandra. Like Laocoon, she is not
believed (246–7). Again, the narrator signals this next dramatic event
with *ecce* (270). In his dream, says Aeneas, 'I seemed to speak to him'.
His words show how complete was his temporal and spatial dislocation
from reality. He has forgotten how Hector died, and seemed also to
have forgotten recent events, to which he refers vaguely: 'so many

deaths and tribulations undergone by the city and her people.' Aeneas
retains this strange sense of dislocation in narrating his dream to Dido.
His famous words

> ei mihi, qualis erat, quantum mutatus ab illo
> Hectore qui redit exuuias indutus Achilli   (274–5)

though addressed to Dido, belong to the confusion and delusion of
his dream, for they imply that he last remembers Hector when he had
just killed Patroclus. In projecting his surprise that Hector has been
mutilated, Aeneas and the implied author reinforce the sense of Trojan
bewilderment with a pathos no less effective for being completely
unreal. Aeneas' questions to Hector are thus irrelevant, since they
relate solely to his appearance and to Aeneas' confused feeling that
the light and hope of Troy has somehow, inexplicably, deserted her.
Then, at line 287

> ille nihil, nec me quaerentem uana moratur

Aeneas suddenly brings his narrative up to date, back into reality. The
implied author has a moral and structural plan in composing this
passage. Hector's role is a prophetic one, like Laocoon's and Cassandra's. Ignoring his irrelevant questions, Hector brings Aeneas once
again face to face with the truth.

> 'heu fuge, nate dea, teque his' ait 'eripe flammis.
> hostis habet muros; ruit alto a culmine Troia.
> sat patriae Priamoque datum; si Pergama dextra
> defendi possent, etiam hac defensa fuissent.
> sacra suosque tibi commendat Troia penatis;
> hos cape fatorum comites, his moenia quaere
> magna pererrato statues quae denique ponto.'   (289–95)

'Troy is falling. If any hand might have saved her, mine would have.
Now she commends her *sacra* and her penates to your protection.
Leave now.' These crucial words represent Aeneas' sanction to escape.
Virgil has postponed Aeneas' flight from its traditional moment, after
Laocoon's death. The narrative reason for this is clear: Aeneas must
be the eye-witness through whom the epic narrator can present to
Dido and the reader a treatment of the destruction of a city which
remains unsurpassed in its power and immediacy. There are some
crucial episodes to come – the deaths of Panthus and Priam, the spurious
Helen passage, the epiphany of Venus and the theophany, and the
death of Creusa – but Aeneas now carries in Hector's words a mandate
for his eventual and inevitable departure. He has a new role. His role
as *dux* is temporarily in abeyance, to be resumed after he lands in
Italy. Paramount now is his role as *penatiger*, as guardian of the *sacra*.

One priest, Laocoon, has died already; Panthus is next; Priam is killed seeking sanctuary, like Cassandra, in vain. Only Aeneas can take over the priestly role, and he only if he escapes. Dryden pointed out in his *Dedication to the Aeneis* that Virgil here 'plainly touches at the office of high priesthood, with which Augustus was invested. . . . That office . . . was made vacant by the death of Panthus for Aeneas to succeed to it, and consequently for Augustus to enjoy.'

The appearance of the mutilated figure of Hector has affinities with the appearance of Deiphobus in the underworld (6.494–547). His mutilation is described even more violently than Hector's. When Aeneas asks how he was wounded, he tells how, on the last night of Troy, Helen (in whose bed he had succeeded Paris) betrayed him to Menelaus and Ulysses. There too a dead and mutilated Trojan hero advises Aeneas to go forward to a better destiny than his own (*i, decus, i nostrum: melioribus utere fatis*, 546).

Awakening from his dream of Hector, Aeneas goes at once to his father's house, where he ascends to the roof and sees Deiphobus' house in ruins. Presumably the grim scene of betrayal and death described later by Deiphobus has already been enacted. Now, with another signal of *ecce autem* (318), comes the passage in which Panthus, Apollo's priest, is trying to escape taking with him the *sacra*, Troy's defeated gods (the penates) and his small nephew: a clear prefiguration of Aeneas himself. But not even his great *pietas* nor his priestly ribbon could save him, says the narrator. His bid to save the *sacra* had failed. He died along with Coroebus, who had come to Troy to woo Cassandra and tried in vain to save her from being dragged off into slavery from the inner shrine of the temple of Minerva. All these scenes, culminating in the death of Priam himself, slain at his own altar, mutilated like Hector and Deiphobus, add up to an indictment of Greek sacrilege and depravity. From Hector's death (albeit long ago in the *Iliad*, and for this reason recalled in the dream-scene in *Aeneid* 2) to Priam's we encompass the entire degradation and downfall of Troy; neither her greatest champion, nor her walls, nor her priests, nor the gods to whom she has so assiduously sacrificed, can save her. Holy Ilium survives now only in the symbolism of her displaced *sacra*.

But if Aeneas is to remain in Troy, if he is to postpone his rescue of the *sacra*, he must stay on as more than a reporter. If he stays, he must fight. And for a brief moment he leads a counter-attack, born of the desperation of someone who no longer cares for life. The motif of Aeneas' death-wish, *moriamur ... una salus uictis nullam sperare salutem ... uadimus haud dubiam in mortem* (353–4, 359), is strongly heard in the Panthus episode. It is after Panthus' death, and before Priam's, that Aeneas expresses with extreme eloquence his feeling that

fate has protected him from the death in battle he had both courted
and earned.

With the deaths of Coroebus, Rhipaeus, and Panthus, and with
Aeneas' decision to try to defend Priam's palace, the narrative becomes
complicated, particularly from v. 458, when Aeneas climbs to the palace
roof (his second such ascent, closely resembling vv. 302–3, when he
climbed the roof of his father's house), down to 632 (*descendo ac ducente
deo*) when he returns to his father's house. This last phrase is in direct
response to Venus' exhortation, *eripe, nate, fugam* (619), an echo of
Hector's advice at v. 289 which brings the narrative full circle. In
Quintus Aeneas escapes to Mount Ida much earlier, after Laocoon's
sons are killed and under the guidance of Venus. It is strange that
Virgil should have written *deo* just after the epiphany of Venus, and
it is here that the unrevised state of book 2 is most evident. If we
excise the Helen episode as spurious and regard the Venus episode as
a later addition which Virgil had not yet integrated into the narrative,
then we proceed directly from 566, when Aeneas realizes he is alone
and that his family need him, to 624, when he comes down from the
roof of Priam's palace and returns home. This would leave 458–566
as a first draft of what would presumably have emerged finally as
'Aeneas' last stand'.[9] In his commentary on the Deiphobus passage in
book 6 Norden rightly points out that we do not need to use metrical
trivia (*metrische Kleinigkeite*) to condemn the Helen episode in book 2.
In the Deiphobus passage we have an authentic and powerful treatment
of the role of Helen on Troy's last night as it was in the *Iliou Persis*.
Whether she was a symbol, as she stood with her flaming torch on the
citadel of the doomed city, of that moonlight in which Troy was
betrayed, or whether her Bacchic torch was the pretext for a fire-signal
(perhaps reinforcing Sinon's), there is in the entire scene a certainty
of touch which places the scene firmly in the mainstream of the *Iliou
Persis* and of *Odyssey* 8, where the role of Menelaus and Odysseus in
killing Deiphobus with Helen's connivance is also attested (517–18).
And in the humiliation and mutilation of Deiphobus we have supporting evidence for the presentation of Hector in book 2.

The most distinguished defender of the Helen episode is Austin.
But the number of times he finds himself obliged to repeat the words
'there is no precise parallel in Virgil' is almost indictment enough of
itself. Words and phrases thus signalled out are: *praemetuens, aspicio,
exarsere ignes, sceleratas sumere poenas, subit ira … ulcisci*. To this may
be added the strong suspicion that *Tyndarida* in 569 is a clear borrowing
from 601, the Venus passage, the only occurrence of the form in the
Aeneid.

But even if we agree that on grounds of language and style the Helen

episode is un-Virgilian, and does not really belong to the narrative as
we have it, that is not quite the end of the matter. If we look at Quintus'
version, we find that he has followed, not the *Iliou Persis* but the *Little
Iliad*, which told how Helen ran away and hid in the palace where
Menelaus found her 'cowering from the anger of her lord'. Menelaus
contemplates killing her but is prevented by Aphrodite, as the result
of which he feels only love for Helen, yet continues to threaten her in
order to make his act look convincing to the Achaians, so that it is
ultimately Agamemnon who says

> Cease your anger, Menelaus, for it is not fitting
> To kill your wedded wife for whose sake we
> Have suffered much affliction, while we sought
> Vengeance on Priam. Helen was not to blame,
> But the guilt is Paris', who slighted
> Zeus Xenios and your own hospitality.

It seems clear that whoever wrote the Helen episode in *Aeneid* 2 was
adapting this version of the cycle. But the strongest condemnation of
the episode is surely to be found in the transfer of Menelaus' anger to
Aeneas. Would Virgil seriously have contemplated this, when Menelaus
was a villain ready to hand, with a much stronger motive for anger
against Helen than Aeneas had?

It is with something like relief that we turn from this dark and
confusing passage to the epiphany of Venus which, in our text, immediately follows it, a passage signed with Virgil's name in every phrase
and every line. There are no awkward expressions or *hapax legomena*.
The discourse flows eloquently and passionately. The theophany which
Venus reveals to Aeneas is one of the most striking passages in the book.
The words of Panthus, *ferus omnia Iuppiter Argos transtulit* (326–7),
becomes visibly true. Venus' speech is *not* a reproach to Aeneas for
trying to kill Helen, though one can see how the Helen episode might
have been written to explain a too-hastily digested reference to Helen
in Venus' speech, which is much more subtle than that. Its primary
purpose is to show Aeneas the pointlessness of further fighting. Her
words *eripe, nate, fugam, finemque impone labori* (619), reinforce those
of Hector. It also serves to support her guarantee in book 1: *nusquam
abero et tutum patrio te limine sistam* (620). Aeneas himself had also
said to the unidentified figure of the goddess

> sum pius Aeneas, raptosque ex hoste penates
> classe ueho mecum ...
> matre dea monstrante uiam data fata secutus. (1. 378–9, 382)

In the two epiphanies of Venus, in books 1 and 2, the reader feels an
overwhelming sense of the discrepancy between Aeneas' *pietas* and the

divine love and protection afforded him by the gods, and the sheer size and weight of his misfortunes.

Throughout book 2, Virgil's chief narrative problem – and one that he evidently had not completely solved when he died – was how plausibly, and how protractedly, to defer Aeneas' departure. If too soon, it would diminish the hero in Dido's and the reader's eyes. If too late, it would seem like folly or, worse, blind *furor*, to detain him in the doomed city fighting a rearguard action which would not merely achieve nothing but might have the negative result of letting the hero's family die unprotected. Venus actually says she herself has intervened to protect Anchises, and reproaches Aeneas for neglecting his familial responsibilities. Aeneas' last recorded thought before the supervention of the Helen scene was for his father, of whom he was reminded when he saw Priam die. This further indicates a lacuna between the narrative from 458 (Aeneas on the palace roof) to 566 (Aeneas alone, aware for the first time, with Priam dead, that the situation is past saving: *me tum primum saeuus circumstetit horror*, 559) – and the short passage which follows the theophany, when the hero comes down from the roof of the palace and hurries through the now blazing city in search of his family (624–31). Anchises at first refuses to leave. He feels that he is too old to start a new life of exile. This last delay to Aeneas' departure is extremely plausible both as narrative and as an instance of the implied author's insight into the psychology of the old. The phenomenon of the fire on his grandson's head – *innoxia flamma* in striking contrast to the destructive fire which is sweeping through Troy – causes him to pray to Jupiter, who sends the omens which finally persuade him to leave: the thunderclap and the star which, like Venus herself, shows Aeneas the way to Mount Ida and safety. It is to Anchises now that Aeneas entrusts the *sacra* and the penates, for his own hands are stained with blood. The mission prophetically entrusted to him by Hector gets under way at last.

The postscript in which Aeneas returns alone to the beleaguered city is perhaps the most moving ending of any of the twelve books of the *Aeneid*. The reader has a crucial role here: that of remembering that Aeneas is still talking to Dido. He is telling her how, without any hesitation, he went back for his wife, momentarily forgetting and defying his mission, putting personal feelings first for perhaps the only time in the poem. It takes the shade of Creusa herself to convince him that he is doing the wrong thing: her words at v. 776, *quid tantum insano iuuat indulgere dolori*, recall the cry of *quae tanta insania* uttered by Laocoon (in vain). She foretells now the long journey across the sea of exile to Italy. She commends Aeneas to the future, and to another woman, with her blessing. From Dido in the structurally correspondent close of book 4 Aeneas will depart without turning back, to receive from her not the blessings of history but its curse.

NOTES

1. This paper was delivered at the Annual Conference of the Classical Association in April 1984. I am indebted to my colleague Mr Peter Mack for drawing to my attention the discussion of Sinon's speech by Rudolph Agricola cited below, and also for suggesting a possible analogy between Sinon and Iago.

2. For the surviving fragments see E. Bethe, *Homer, Dichtung und Sage*, vol. 2 (Berlin, 1922), pp. 167–81, and C. Zintzen, *Die Laocoon Episode bei Vergil* (Mainz, 1983). For information on Proclus' *Chrestomathy*, a chronicle of post-Iliadic events which seem to have been based on the epic cycle, see G. L. Huxley, *Greek Epic Poetry* (London, 1969), pp. 123–6, 144–7.

3. See Malcolm Campbell, *A Commentary on Quintus Smyrnaeus, Post-Homerica XII* (Leiden, 1981). I shall not be concerned with the question of whether Quintus knew Virgil; if he did, as Campbell remarks, he forgot or ignored almost all that is remarkable in Virgil's narrative.

4. For this story see J. Griffin, *JHS* 97 (1977), 45. I discuss the passage in detail in connection with the pseudo-Virgilian Helen episode and the version in Quintus: see below.

5. In Triphiodorus' *Capture of Troy*, a brief text of less than seven hundred lines which, like Quintus' poem, must have used cyclic as well as Hellenistic material, Sinon also appears after the debate has started. See the Budé edition by B. Gerlaud (Paris, 1982).

6. *Ecce* occurs eight times in book 2, more often than in any other book of the *Aeneid*. It signals the appearance in the narrative of Sinon, the snakes, Hector, Panthus, Cassandra, Polites, Creusa, and the flames round the head of Iulus.

7. This point was made in the late fifteenth century by the renaissance scholar Rudolph Agricola in his *De Inventione Dialectica*, which includes a detailed and extremely modern reading of the Sinon episode.

8. Homer (*Odyssey* 8) says it was built with the aid of Pallas herself (cf. Virgil's *dona Mineruae*, 189).

9. On this question, and on the Helen episode, see further G. P. Goold, *HSCP* (1970), 101–68.

ADDITIONAL NOTE (1989)

Page 122 line 4
For 'the implied author' read 'the author'

Page 122 line 8
For '*richnesse*' read '*richesse*'

Page 130 line 3
For 'Rhipaeus' read 'Rhipeus'

Page 130 line 29
For 'entire scene' read 'entire passage'

DIDO, AENEAS, AND THE CONCEPT
OF *PIETAS*

By KENNETH MCLEISH

Various attempts have been made, over the years, to assess the character of Dido, and explain her presence in, and extraordinary influence on, the *Aeneid*. Some critics have seen her as the heroine of an Aristotelian tragedy; others believe that Virgil emulated Pygmalion, and fell in love with his own creation; the most perverse of all call her a digression, a fatal flaw in the construction of the poem, and one which irretrievably weakens our view of Aeneas himself.

But Virgil was far too accomplished a craftsman to make blunders of that sort. It is as ludicrous to assume that he was carried away, and ruined the shape of his work from inadvertence or incompetence, as it is to say that the Porter in *Macbeth* or the handkerchief scene in *Othello*[1] are excrescences that Shakespeare would have regretted if he had lived in a more self-critical age.

Dido is there because Virgil—a great poet, a consummate craftsman— wanted her there. Everything she says or does is part of the design, and her presence in the *Aeneid* must deepen our understanding, not lessen it. The contrary view, that she is the centre of some tongue-in-cheek anti-epic, a satire by Virgil against Augustus, simply collapses in the face of the *Aeneid* itself, a masterpiece full of the highest poetic inspiration, and with an inner logic, an adherence to its own artistic truth, that lift it high outside the realms of 'debunking' literature.

The oldest, simplest view of Dido seems to be the best: poetry apart, she is in the *Aeneid* principally to emphasize Aeneas' *pietas*. Books iv, v, and vi deal with different aspects of *pietas*, which is closely linked every time it appears with Aeneas' destiny, and the progression through Roman history to Augustus himself. The *pietas* in Books v and vi is easy to see; but in Book iv it is obscured—some say obliterated—by the character of Dido.

In parenthesis, it is worth considering this 'character'. To us Dido is a three-dimensional character, a real person whose emotions and actions have a roundness, a wholeness, that often seems missing in Aeneas himself. But we are post-Romantics: our view of Dido is filtered through Purcell, Dryden, Berlioz, and a hundred other interpreters. To a Roman of Virgil's day she was probably nothing more than an unbalanced barbarian queen, a definite encumbrance in Aeneas' way. Virgil's avowed purpose in undertaking the *Aeneid* was to present Aeneas as the founder of the Roman race and precursor of Augustus. He is far more important than any of the obstacles placed in his path. In such a context (and again,

leaving poetry aside) Dido might seem to have no larger a part to play than
Scylla, Charybdis, or Polyphemus himself.

Except, of course, for *pietas*, the theme that runs through her whole
relationship with Aeneas. Of the other qualities of a Roman hero, Aeneas'
gravitas and *dignitas*, his private and public integrity, suffer severe blows[2]
in the course of the work; only his *virtus* (particularly in Books ii and ix–
xii) and *pietas* remain intact, and in the end make it possible for him to
reach his destination and found his city. (And *virtus*, whenever it appears,
is closely linked to *pietas*—consider for example his stirring words to his
followers during the sack of Troy (ii. 348–54), or more interestingly the
very end of the *Aeneid*, where it is only *pietas* for the dead Pallas that can
bring Aeneas, after so many brave and heroic deeds, finally to kill Turnus
and fulfil his destiny (xii. 938–52).)

Even before Aeneas meets Dido in Book i, his *pietas* is heavily
emphasized. He is *insignem pietate virum* (i. 10); when he weeps for the
friends he thinks drowned (i. 220 ff.), stays awake planning for the future
(i. 305), or introduces himself to his own mother (i. 378), he is described as
pius Aeneas. His tears when he sees the decorations of Dido's temple (i.
456 ff.) could be instanced as a sign of his humanity, and his concern for
his dead comrades and living followers. But, interestingly, when he first
tells *Dido* his name, the description is purely factual (i. 595–6):

> adsum,
> Troius Aeneas, Libycis abreptus ab undis—

a marked contrast with Ilioneus' earlier words to the queen (i. 544–5):

> rex erat Aeneas nobis, quo iustior alter
> nec pietate fuit, nec bello maior et armis.

Dido's first appearance contrasts strongly with that of Aeneas. To Aeneas
himself she seems enviable simply because her kingdom is sure and
established (i. 437); but to us, the readers, she is first presented in a scene
of remarkable splendour, closely foreshadowing her entrance for the hunt
in Book iv:[3]

> haec dum Dardanio Aeneae miranda videntur,
> dum stupet obtutuque haeret defixus in uno,
> regina ad templum, forma pulcherrima Dido,
> incessit magna iuvenum stipante caterva.
> qualis in Eurotae ripis aut per iuga Cynthi
> exercet Diana choros, quam mille secutae
> hinc atque hinc glomerantur Oreades; illa pharetram
> fert umero gradiensque deas supereminet omnes
> (Latonae tacitum pertemptant gaudia pectus):
> talis erat Dido, talem se laeta ferebat
> per medios instans operi regnisque futuris.

tum foribus divae, media testudine templi,
saepta armis solioque alte subnixa resedit.
iura dabat legesque viris, operumque laborem
partibus aequabat iustis aut sorte trahebat.   (i. 494–508)

The simile here contrasts with the similes used later, when Aeneas casts off the cloud of invisibility and is first revealed to Dido (i. 586–93). Dido is compared to a goddess striding along in the midst of her excited followers; the emphasis is on bustle and movement; Aeneas on the other hand is given no attributes but handsomeness, a singularly static quality. When we compare this with the 'personal' similes in Book iv (see below), and particularly with iv. 141–50, where Aeneas/Apollo stands apart from barbaric bustle and movement, the pattern of Virgil's thought becomes clear.

The relationship between Dido and Aeneas in the rest of Book is largely formal—but even so the seeds of future destruction are carefully sown: cf. i. 613, Dido's first sight of Aeneas; i. 631–42, the banqueting-scene; the drinking of toasts in i. 734–40, picked up so superbly in i. 749. In fact, by the end of Book i, perhaps even before the gods plant the seeds of love in Dido's heart, she is shown as (a) un-Roman and (b) untouched by or oblivious to the very qualities in Aeneas that make him a 'Roman' hero. Aeneas on the other hand is presented with some care as a man of destiny, not unacquainted with grief, but above all solicitous for his followers and the will of the gods.

Books ii and iii are concerned with Aeneas' narration of the Fall of Troy: there is *pietas* here, and *virtus* in plenty; but the only point we need mention is the introduction to his speech (ii. 1–2), where he is conventionally described as *pater Aeneas*, and the very pointed repetition of the same phrase (coloured by all that has gone between) in the lines describing the end of his narration (iii. 716–18).

If the poem is read aloud, and only a small pause is made between Books iii and iv, the contrast between Aeneas and Dido is immediately obvious, the contrast that occupied Virgil for the greater part of Book iv. Aeneas is calm, quiet, and decisive:

sic pater Aeneas intentis omnibus unus
fata renarrabat divum cursusque docebat.
conticuit tandem factoque hic fine quievit.   (iii. 716–18)

Dido, on the other hand, is already in deep distress;

at regina gravi iamdudum saucia cura
vulnus alit venis et caeco carpitur igni.   (iv. 1–2)

Thus, at the very start of Book iv, all we know of the relationship between Dido and Aeneas is that she is wildly and fatally in love, impulsive and romantic, whereas he is detached and unconcerned, his mind more on the past and future than on the present. Dido's *pietas* (so far) consists solely in welcoming the Trojans instead of destroying them; Aeneas', on the other hand, has been revealed often and in many different ways.

This is the fatal difference, and it is pointed up still further in the opening dialogue of Book iv, where Dido seriously discusses with her sister whether or not to abandon the *pietas* she owes her dead husband Sychaeus. At first she is adamant:

> si mihi non animo fixum immotumque sederet
> ne cui me vinclo vellem sociare iugali,
> postquam prius amor deceptam morte fefellit;
> si non pertaesum thalami taedaeque fuisset,
> huic uni forsan potui succumbere culpae ... (iv. 15–19)

> ille meos, primus qui me sibi iunxit, amores
> abstulit; ille habeat secum servetque sepulchro. (iv. 28–9)

But Anna's practical advice, and the 'love that eats at her heart and gives her no rest', weaken this resolve, so that she asks the gods to settle the matter. This in itself is an act of *pietas*, and it might be argued that the gods' negative answer, suggested in Virgil's comments in iv. 65–7:

> heu, vatum ignarae mentes! quid vota furentem,
> quid delubra iuvant? est mollis flamma medullas
> interea et tacitum vivit sub pectore vulnus,

makes her a tragic figure, in the Aristotelian or indeed any other sense. Dido is doomed, and her helplessness is stressed by the first of the five 'personal' similes[4] in this book (iv. 68–73): she is like a deer wandering the woods, not knowing that she has a poisoned arrow in her side. Her behaviour in this whole passage (iv. 68–89) is already that of an unbalanced, doomed woman. In no more than 80 lines her *pietas* to Sychaeus has begun to weaken, and already her actions are becoming paranormal. The point is not laboured, but it is clearly made.

There follows a brief interlude (the conversation between Juno and Venus), and then come two of the most powerful and significant passages in the whole book. The first concerns Dido:

> Oceanum interea surgens Aurora reliquit.
> it portis iubare exorto delecta iuventus,
> retia rara, plagae, lato venabula ferro,
> Massylique ruunt equites et odora canum vis.
> reginam thalamo cunctantem ad limina primi
> Poenorum exspectant, ostroque insignis et auro
> stat sonipes ac frena ferox spumantia mandit.
> tandem progreditur magna stipante caterva
> Sidoniam picto chlamydem circumdata limbo;

> cui pharetra ex auro, crines nodantur in aurum,
> aurea purpuream subnectit fibula vestem.   (iv. 129–39)

The main impression here is of opulence, colour, and a quite un-Roman kind of splendour. Dido is at the centre of the scene—in fact, by delaying, she is the very cause of its existence. But it is contrasted immediately with the second simile, that comparing Aeneas to Apollo:

> ipse ante alios pulcherrimus omnes
> infert se socium Aeneas atque agmina iungit.
> qualis ubi hibernam Lyciam Xanthique fluenta
> deserit ac Delum maternam invisit Apollo
> instauratque choros, mixtique altaria circum
> Cretesque Dryopesque fremunt, pictique Agathyrsi:
> ipse iugis Cynthis graditur mollique fluentem
> fronde premit crinem fingens atque implicat auro,
> tela sonant umeris: haud illo segnior ibat
> Aeneas, tantum egregio decus enitet ore.   (iv. 141–50)

Here, although the simile is superficially like that in i. 437 ff., the god keeps aloof from his exotic and barbarian followers; the simile *is* chiefly concerned with his handsomeness, but at the same time, and unlike Diana, he chooses to leave his worshippers and walk alone.[5]

After this events move swiftly: the hunt, the storm, the marriage, Rumour, the delivery of Jupiter's warning to Aeneas, and Aeneas' immediate decision to leave Carthage—all happen in the space of 135 lines. In passing we may notice that it is *pietas* that is urged on Aeneas: *pietas* to the will of the gods, to his followers, and above all to Iulus, the eventual founder of Augustus' line (iv. 227–38, 267–76); and Aeneas' reactions show *pietas* both to his followers (iv. 281, 288–91), and to his own relationship with Dido (iv. 291–4).

Immediately after this passage—where Aeneas' obedience to the gods makes him move with an almost ludicrous haste—the third simile is placed (iv. 300–4). Dido is compared to a Bacchant, that is to say to a woman in the grip of a frenzy from which release is still possible. By the time of her next simile (iv. 469–73) this possibility is gone—she is like mad Orestes, or Pentheus on the stage.

Now comes the central part of the book, the section some critics regard as the tragic *peripateia*. It is here, if anywhere, that the crucial point must be made, if Dido's presence in the *Aeneid* is to be justified on purely logical grounds. It is here above all that her ever-increasing madness must be contrasted with Aeneas' *pietas*—and contrasted in such a way that the reader is left in no doubt where his sympathies should lie.[6]

Virgil—as many writers have noted—composed this section with great care. It consists of just under 300 lines, and ends with the Trojans' departure (iv. 583). In it are embedded three personal similes, and two conversations framing three 'solo' speeches from Dido. The form is that of an arch, and its keystone is the refusal of Aeneas to give way (iv. 437 ff.) and Dido's consequent decision to commit suicide (iv. 450 ff.).

Let us first examine the similes. They occur, as always, at the crucial points of the narrative. There are three, two involving Dido, and one—the central one in the book—describing Aeneas. In iv. 301–4 Dido is compared to a Bacchant (see above); in iv. 441–9 Aeneas is compared to an oak; and finally, in iv. 469–73 Dido is compared to two notorious stage madmen, both punished by the gods and hounded by the Furies. When these similes are set against the earlier pair (iv. 68–73 Dido = deer; iv. 141–50 Aeneas = Apollo), the progression in Virgil's mind is obvious. Just as Dido was doomed from the start, and her decline into madness and suicide is logical and foreordained, so Aeneas' reactions from the beginning are single-minded, and follow the pattern laid down for *him* by destiny.

When we move from similes to speeches, the immediate point of interest is the symmetry with which they are grouped. None the less the effect is not of an ordered, formal debate, where each side states its case with exactly equal weight. Virgil avoids this by grouping his speeches in threes, not twos. A chart can be made thus:

> 9–29 Dido; 31–53 Anna.
> 94–104 Juno; 107–14 Venus; 115–27 Juno.
> 204–18 Iarbas; 222–37 Jupiter; 265–76 Mercury.
> 305–30 Dido; 333–61 Aeneas; 365–87 Dido.
> 416–36 Dido; 477–98 Dido; 534–52 Dido.
> 560–70 Mercury; 573–9 Aeneas; 590–629 Dido.
> 634–40 Dido; 651–8 Dido; 659–62 Dido.
> 675–85 Anna; 702–3 Iris.

It is immediately clear that Dido has far more to say than Aeneas. His last words to her occur as early as iv. 361—'Italiam non sponte sequor'—and contrast most interestingly with his last words of all, which are a prayer to Mecury to guide the Trojans safely on their way. This prayer, with its implications that the gods' will has been accepted, itself contrasts with *Dido*'s last words (iv. 660 ff.), a curse on Aeneas, the violent expression of a mind overborne beyond redemption.

In fact one can trace in the speeches given to the two main characters Virgil's whole purpose. Aeneas has no need of length; Dido has, and protests too much. Once again our historical perspective is distorting: we pity Dido's predicament, and are moved by her grief until we overlook the violent, unbalanced nature of most of her utterances. Aeneas, on the other hand, because he says little, seems cold and unsympathetic. But the Romans—and the Augustans in particular—prized moderation; to them Dido's behaviour must have seemed excessive and over-dramatic—not for nothing is she compared, at the height of her madness, to stage characters. The world of Senecan melodrama is not far away.

Aeneas speaks only twice in Book iv, if we discount the commands given indirectly in iv. 288–94. His first speech (iv. 333–61) is a measured answer to Dido's first impassioned attack. Her words end with *dixerat* (iv. 331), the pluperfect of finality, used of Jupiter in iv. 238 and after Dido's last words on earth (iv. 663). In other words, no answer is expected; but nevertheless Aeneas gives one. In it, although he speaks with affection of Dido, he specifically denies that he entered into any marriage (iv. 339)—an alliance which would have involved the claims of *pietas*. He then turns to matters in which his *pietas is* involved: Troy and his dead friends' memory; Italy, the goal ordained for him by Jupiter; his father's ghost and the son he is cheating of his destiny; and finally, clear orders sent from Jupiter himself. *These* are the things that motivate Aeneas, and the things Virgil's audience would understand. Compared to them, all Dido's reproaches are no more than *querelae* (iv. 360), irrelevant hysteria remote from the realities of life.

Then there are the last words of his speech, his last words to Dido: 'Italiam non sponte sequor' (iv. 361). How much they reveal of his emotion, and his *pietas*! His pursuit of Italy has become a burden, largely because of his love for Dido, but it is still a sacred duty which he cannot and will not abandon. This is hammered home in iv. 393 ff., after Dido's violent answer to him. He longs to comfort her, but despite his anguish he obeys the gods' orders and goes back to his people. And here—as the book approaches its climax, the keystone of its arch, the oak-tree simile (iv. 441–9)—is the only place in Book iv where Aeneas is actually given the adjective *pius* (iv. 393). The whole point of Book iv is there, emphatically and clearly made.

Aeneas' second speech comes after an interesting passage involving sleep. In iv. 522 ff. everything in the world is asleep—except Dido. She is filling the air with *questus* (iv. 553; cf. *querelae* above). But Aeneas *is* asleep; his mind is made up (*certus eundi*, iv. 554), he is enjoying his rest (iv. 555) not because he is callous or indifferent to Dido, but because his *pietas* has carried him through, and he is filled with the serenity of a man at peace with fate. So, when Mercury awakes him, it is not this time to remind him of his duty, but simply to point out the Trojans' danger and the need for haste. At once Aeneas moves with the swiftness one would expect from such a leader: the crew are at the oars, the anchor-rope cut, and the ritual prayer for fair wind said and done with, all in the space of 9 lines. Aeneas' inner conflict is over and won; like an oak, his *pietas* has been battered by the winds of conflicting emotions, and shaken to its roots, but has emerged all the stronger from its ordeal.

For Dido, on the other hand, her initial act of *impietas* against Sychaeus can only end in madness and death. As she herself says:

infelix Dido, nunc te facta *impia* tangunt?
tum decuit, cum sceptra dabas.   (iv. 596–7)

The speech containing these lines is a violent vengeance-aria culminating
in the prophecy of Hannibal arising from her ashes—but it contains many
signs of madness, and more than a touch of theatricality. Medea's
soliloquies comes to mind, at iv. 595, iv. 600–3, and above all in the
invocation to Hecate and the other gods (iv. 607–12).

At the very end, however, Dido does recover a little sanity: her final
speech on the funeral-pyre—apart from its closing words—is both digni-
fied and full of real pathos. There is—at last!—some queenly *dignitas* in iv.
653 and iv. 655 ff. This is the royal Dido glimpsed briefly in Book i, before
she met Aeneas. Her death, like her reign, was noble: it is right that the
Funeral Games in Book v (in fact an act of *pietas* by Aeneas to his father)
should seem *emotionally* to be held in her honour.

Aeneas' relationship with Dido, then, preserves a symmetrical and
logical pattern from its beginning in Book i to its beautiful 'dying-fall'
ending in Book vi (lines 450–71). Both characters are rounded and three-
dimensional; both preserve their integrity as creations of the mind, their
unity of motive, feeling, and action. And, most importantly, the *pietas*
which is the key to the character of *Virgil's* Aeneas (as distinct from
anyone else's) is expounded, strengthened, and developed, through his
affaire with Dido, in a way that commands our great respect for his
creator's mind. Virgil took a risk, but it was a calculated risk, and it came
off brilliantly.

NOTES

1. Criticized as melodramatic by Shaw in *Plays and Players*.
2. Cf. his behaviour in the storm (i. 92 ff.); his inner torment after the ships are burnt (v. 700
ff.), or the gross indignities (disobedience by his men, wounding) he suffers before the final
conflict (xii. 311 ff.).
3. See below for comments on how this passage differs from its near-twin in iv. 141–50. Both
Dido and Aeneas are presented to us as god-like beings—with the single absence of *pietas* to
distinguish her from him. (One might also note that they are not only god-like, but god-
dominated as well. In Book iv Aeneas is described as *certus eundi* [554], whereas Dido is *certa mori*
[564]. Their destinies are set out for them, whatever their characters or actions.)
4. The 'ant-simile' (iv. 402 ff.) is not strictly relevant to our purpose, as it is concerned more
with the external appearance of movement than with inner emotion.
5. This simile is also reminiscent of ii. 304–8, where Aeneas compares himself to a lone
shepherd on a hill top, watching flames or a flood engulf the farmlands below. The imagery is
once again metaphorically significant.
6. It is here too that the great critical dilemma occurs. Book iv is poetically very fine, and Dido
emerges from it as a real person, perhaps more sympathetic even than Aeneas himself. How much
Virgil's head was at odds with his heart, has been the subject of speculation for centuries. The
present article argues that in one respect at least his head remained fully in control. At the same
time, the whole treatment of Dido and Aeneas in this book shows a depth of human understanding that makes nonsense of the black-and-white judgements critics are so often compelled to
make.

ARISTOTLE AND DIDO'S *HAMARTIA*

By J. L. MOLES

Scholars have long recognized that the story of Dido in the *Aeneid* is structured like a Greek tragedy and that several of Aristotle's concepts in the *Poetics* can profitably be applied to it. Here I return to an old question, to which no answer yet given has commanded general assent: if Dido is a tragic heroine, what, in Aristotelian terms, is her *hamartia*? I shall argue that Aristotle's model of tragedy provides a useful blueprint for gauging both Dido's moral responsibility for her downfall and the moral and emotional response to it which Virgil expects from his readers.[1] These matters have indeed been very extensively discussed by very distinguished scholars, but in many areas of classical literature – and nowhere more than in the *Aeneid* – modern criticism has become so sophisticated and so attuned to the detection of subtleties such as irony, ambiguity, and ambivalence that it sometimes misses the significance of what is simple and obvious. Aristotle's model of tragedy, while not a refined critical tool,[2] helps us to isolate some basic truths about the tragedy of Dido.

I begin with an exposition of the relevant parts of Aristotle's analysis,[3] because even today much of it is often imperfectly understood.

Aristotle, quite reasonably, takes it for granted that the plot of most tragedies revolves round a single central figure, and that it is primarily his or her change of fortune or *metabasis* (a change usually, though not necessarily, from good fortune to bad) which arouses the requisite pity and fear in the audience. (This does not imply that other figures in the drama are of no significance. The actions and sufferings of the central figure have to be seen in relation to those of others.) The central figure must be 'of high repute and great good fortune' (*Poe.* 13.1453a 10), so that his change of fortune may be more extreme, hence more dramatic. That apart, the successful arousal of pity and fear depends on two main factors: (1) the audience must be able to identify with the central figure, so that they are emotionally affected by his sufferings and (2) the central figure's change of fortune must broadly satisfy what Aristotle describes as τὸ φιλάνθρωπον (*Poe.* 13.1452b 38, 1453a 2–3) – 'human feelings', or, in effect, the sense of natural justice that we feel as human beings.[4] These two requirements have profound implications for the characterization of the central figure.

Aristotle seems to believe that as a general rule we identify with people who are neither *very* good nor *very* bad, but somewhere in between, people who are 'like ourselves' (ὅμοιος, *Poe*. 13.1453a 6).[5] But it is desirable that the central figure should be 'better rather than worse' (*Poe*. 13.1453a 15–16): the emotion generated by the downfall of such a person will be greater because it is human nature to be more affected by the downfall of the good. Since also pity is aroused by *undeserved* suffering (*Poe*. 13.1453a 4, ἀνάξιον ... δυστυχοῦντα), there must be a degree of *disproportion* in the sufferings of the central figure: he must suffer beyond his deserts. Yet this disproportion must have a limit, otherwise the affront to our sense of natural justice becomes too great and we feel 'moral revulsion' (τὸ μιαρόν, *Poe*. 13.1452b 36) rather than pity and fear.

The ideal tragic figure is therefore 'the man between these' (sc. the poles '*very* good' and '*very* bad'). 'He is one who is not pre-eminent in moral virtue, who passes to bad fortune not through vice or wickedness, but because of some *hamartia*' (*Poe*. 13.1453a 7–8); again, 'the change of fortune should be produced not through wickedness, but through some great *hamartia*, on the part of such a person as I have described, or a better one rather than a worse' (*Poe*. 13.1453a 15–17).[6]

Here we confront the notorious problem: what does Aristotle mean here by *hamartia*? The old view was that *hamartia* refers to a 'flaw of character', the modern view (at least until recently) that it means 'error', 'mistake of fact', that is, an act done in ignorance of some salient circumstances, in effect an error of identity (e.g. Oepidus' killing of Laius in ignorance of the fact that Laius was his father). But our understanding of Aristotle's concept of *hamartia* has been greatly advanced by an excellent study by T. C. W. Stinton, which appeared in 1975.[7] Stinton demonstrates conclusively that *hamartia* can have a very wide range of application indeed. It can refer not only to 'mistakes of fact', but also to acts done under the influence of passion, to acts done through weakness of will (ἀκρασία), to 'mixed acts' (i.e. wrong acts done for the sake of a greater good), and/or to the various dispositions or characters that correspond to these various kinds of acts.

So interpreted, *hamartia* fulfils the general requirements of *Poetics* 13 in the following ways:

(1) There is a direct causal connection between the actions of the tragic agent and his downfall – his downfall is not arbitrary (this does not *necessarily* imply that he is morally culpable to any degree).

(2) Whatever the precise nature of his *hamartia* (and, as we have seen, the range of possibilities is large), in every case it must fall short of 'vice or wickedness' and it must be possible to make a plea of mitigation for it. In some cases (certain kinds of 'mistakes of fact'), no moral culpability at all may attach to the *hamartia* of the tragic agent. In most cases, there will be some moral culpability, which will vary

according to the particular circumstances, but in all cases there must be *some* exonerating factors.

(3) Our sense of natural justice is satisfied, because:

(a) in *all* cases there is a causal connection between the central figure's actions and his downfall;

(b) in cases where some moral culpability attaches to the agent, we feel that his downfall is, to some extent, just;

(c) in cases where no moral culpability at all attaches to the specific *hamartia* of the tragic figure, he is given some unattractive qualities (e.g. Oedipus' tyrannical bent and volcanic temper) which ensure that we are not *outraged* by his fall into misfortune, even if, on a cool assessment, it would seem unjust.

(4) We nevertheless feel that the central figure has suffered beyond his deserts, is ἀνάξιος δυστυχῶν, because in all cases there are some mitigating circumstances for his actions.

Aristotle's model therefore takes account of many different types of tragic situation. His emphasis on the *hamartia* of the tragic agent also focuses on one of the most important concerns of tragedy – at any rate, of great tragedy: *moral choice*. For his model requires the audience in turn to make moral judgements about the rightness or wrongness of the tragic figure's behaviour and the justice or injustice of his fate.[8] This necessarily involves consideration of the tragic agent's *hamartia*, which in turn requires scrutiny of his motivation in committing the *hamartia* and hence also of his character (on Aristotle's definition, character – *ethos* – is 'that which makes plain the nature of the *moral choice – prohaeresis* – the personages make', *Poe.* 6.1450b 8–9).

Let us now apply Aristotle's prescriptions to the tragedy of Dido.

In the story of Dido and Aeneas the focus is primarily upon Dido: she corresponds to the central tragic figure of the Aristotelian model. As a queen and the founder of a city, whose downfall is great, she fits into the category of 'those who are of high repute and great good fortune' but 'pass to bad fortune'. Her character has of course been very variously assessed, yet most of us will agree that, in Aristotelian terms, she is 'like us', in being somewhere 'between' the poles '*very* good' and '*very* bad'. On the one hand, she is a dutiful ruler, she treats Aeneas and the Trojans with sympathy, kindness, and hospitality, she is devoted to her sister and feels love and loyalty to the dead Sychaeus, and so on; on the other, she is over-emotional, neglects her public duties in her distraction over Aeneas (*Aen.* 4.86ff.), succumbs to 'furor', engages in dubious magical rites, and curses Aeneas at the end. Yet, on balance, she is surely 'better rather than worse'.

What is her *hamartia*?

She has fallen in love with Aeneas, but this indeed is hardly her fault, for it has been brought about through direct divine intervention and forced upon her. It is true that her passion for Aeneas is also psychologically plausible on the human plane, but on either level this is a love from which there is no escape – 'moral choice' (*prohaeresis*) does not come into it. But, given that she has fallen in love, she now has to make a decision: what should she do about it? – and this question is extensively discussed by her and her sister. This is indeed a matter for 'moral choice', on the Aristotelian model. And Dido makes her choice when she and Aeneas meet in the cave:

> speluncam Dido dux et Troianus eandem
> deveniunt. prima et Tellus et pronuba Iuno
> dant signum; fulsere ignes et conscius aether
> conubiis, summoque ulularunt vertice Nymphae.
> ille dies primus leti primusque malorum
> causa fuit; neque enim specie famave movetur
> nec iam furtivum Dido meditatur amorem:
> coniugium vocat, hoc praetexit nomine culpam.
> (*Aen.* 4.165–72)

Since the story of Dido and Aeneas as a whole is conceived as a tragedy, it seems legitimate to analyse this key scene in specifically tragic terms.[9] Here we have the climactic moment, the moment of decision. The decision is made, and Virgil himself steps out of the narrative and pronounces his own judgement, almost in the style of a tragic chorus. As in tragedy, the author demands a moral response from his audience. The sentiment 'ille dies primus ... malorum causa fuit' also reflects the ἀρχὴ κακῶν ('beginning of evils') motif so basic to the thought and narrative patterning of Homeric epic and Greek tragedy.[10]

In itself the word 'culpa' can cover a wide range of failings – from the trivial to the great,[11] and it takes its precise meaning from its context. In both respects it resembles *hamartia*. Since (a) the whole story of Dido and Aeneas is a 'tragedy', (b) the specific context responds to 'tragic' analysis, and (c) 'culpa' is a suitable Latin equivalent for *hamartia*, Virgil here seems to be telling us, almost in so many words, that Dido's 'culpa' was her *hamartia*.[12]

What, then, is it? In context it makes no sense to think of some general 'moral flaw': one cannot 'praetexo' a 'moral flaw' by calling it 'coniugium'! Quite clearly, her 'culpa' is her act in giving herself to Aeneas. But in what respect is this a 'culpa'? One popular interpretation has been that the 'culpa' lies in her abnegation of her oaths to Sychaeus. Yet this makes no sense in context. To defend herself against criticism Dido calls her 'culpa' a 'coniugium'. Her 'culpa' cannot be disloyalty to Sychaeus, for *any* association with a man, whether licit or illicit, *necessarily* involves abnegation of her oaths to Sychaeus and to protest

that her association with Aeneas was a 'coniugium' does nothing at all
to meet that charge,[13] as indeed Dido herself has already recognized
(*Aen.* 4.15–19). In a more refined version of the interpretation of 'culpa'
as = 'disloyalty to Sychaeus', Gordon Williams argues that 'the words
can just as well mean this: what Dido was doing was culpable, but this
fact was concealed by her regarding it as marriage'.[14] But this still fails
to meet the logical objection that Dido's regarding what she was doing
as marriage has no bearing on her feelings of obligation to Sychaeus.
Even more important, Virgil's words clearly imply that Dido is
behaving badly and knows it: she 'is no longer influenced by appear-
ances or reputation; no longer is it a secret love she practises. She *calls*
it marriage – with this *name* she *conceals* her "culpa".' Dido, now
shameless, *says* something (she does not just 'regard' it) which is not
true. Virgil draws a clear contrast between Dido's *outward* behaviour
and the *inner* reality.

The obvious meaning of Virgil's words is that the 'culpa' consists in
the *illicit* nature of her love-making with Aeneas, which Dido, to defend
her reputation, tries to present as proper 'coniugium'.[15] 'Culpa' of
course very often refers to sexual misbehaviour[16] – a thoroughly
appropriate implication in a context where two people have just made
love and the woman is criticized for shamelessness. Some scholars,
indeed, preeminently Gordon Williams, have strenuously resisted this
simple conclusion. Williams[17] argues that (a) Juno refers to the union
of Dido and Aeneas as a proper marriage (*Aen.* 4.99, 103–4, 125–7); (b)
the responses of the elements, Juno, and the nymphs to the 'wedding'
are ritually correct; (c) in Roman law and social practice cohabitation
and consent were sufficient to validate a marriage; (d) Dido later regards
her relationship with Aeneas as marriage; (e) in Ovid's treatment of the
incident in the cave (*Heroides* 7.93–6) Dido at the time sincerely regards
herself as having become Aeneas' wife. All these observations are
correct in themselves, but they do not validate the conclusion that Dido
is acting in good faith. For her own purposes Juno desires the union of
the two lovers to be a permanent marriage: this does not amount to an
objective statement of the nature of their union. While the divine
responses to the 'wedding' are indeed ritually correct, the *emotional*
effect is of a ghastly parody of the norm, suggesting rather that this
marriage presided over by Juno is not a true marriage at all.[18] As for
the point about Roman marriage practice, at this juncture in the
narrative Dido and Aeneas are not yet cohabiting: they have only made
love once! Nor, as we learn later, even as time passed, did Aeneas ever
give his consent. Nor are Dido's *subsequent* thoughts about her *prolonged*
cohabitation with Aeneas relevant to the immediate context. Finally,
though Ovid is certainly recycling Virgilian material in *Heroides* 7, it is

wholly illegitimate to invoke his 'authority' in support of a contentious interpretation of Virgil's meaning: Ovid is not bound to follow Virgil in every respect.

In sum, Virgil's wording in verses 165–72 shows quite clearly (a) that the union of Dido and Aeneas is *not* a proper 'coniugium', (b) that it is a 'culpa' (in the sense 'sexual misdemeanour'), and (c) that at this point Dido knows that she is not married to Aeneas but pretends to the world that she is to avoid disgrace. Dido's 'culpa' or *hamartia*, then, consists precisely in her submitting sexually to Aeneas out of wedlock. In Aristotelian terms, this may be defined as a wrong act committed through weakness of will because of her passion for Aeneas. It is this *hamartia* which sets in motion the chain of events which produces her 'change of fortune' to ill fortune, as Virgil himself indicates ('ille dies ...'). There is a direct causal link, as Aristotle requires, between Dido's *hamartia* and her *metabasis*. Her act is culpable, but it is not an act of 'vice or wickedness': there are some exonerating circumstances and a fair plea of mitigation for her conduct can be made (she is in love, not fully in control of herself, and so on). But Dido's 'passing' into 'misfortune' does fulfil the requirement of 'human feeling', for her downfall is to some extent the result of her own wrong-doing: it is basically just. Yet there is also the necessary tragic *disproportion* between fault and fate to arouse our *pity* (*Aen.* 4.696, 'quia nec fato merita nec morte peribat'; cf. 4.693, 'tum Iuno omnipotens, longum *miserata* dolorem').

All this is of course a considerable simplification of the tragedy of Dido. Nevertheless, we can see that the Aristotelian model of tragedy does enable us to pin-point the essential nature of Dido's 'culpa'/ *hamartia* and to establish the broad parameters of the moral and emotional response to her downfall which Virgil wants from us.

Finally, a few brief observations on the reasons why Virgil chooses to represent the liaison of Dido and Aeneas, whatever its ultimate status, as beginning in sexual misconduct. Such a detail might seem gratuitous: after all, any emotional entanglement between Dido and Aeneas is bound to end unhappily. In fact it serves several purposes. It is inconceivable that Aeneas could have considered marriage with Dido had it been offered to him in the proper way, whereas it is both realistic and psychologically convincing that he should drift into a relationship with Dido after both have succumbed to temptation in the cave. From the point of view of the plot Dido's seduction is in fact a *sine qua non* of Aeneas' staying on with her in Carthage at all. Again, the fact that their liaison begins with seduction sheds a critical light on Dido's love for Aeneas, Aeneas' response, and indeed upon the emotion itself: however sympathetically Virgil may portray its victims, love is a passion, often destructive in its effects and ignoble in its manifestations. The statesman must avoid it, or, if he becomes enslaved by it, free himself from its toils as soon as possible. Hence *Aen.* 4.393: 'At pius Aeneas.' Those words are no aberration but the emphatic judgement of Virgil the moralist at his most explicit.[19]

NOTES

1. For the relevance of tragedy and Aristotle's prescriptions to the Dido story, see most recently F. Muecke, *AJP* 104 (1983), 134–55 (with full bibliography). N. Rudd, *Lines of Enquiry* (Cambridge, 1976), pp. 32–53, surveys various interpretations of Dido's 'culpa'/*hamartia* and concludes on an agnostic note. Whether Virgil had read the *Poetics* naturally cannot be established. It is chronologically possible that he had, even if one believes that Aristotle's major treatises went out of general circulation in the Hellenistic period: cf. D. Earl, *ANRW* I.2 (1972), pp. 850ff. on the date of their re-emergence in Rome. On the other hand, C. O. Brink, *Horace on Poetry* I (Cambridge, 1963), p. 140 finds 'no evidence of any first-hand knowledge of Aristotle's *Poetics* in Horace's time'. What matters here is that Aristotle's prescriptions seem to work both with Greek tragedy and the story of Dido and that they *had* currency in early Augustan Rome, though perhaps only through intermediaries such as Neoptolemus.

2. It is of course not meant to be: Aristotle is trying to define the essence of tragedy, necessarily a process of simplification and generalization.

3. I here follow the views of T. C. W. Stinton, *CQ* 25 (1975), 221–54, with my own modifications in *CQ* 29 (1979), 77–94.

4. For this interpretation of τὸ φιλάνθρωπον, cf. M. E. Hubbard in *Ancient Literary Criticism* (Oxford, 1972), p. 106 n. 2; Stinton (n. 3), 238 n. 2.

5. ὅμοιος certainly implies 'not very bad'; whether it also implies 'not very good' (as usually argued) is less clear: see my discussion (n. 3), 92–4.

6. Translated by Hubbard (n. 4), pp. 106–7, except that I have left ἁμαρτίαν as it stands.

7. Cf. n. 3 above.

8. I stress here (since this is often misunderstood) that Aristotle's view of the moral element in tragedy is radically different from Plato's. Aristotle does *not* require that tragedy should be morally improving: his point is that if the plots of tragedy do not harmonize, more or less, with the audience's moral sense, this interferes with the *aesthetic* purpose of tragedy – the arousal of pity and fear.

9. Cf. the interesting observations of J. Foster, *PVS* 13 (1973–4), 32.

10. According to G. Williams, *Tradition and Originality in Roman Poetry* (Oxford, 1968), p. 379, the wording echoes 'the last words of the Spartan ambassador at the end of the last peace conference before the Peloponnesian War (Thucydides ii. 12.3)'. Maybe so, but the colouring of the Spartan ambassador's words is itself epic/tragic, and this colouring is what is important in our passage.

11. See *ThLL* and *OLD* s.v.

12. Most scholars assume this equivalence.

13. For similar arguments, cf. R. C. Monti, *The Dido Episode and the Aeneid* (Leiden, 1981), p. 106–7 n. 29.

14. Williams (n. 10), p. 379.

15. Cf. Monti (n. 13), loc. cit.

16. *ThLL*, s.v., IV, col. 1302, 67–1303, 18.

17. Williams (n. 10), pp. 378ff.

18. Page, ad loc. has some characteristically good observations.

19. It will be clear why I completely disagree with the arguments of S. Farron, 'The Aeneas-Dido Episode as an Attack on Aeneas' Mission and Rome', *G & R* 27 (1980), 34–47. Nor can I accept the 'morality is irrelevant' attitude of D. Feeney, *CQ* 33 (1983), 205 n. 10 ('it is not a matter of "judging", still less of deciding which "side" we favour'). In Book 4, vv. 169–72 a̲ d̲ 393 are *explicit* moral 'sign-posts'.

LACRIMAE ILLAE INANES

By A. HUDSON-WILLIAMS

Ire iterum in lacrimas, iterum temptare precando
cogitur et supplex animos summittere amori,
ne quid inexpertum frustra moritura relinquat.

talibus orabat, talisque miserrima fletus
fertque refertque soror. sed nullis ille mouetur
fletibus aut uoces ullas tractabilis audit;
fata obstant placidasque uiri deus obstruit auris.
ac uelut annoso ualidam cum robore quercum
Alpini Boreae nunc hinc nunc flatibus illinc
eruere inter se certant; it stridor, et altae
consternunt terram concusso stipite frondes;
ipsa haeret scopulis et quantum uertice ad auras
aetherias, tantum radice in Tartara tendit:
haud secus adsiduis hinc atque hinc uocibus heros
tunditur, et magno persentit pectore curas;
mens immota manet, lacrimae uoluuntur inanes.

(Virgil, *Aeneid* 4.413–15 and 437–49)

The source of the tears mentioned in the much quoted final line (449) has been the subject of diverse views. That the shedder of the tears is not specifically designated has been felt to create an ambiguity, and critics have been tempted to conjecture his or her identity according to their personal whims or prejudices. The point is of more than passing interest and is of relevance in the assessment of Aeneas' character and the understanding of Book 4. The tears have been variously assigned: to Aeneas (so Servius, Augustine, *C.D.* 9.4 fin.,[1] and a number of modern critics[2]); to Dido and Anna (Heyne-Wagner, Conington-Nettleship), or Dido (Sidgwick, Page); to Aeneas, Dido, and Anna (R. Lesueur, *L'Énéide de V.* (Toulouse, 1975), p. 404). R. G. Austin (ed. *Aen. IV*, Oxford, 1955, p. 135) thinks it wrong to probe: 'Virgil is purposely ambiguous, and why may he not remain so? The line is ruined by a chill analysis . . . These tears could not be denied to Aeneas: but . . . few could withhold them for ever from Dido.' The position is summed up in Servius *auctus*: 'quidam . . . *lacrimas inanes* uel Aeneae uel Didonis uel Annae uel omnium accipunt', to which we may add '⟨uel totius generis humani⟩': cf. 'Virgil has not said whose tears; by not specifying he widens the area of sorrow, generalises this particular conflict into the universal conflict of pity with duty' (R. D. Williams (ed.), *Aen I–VI* (London, 1972), p. 373; cf. too W. F. Jackson Knight, *Roman Vergil* (London, 1944), p. 205). That Virgil should in truth have intended such puzzling obscurity seems hard to credit. It is being assumed that in a detail of his narrative which closely concerns the leading characters and which cannot but excite the reader's interest this master artist is guilty of a vagueness for which another writer would be censured as negligent, if not inept. It appears to me that the evidence presented by the poet himself is nowadays commonly ignored, and, outmoded as the process may seem, a reasoned consideration of the actual Latin text may not be out of place.

Dido appears before the reader as an undisciplined and unstable woman who makes little or no attempt to curb or conceal her emotions (cf. 68 ff., 'uritur infelix Dido totaque uagatur | urbe furens . . .'; 300 ff., much as the demented Amata in 7.377), and these find an outlet in frequent fits of weeping: 30, 'sic effata sinum lacrimis impleuit obortis'; 314, 'per . . . has lacrimas dextramque tuam'; 369, 'fletu . . . nostro'; 413, 'ire iterum in lacrimas . . . cogitur'; 437–9, 'fletus . . . fletibus' (above); 548, 'tu lacrimis euicta meis'; 649, 'paulum lacrimis et mente morata.' Throughout the book tears are a prominent and inseparable feature of Dido's behaviour; they form an essential ingedient of her supplications.

It is otherwise with Aeneas. So prone to tears elsewhere, in no single place of Book 4 is he specified either as weeping or as close to weeping. Indications of emotion, indeed, are few and brief. His reactions to Dido's first impassioned appeal (305–30) are thus described (331 f.): 'ille Iouis monitis immota tenebat | lumina et obnixus curam sub corde premebat' (cf. 1.208 f., 'curisque ingentibus aeger | spem uultu simulat, premit altum corde dolorem'); his heart was grieved, but he kept his eyes motionless— they shed no tears. There follows the prim apologia of 333–61 (cf. 'pro re pauca loquar', 337, etc.). After a bitter invective (365–87), Dido leaves Aeneas stammering and embarrassed (390 f.); he is described as 'multa gemens magnoque animum labefactus amore' (395; cf. 5.869, 'multa gemens casuque animum concussus amici'); *gemitus*, certainly, but no *fletus*, no *lacrimae*. Moreover, in 369 f. Dido actually castigates Aeneas for their absence: 'num fletu ingemuit nostro? num lumina flexit? | num lacrimas uictus dedit aut miseratus amantem est?' (even her rhetoric could hardly ignore obvious weeping). In 448 (above), 'magno persentit pectore curas', the language suggests grief, but not overpowering emotion, not rolling tears. The love of Aeneas does not match that of Dido. Illuminating are the two vividly contrasted later scenes, the one depicting Dido's night of anguish (522 ff.), the other Aeneas' calm repose (554 ff.)—a repose to be rudely shattered by the peremptory injunctions of Mercury to be off forthwith. To sum up: in Book 4 Dido is ever shedding tears; none are certainly imputed to Aeneas.

The second of the above passages (437–49) follows on Dido's request to her sister (424 ff., 'i, soror, atque hostem supplex adfare superbum . . .') to entreat Aeneas on her behalf at least to delay his departure; the terms of her entreaty are expressed in 425–36. In this highly compressed piece of narrative we must picture a series of tearful appeals addressed to Aeneas by Dido, but actually conveyed by Anna (438, 'fertque refertque soror'). We are nowhere told that the latter wept, though she may well have done so. Whether she did or did not, is of no consequence. Anna is a mere instrument of communication and in this sketch her personality does not appear. The only claimants to authorship of the *lacrimae inanes* that merit any consideration are Dido and Aeneas. That explicit reference has already been made to Dido's tears earlier in the passage (437–9) and none to tears of Aeneas either here or anywhere else in 4, is not a point on which critics tend to dwell: in itself it suggests the verdict; a study of the lines supplies corroboration. In respect of style, the passage is a good example of the verbal dexterity that was understood and appreciated by the cultivated reader of Virgil's day. The brevity is artistic and admirable, the arrangement and finish meticulous. Particularly in the prominence of point and balance, the influence of rhetoric, though restrained, is plainly seen. Towards the modern reader's comprehension of what Virgil was about, commentators and critics proffer but small aid and an examination of the contents seems desirable.

The key to an appreciation of the lines is provided by the previous 413–15 (quoted above), which immediately precede Dido's address to her sister. To be noted are the two closely allied elements in Dido's entreaty, viz. prayers, i.e. words, and tears; the former are subsequently specified (425 ff.), the latter are to be imagined as concomitant. For this combination, much favoured by subsequent poets, cf. 3.599, 'cum *fletu precibus-que*'; *Georg.* 4.505, 'quo *fletus* Manis, quae numina *uoce* moueret?'; also, in the later Dido episode, 6.467 f., 'talibus Aeneas ... lenibat *dictis* animum [Didonis] *lacrimas*que [sibi] ciebat' (see below).[3] It is with reference to these two elements that the long passage begins. The arrangement of the clauses is chiastic, the thought centring on the two elements: *talibus* (*dictis*, cf. 219, 6.124) *orabat* (cf. *oro* 431, 435)—*fletus*—*fletibus*—*uoces*; 'in such words she kept beseeching, and such was the tale of tears that her sister sadly took and took again. But by no tears was he moved, he would not be managed and gave ear to no words' (Austin). In 437 *fletus*, like *fletibus* 439, which is clearly contrasted with *uoces*, reflects the *lacrimae* of 413, just as *talibus orabat* corresponds to *temptare precando*. The *uoces* of 439 and 447 signify Dido's prayers as conveyed by her sister; cf. *talibus* (*dictis*). We should compare the situation in Val. Flacc. 7.268–70 (surely influenced by Virgil; for 263, 268, 273, cf. *Aen.* 4.141, 621, 436), where Venus, appearing to Medea as Circe, her aunt, reports an entreaty which she says Jason has asked her to convey (cf. *Aen.* 4.424): 'haec precor [ait Iason], haec dominae [tuae] *referas* ad uirginis aurem. | tu *fletus* ostende meos; illi has ego *uoces* (271 ff.) . . . hasque manus . . . tendo' ('*fletus ostende*: id est, narra tam plane et efficaciter, ut uidere se putet', Burman). Compare too the letter addressed by Phaedra to Hippolytus (Ov. *Her.* 4.175 f.): 'addimus his *precibus lacrimas* quoque: *uerba precantis* | perlegis et *lacrimas* finge uidere meas.' Virgil's arrangement is forceful and effective. Aeneas repels both words and tears. Fate, we learn, stands in the way and the god stops his ears so that they are at peace;[4] heaven is on the watch and takes no risks (cf. 331).

There follows the simile of the stalwart oak (Aeneas) that stands firm against the blasts of the winds (Dido's hurricane of words and tears), *flatibus* in 442, it may well be, allusively reminiscent of *fletibus* in 439 (cf. D. West, art. cit. 45).[5] The last three lines (447–9) return to the thought of the three first (437–9). In 447 *uocibus* corresponds to the *uoces* of 439. By these Aeneas' ears are unceasingly pounded, *adsiduis* repeating the notion of frequency contained in *fertque refertque* in 438. In 449 the expression *immota manet* further emphasizes the immovability already stressed in *nullis moueter f.* in 438. I do not see how it can be doubted that in the *lacrimae* which roll to no purpose (449) we return to the *fletus, fletibus*, of the initial lines. As the *uoces* by which Aeneas is battered (447) are those of Dido, it seems mere perversity to regard their associated partner, the *lacrimae*, as shed by anyone but her; the last line manifestly reflects the thought of 438–9; cf. 12.400, 'lacrimis [iuuenum] immobilis [Aeneas]'. The arrangement is again chiastic, the corresponding or contrasted ideas being grouped around *uocibus—pectore—mens—lacrimae*: 'even so, by ceaseless words from this side and that is the hero battered, and his great heart feels deep sorrow; yet his mind remains unmoved, the tears roll in vain.' Aeneas, though pained, remains (as) inflexible (as the oak), Dido's words and tears are (as) ineffectual (as the buffeting winds). The addition of any word specifically designating the author of the tears could only be the work of a novice; to the attentive reader the poet's careful language presents no ambiguity. Henry's notion (so Pease on 30) that the *lacrimae* should belong to the same person as the *mens* is groundless. In such cases much must depend on the context, much on the reader's good sense: cf. 82 f., 'sola domo maeret uacua *stratisque relictis* | incubat', where (*pace* Heyne-Wagner) the meaning must be *relictis ab Aenea* (cf. 1.699 f.); but in Luc. 5.790 f., 'sic fata *relictis* | exiluit *stratis*' (compared by H.-W.), we understand *r. a se*. Adjudgement of the tears to Aeneas removes an integral part of the structure and substitutes an irrelevance. The final verse, forcefully underlining the utter hopelessness of Dido's position, prepares the reader for the account, which now follows, of her desire for death.

For the general arrangement of the passage we may compare 1.142–56, where again the thought of the words which precede the simile is repeated and emphasized in those which follow: thus 'cunctus pelagi cecidit fragor'

(154) corresponds to 'tumida aequora placat' (142) and 'temperat aequor' (146); 'caelo ... aperto' (155) to 'collectas ... fugat nubes solemque reducit' (143); 'flectit equos curruque uolans dat lora secundo' (156) is but a poetic equivalent of 'rotis summas leuibus perlabitur undas' (147); cf. Conway on 156. So in 4.141–50, after the simile the words 'haud illo [Apolline] segnior ibat | Aeneas, tantum egregio decus enitet ore' (149 f.) recall the reader to the stately movement and beauty of Aeneas alluded to in 141 f., 'ipse ante alios pulcherrimus omnis | infert se socium'; likewise 7.376–84, 11.806–15.

Thus the lachrymose Stoic whom many have detected in 449 suffers, it is hoped, a timely demise, the coy alliance of the iron will and the rolling tear falls apart; such assertions as 'Aeneas is affected—his tears still flow— but he is now the immovable oak' (Brooks Otis, op. cit., p. 84) have, in respect of the tears, no basis in Virgil. Aeneas' eyes are as *immota* as his *mens*, just as they were on the earlier occasion, 331 f., 'immota tenebat lumina'. Aeneas was impervious to Dido's tears when he actually beheld them; as reported by Anna they have no hope of success; of this heaven has made sure beyond doubt (440). Applied to Dido's tears, the epithet *inanes* has a relevant and natural force (in 10.465, '[Alcides] lacrimas ... effundit inanes', the situation is different; cf. too *Georg.* 4.375, 'nati fletus cognouit inanis'); those who give the tears to Aeneas have to assume a meaning that is forced or feeble. Compare Pöschl (op. cit. p. 46), 'the *lacrimae inanes* are the tears which Aeneas sheds in vain; they have no effect on his unshakable resolution': in normal circumstances, the tears which affect or do not affect a person's resolution are someone else's, not his own.[6] To illustrate his point, Augustine (so E. V. Arnold, *Roman Stoicism* (Cambridge, 1911), p. 391) would have done better to appeal, not to the specious charms of the line 'mens ... inanes' wrested from its context,[7] but to the sharply antithetical clauses 'magno persentit pectore curas [= Aug.'s *perturbationes*]; mens immota manet'; cf. the opposition between *sentit* and *uincit* in Sen. *Dial.* 1.2.2 (see n. 4) and *Epist.* 9.3, 'noster sapiens *uincit* quidem incommodum omne, sed *sentit*' (quoted by Pease).

To the simile of the oak-tree battered by the winds a bizarre twist has been imparted by several critics,[8] who, following one of Servius' less felicitous pronouncements[9] and seemingly unfamiliar with the aspect of rolling tears, find in the mention of the lofty leaves that strew the ground (443 f.) a reflection of the tears of Aeneas and assume that the *lacrimae* of 449 are shed by him. Quite apart from the considerations discussed above, it is hard to believe that a thought so alien to Virgil's sense of propriety could ever have occurred to him. Compare Mackail's astonishing comment, 'the unusual *lacrimae uoluuntur* [so 10.790 'lacrimae ... per ora uolutae'] emphasizes the analogy of the tears with the whirling leaves of 444'; significantly, we read of ἔπεα, but not of δάκρυα, πτερόεντα. The introduction of the leaves serves but to lend interest to the image, suggesting that the only effect of the winds on the tree is the loss of its *altae frondes*; very similar is *Anth. Pal.* 9.291.5 f., οὕτως καὶ ἱεραὶ Ζηνὸς δρύες ἔμπεδα ῥίζαις | ἑστᾶσιν, φύλλων δ'αῦα χέουσ' ἄνεμοι.[10] A corresponding reference to the leaves occurs indeed in the tree simile of 2.626 ff., where the sinking of the enflamed Troy is compared to the fall of an aged ash beneath the axe, 'illa usque minatur | et *tremefacta comam* concusso uertice nutat'.[11] The lofty leaves that strew the ground in 444 bear no more relation to the rolling tears than do the aged timbers of the oak (*annoso robore*)[12] to the person of the comely and nubile Aeneas (cf. 141, 150).

It seems, accordingly, proper to state that Book 4 presents no instance of a tearful Aeneas: if we are to judge from the narrative itself, he remains throughout as *illacrimabilis*, if not as unfeeling, as Pluto himself. That he wept on meeting Dido in the underworld is noteworthy and lends confirmation to our interpretation of 4.449: cf. 6.455, 'demisit lacrimas dulcique adfatus amore est', 468 (see below), 476, 'prosequitur lacrimis longe et miseratur euntem'. It is to be remarked that the passage contains three references to the *lacrimae* of Aeneas. In this episode the mood of Aeneas is changed; in 4 stern resignation and inexorable resolve are the dominant elements, in 6 tenderness and compassion. Unhampered by the attentions of fate and Olympus, his emotions follow their normal course; Aeneas is himself again. The situation of 4 is now strikingly reversed: in 6 it is Dido who is tearless and inflexible, Aeneas who weeps and appeals (cf. Norden on 456 ff.). This reversal in the roles of the two adds a piquancy and force to the narrative of 6. Note 6.467 ff., 'talibus Aeneas ... torua tuentem | lenibat dictis animum lacrimasque [sibi] ciebat. | illa solo fixos oculos auersa tenebat | nec magis ... uultum ... mouetur | quam si dura silex aut stet Marpesia cautes' (for *lacrimas ciebat* see Norden ad loc., *OLD cieo* 5). Here again occurs the combination of words and tears (cf. 455),[13] but now they belong, not to Dido, but to Aeneas, and here again they are ineffectual.

In view of Aeneas' notable addiction to weeping in other parts of the poem (see Pease on 4.449, p. 368), his complete abstinence from tears in so emotional a book as 4 is remarkable, and such abstinence cannot be the result of chance. In this episode the poet wishes to represent Aeneas as a man who rises superior to his personal emotions, inflexibly resolved to discharge the world task commissioned by heaven and displaying therein an uncompromising and unshakable front. The demands of duty are inexorable and a woman's tears must roll in vain. 'Lacrimis', observes Ovid, 'adamanta mouebis': adamant, perhaps, but not Aeneas.

NOTES

1. 'Ita mens, ubi fixa est ista sententia, nullas perturbationes, etiamsi accidunt inferioribus animi partibus, in se contra rationem praeualere permittit; quin immo eis ipsa dominatur eisque non consentiendo et potius resistendo regnum uirtutis exercet. talem describit etiam Vergilius Aenean, ubi ait "mens . . . inanes".'

2. J. Henry, *Aeneidea* (Leipzig, Dublin, Meissen, 1873–92), ii. 749 f.; J. W. Mackail (ed.), *Aeneid* (Oxford, 1930), p. 151; T. R. Glover, *Virgil*[6] (London, 1930), p. 197; E. K. Rand, *The Magical Art of V.* (Cambridge, Mass., 1931), pp. 361 f.; A. S. Pease (ed.), *Aeneid IV* (Cambridge, Mass., 1935), pp. 365–8; V. Pöschl (*Die Dichtkunst Virgils*, Innsbruck, 1950), *The Art of V.* trans. G. Seligson (Michigan, 1962), pp. 45 f.; K. Quinn, *Latin Explorations* (London, 1963), pp. 40 f.; Brooks Otis, *V.*, *A Study in Civilized Poetry* (Oxford, 1964), pp. 84, 269; J. Perret, *Virgile*[2] (Paris, 1965), p. 140; W. S. Anderson, *The Art of the Aeneid* (Englewood Cliffs, N.J., 1969), p. 48; D. West, *JRS* 59 (1969), 44 f.

3. Cf. Ov. *Her.* 4.175 f.; 20.76; *Met.* 11.387, '*uerbis*que precatur *et lacrimis*'; 444, 'talibus Aeolidis *dictis lacrimis*que mouetur'; 13.586, 'genibus procumbere . . . Iouis *lacrimis*que has addere *uoces*'; *Pont.* 3.1.157 f., 'nec tua si *fletu* scindentur *uerba* nocebit: | interdum *lacrimae* pondera *uocis* habent'; Sen. *Phoen.* 500 f.; Val. Flacc. 4.11, '*precibus* . . . *lacrimis* et supplice dextra'; 42, '*lacrimis* . . . *uoce*'; 7.269–70; Stat. *Theb.* 5.275 f., 'nec *dictis* supplex quae plurima fudi | ante Iouem frustra *lacrimis*que auertere luctus | contigit'; 6.196, 'talia *fletu uerba* pio miscens'; 10.719, 'nec *lacrimae* nec *uerba* mouebant'. Thus the vocabulary is *uoces (uox)*, *uerba*, *dicta*, or *preces*; *fletus* or *lacrimae*. Among prose writers the combination *preces* + *lacrimae* occurs several times in Cicero's speeches and in Livy: cf. *Thes. Ling. Lat. lacrima* 837.60 ff. (*uerba* etc. + *lacrimae* I do not find noted).

4. The meaning 'kindly ears' attributed by some to *placidas auris* (cf. T. E. V. Pearce, *CR* 82 (1968), 13 f.) seems, in view of Aeneas' inexorable rejection of all Dido's pleas, highly unnatural (cf. Dido's words 428, 'duras . . . auris'). The use of *placidus* is illustrated by Sen. *Dial.* 1.2.2, 'nec hoc dico: non sentit [uir bonus] illa [omnia externa], sed uincit et alioqui *quietus placidus*que contra incurrentia attollitur' (cf. Cic. *Tusc.* 4.5.10); for the prolepsis, cf. *Aen.* 10.103, 'premit placida aequora pontus'.

5. It may be noted that the form *fletibus* occurs nowhere else in V., *flatibus* only in *Georg.* 2.339.

6. Cf. too Quinn, op. cit., p. 41, 'used of Aeneas' tears, the word [*inanes*] implies tears of frustration because A. is not free to go against fate'.

7. A notorious example of words of Virgil subject to misunderstanding and misleading quotation is 1.462, 'sunt lacrimae rerum', where *hic etiam* must be supplied from 461 and the genitive is objective: the meaning cannot be anything like 'tears are universal' (Henry and others). Cf. too 6.126, 'facilis descensus Auerno' quoted without reference to what follows.

8. e.g. Mackail, Rand, Pease, Pöschl, Quinn, West: see n. 2.

9. On 444, 'frondes: sicut lacrimae Aeneae.' Servius' occasional fantasies are illustrated at 30, 'sic effata sinum lacrimis impleuit obortis', where some have strangely attributed the bosom to Anna (so Peerlkamp) and Servius, even more strangely, does not consider *sinum* to be a bosom at all, but refers it to the eyes (= *palpebras*), 'about which interpretation', comments Henry, 'the less said the better'.

10. A. S. F. Gow–D. L. Page (*Greek Anth., Garland of Philip* (Cambridge, 1968), ii. 239; cf. i. 215) on φύλλων . . . ἄνεμοι suggest that 'the detail may be significant, not merely decorative; as the wind scatters the leaves though the oak remains steadfast, so Rome under Caesar will stand firm though the storm of battle strips her of men'. Would the poet be likely to symbolize Rome's fighters by 'withered leaves'?

11. Besides the mention of the leaves, the two similes have these features in common: 4.441, '*annoso* . . . robore quercum', and 2.626, '*antiquam* . . . ornum'; 4.443, '*eruere* inter *se certant*', and 2.628, 'instant | *eruere* . . . *certatim*'; 4.444, '*concusso* stipite', and 2.629, '*concusso* uertice'.

12. Cf. *Georg.* 3.332, 'antiquo robore quercus' and echoes in subsequent poets; for these and for further references to aged trees in V. and elsewhere, see Pease on 441.

13. Note, again, the chiastic arrangement of the clauses, to which Austin (ed. *Aen. VI* (Oxford, 1977)) at 6.468 calls attention. The ideas centre on *lacrimas—adfatus* (455)—*dictis—lacrimas* (468), the two parts being separated by Aeneas' words.

ADDITIONAL NOTE (1989)

A passage, but briefly mentioned above, that has an interesting affinity with 4.447–9 is 12.398–400 (cf. Maguinness ad loc.): 'stabat acerba fremens . . . | Aeneas [grauiter saucius] magno iuuenum et maerentis Iuli | concursu, *lacrimis immobilis*'; Aeneas is impatient for battle and is 'unmoved by their tears' (of sympathy), tears attributed by few critics, I believe, to Aeneas.

LAVINIA'S BLUSH: VERGIL, *AENEID* 12.64–70

By R. O. A. M. LYNE

In the *Aeneid* actions are consistent with character and psychology, indeed indicative of character and psychology. This statement has, I think, general if not universal truth. At any rate, one should not hastily assume otherwise.

Amata begs Turnus not to fight Aeneas. Lavinia is listening. She weeps, she blushes (*Aen.* 12.64ff.):

> accepit uocem lacrimis Lauinia matris
> flagrantis perfusa genas, cui plurimus ignem
> subiecit rubor et calefacta per ora cucurrit.
> Indum sanguineo ueluti uiolauerit ostro
> si quis ebur, aut mixta rubent ubi lilia multa
> alba rosa, talis uirgo dabat ore colores.
> illum turbat amor ...

It is a famous blush, with a famous simile. Two similes, of course – but the second tends to get overlooked. Neither has been properly explained. Nor for that matter has Lavinia's weeping. Why does she weep? And why does she blush?

To most scholars Lavinia is not a character with feelings and emotions.[1] Naturally therefore her own state of mind cannot supply answers to these questions. But some scholars do have a sense of character – in particular, in these lines. Some scholars even sense that Lavinia is in love – but with whom?

If Lavinia were characterized enough to be in love, I would find this a welcome touch of colour, φάρμακον, in the outline of the μῦθος at this point.[2] The poem would be richer. If there was any suggestion that she was in love with, specifically, Turnus, this would be troubling. It would seriously complicate our emotional if not our moral response to the rapidly approaching dénouement. But that is not implausible. Our responses to the dénouement are pretty complex already. And it is in fact the case. Lavinia comes alive in these lines. Lavinia, the text adumbrates, is in love with Turnus.

We should not expect such a disturbing revelation to be floodlit. The future wife of the founder of the Roman people cannot too explicitly have loved another man; it ill suits a proto-Roman *uirgo* to have such emotions at all. But disturbing insinuations, these are pre-eminently in the Vergilian manner. For example, the final victory of the *Aeneid*'s Augustan hero is marred – albeit by a human, honour-

able action:[3] an honourable, human impulse overrides the higher
claims of the new *pietas*: *parcere subiectis* and, for that matter,
pacique imponere morem. And the nubile Lavinia, *plenis nubilis annis*
(7.53), had it seems set her heart on another man (a *iuuenis praestans
animi* in the opinion of an admirable judge, 12.19): it is implicit in our
lines. But let us start at line 55, with Amata.

The passionate Amata appears strangely devoted to Turnus, here and
elsewhere; her relationship to him reminds us of other relationships
besides that of possible future mother-in-law. In her pleading speech
she recalls, of course, Hecuba pleading with her son in the analogous
Iliadic scene (22.82–89); and her words suggest a motherly love, and
accord with a mother's circumstances – more than with her own:
spes tu nunc una, senectae tu requies miserae (57f.).[4] Her words, and
Vergil's description of her, also suggest a more directly passionate
emotion: *flebat et ardentem generum moritura tenebat*: '*Turne, per has ego
te lacrimas* ... (55f.) ... *qui te cumque manent isto certamine casus et
me, Turne, manent* ... (61f.). With this, compare e.g. Prop. 2.20.
18, *ambos una fides auferet, una dies*; and, as so often, Amata recalls
and exhibits the passion of Dido. Here she recalls the *moritura* Dido
beseeching the parting Aeneas: 4.307ff., *nec moritura tenet crudeli
funere Dido?* ... *per ego has lacrimas* (314) ... *cui me moribundam
deseris* ...? (324).[5] Amata is an interesting creation. This is not the
place to probe her psychology. But I can allow myself to say that she
does have a coherent psychology. She is not merely a patchwork of
characters from other books or poems uttering useful prompts at convenient places in the narrative. Vergil's description of her reflects his
understanding of the close interrelation between, even identity of,
many apparently distinct passionate emotions. It would be misleading
to say that Amata is simply 'in love' with Turnus. But some of her
language suggests she is. That fact must have repercussions.

One unexpected, incidental repercussion it has is for Lavinia and
for the plot. Lavinia's sense of propriety, Vergil's sense of propriety,
forbids Lavinia herself to speak. But Amata's words seem in some way
to have spoken for her, to have caught her mood; anyway to have
affected her.[6] She reacts to Amata's words, more particularly (as I
would stress) she reacts *in line* with them. She weeps: *accepit uocem
lacrimis*: like, and with, Amata (and like Dido – and like Delia:
Tibull. 1.3.14). Why? A great many possible reasons suggest themselves. But one not to be excluded (among others) is the one already
adumbrated. She weeps for the same general reason as Amata (and
Dido, and Delia). She weeps in similar response to the same crisis:
a person who arouses passionate emotion in her is meditating leaving
on a dangerous enterprise. It is a natural interpretation. It is also a

natural interpretation that she is weeping for the same person as Amata, with whom she weeps. And is it not plausible? *praestans animi iuuenis* (12.19), *petit ante alios pulcherrimus omnis* (7.55); *iam matura uiro, iam plenis nubilis annis* (7.53). And with Lavinia (and Delia, and perhaps Dido) the passionate emotion can be 'simply' defined: she is 'in love'. Harder evidence follows.

Lavinia blushes as well as weeps: *flagrantis . . . rubor . . . calefacta per ora*. Why? Let us try following the interpretation of the previous paragraph. The psychology works, and a pleasant parallel offers itself. Passion for Turnus has been uttered (by Amata); Lavinia reveals her heartfelt sympathy with that utterance (in weeping). So she reveals her love – this anyway iṣ what she thinks. In consequence she is embarrassed, guilty even: *conscia* and blushing – as modest girls are when caught in such a position: cf. Catull. 65.19–24:

> ut missum sponsi furtiuo munere malum
>   procurrit casto uirginis e gremio,
> quod miserae oblitae molli sub ueste locatum
>   dum aduentu matris prosilit, excutitur,
> atque illud prono praeceps agitur decursu,
>   huic manat tristi conscius ore rubor.

The parallel seems to me a most suggestive one. And from Hellenistic times on, of course, ἔρως has often provoked a maidenly blush. E.g. in Apollonius' Hypsipyle (1.790f.):

> ἡ δ᾽ ἐγκλιδὸν ὄσσε βάλουσα
> παρθενικὰς ἐρύθηνε παρηίδας.

Such blushes are powered by ἔρως, but they also bespeak, to a greater or lesser extent, *pudor* (they are the reaction of a *pudibunda* to ἔρως);[7] and of course Lavinia will not voice her love or act on it – of that we may be even more sure now than before: *ubi enim rubor, obstat amori*. Contrast more brazen heroines, Scylla daughter of Nisus, for example: *nullus in ore rubor: ubi enim rubor, obstat amori. atque . . . fertur* (*Ciris* 180ff.).[8]

Let us concentrate a moment on the phrasing of *flagrantis genas, ignem subiecit rubor, calefacta ora*. It seems a tremendous amount of heat to attribute to a blush. But that is what Vergil seems to say:[9] *cui plurimus ignem/subiecit rubor*, 'in whom a great blush kindled fire' – and produced, presumably, the *flagrantis genas* and *calefacta ora* as well as the *ignem*. Of course Vergil helps to explain the amount of heat by stressing the huge size of the blush: *plurimus*. And we might (I think validly) infer from that that what was being blushed *for* was huge (at least in Lavinia's eyes) – causing the huge blush which caused the huge heat: ultimately, the love. So there is logic in the text – and food for thought. There is also a fine example of ἔμφασις, *significatio* (I am trying to avoid the word 'ambiguity').[10] For fire, as we shall soon recall, is a very significant image of love in the *Aeneid*. By emphasizing the depth of the blush in the symptoms and terminology of fire, Vergil suggests – he almost brings to the surface of his text – its erotic cause. Lavinia with *flagrantes genae*, with *ignis* kindled in her, with *calefacta ora*, is 'on fire'; and the repercussions of that sort of statement about a girl in a Vergilian text are obvious. It is tempting to use the word 'ambiguous'.

The source of the stained ivory simile is well known: the simile describing Menelaus' wound in *Iliad* 4.141ff.:

ὡς δ᾽ ὅτε τίς τ᾽ ἐλέφαντα γυνὴ φοίνικι μιήνῃ
Μῃονὶς ἠὲ Κάειρα . . .

No one can deny that Vergil's choice of simile is quite surprising, its literary purpose unobvious. Of course, the poet is shortly to base a whole scene (the breaking of the truce) on precisely this section of the *Iliad*; and some might maintain that he uses the simile simply because it is present to his mind and attractively decorative. On the other hand, Vergil usually displays profounder artistic principles than convenience, and seeks more in his similes than extrinsic ornament. In fact, the latest full discussion of Vergil's similes tells us that Book 12 exhibits the greatest interdependence between simile and narrative.[11] The same discussion fails, however, to elucidate ours.

Allusion is the key. Readers of Vergil know that the content and context of a Vergilian source are often (not always) to be borne in mind when reading the new fabrication. This is most clearly demonstrable over broad stretches of text. The content and context of Odysseus' wanderings focus and direct our reading of *Aen.* 1–6. But it can be clearly demonstrated in small and specific cases, as Knauer has frequently shown.[12] For example the full significance of *Aen.* 12. 896ff. is not realized unless the Iliadic source or rather sources (primarily Diomedes material) are sensed through the Vergilian lines.[13]

Now the fact that 12.896ff. are part, indeed the climax, of a pattern of more or less well marked Diomedes material helps us to pick up the allusion. The very unexpectedness of our simile prompts us to consider sources, and takes us back to Menelaus and *Iliad* 4. But what is the significance of the allusion, if such it be? What has Menelaus to do with Lavinia? Personally, nothing. The point lies elsewhere.

Two lexical details, in comparison with Homer, are significant. The epithet *sanguineus* is an addition to the Homeric source. *uiolo* is a much

stronger word than μιαίνω. It has (among other things) a strong
moral connotation ('defile') – but some moral connotation ('sully') is
probably always present in the Greek word;[14] and *uiolo* signifies
physical injuring in a way that μιαίνω does not; indeed, in four out
of its eight other uses in the *Aeneid* (all Vergil's examples occur in the
Aeneid) it makes up a formula *uiolauit uulnere, sim.*[15] We could say
that, especially for Vergil, it was a 'wound' word. This nuance
obviously works with *sanguineus*.[16] Thus, paradoxically, these varia-
tions from Homer assist the recall of Homer: they remind us that the
simile originally applied to a wound (Menelaus' wound). And they also
focus our attention upon what in the original context is relevant to our
own: the *wound*.

The simile, in the first place illustrating Lavinia's blush, suggests by
allusion (allusion assisted by diction: *sanguineus, uiolo*) that Lavinia is
wounded. So, by a concatenation of emotions including love, is
Turnus: *Poenorum qualis in aruis/saucius ille ...* (12.4ff.). So, pre-
eminently, was Dido (suggestively linked to Turnus by the specification
Poenorum). Wound, and fire, were dominant and striking images for
Dido's love in Book 4: *at regina graui iamdudum saucia cura/uulnus
alit uenis et caeco carpitur igni* (1–2), and so on, at salient intervals
in the book.[17] Wound and fire: *flagrantis, ignem, calefacta, sanguineo
uiolauerit,* ὠτειλή. Discreetly but perceptibly Vergil reinforces the
suggestion that Lavinia, like Dido, was in love: she was in love with
(it must be) Turnus.

It is not, of course, in Vergil's way to say or suggest things
objectively. His 'subjective style' (Otis's clumsy but now traditional
phrase) instils into the narrative the feelings of the narrator – or one
of the narrator's characters. Here we sense the narrator, Vergil himself. Wound imagery suggests sympathy. Wounds involve suffering,
which we pity: remember how Dido's *tacitum uulnus* was amplified
into the pitiable picture of the wounded hind, and finally realized in
the frightful *uulnus stridens* of her suicide (4.67, 69ff., 689). Fire
imagery is less sympathetic: we remember how Dido's *ignis* switched
fluently to the *atri ignes* of her curse (4.384). Vergil sees an anti-
pathetic as well as a sympathetic aspect to Dido's violently passionate
love. We perceive the same ambiguity in his delicate adumbration of
Lavinia's more delicate passion: wound and fire. But in the final count,
however sympathetic with its victims, Vergil condemns passionate love
itself – he has done so (arguably consistently) since *Ecl.* 2: note
especially *Georgics* 3.209ff. Vergilian disapprobation of love, his dis-
taste, is evident here, in the moral connotation of *uiolauerit*.

Behind the second simile, *aut mixta rubent ubi lilia ...*, is, probably, Apollonius' description of Medea, *Argonautica* 3.297–98:

ἀπαλὰς δὲ μετετρωπᾶτο παρειὰς
ἐς χλόον, ἄλλοτ᾽ ἔρευθος, ἀκηδείῃσι νόοιο.

The imagery itself reminds one (a) of a lover describing his beloved:
cf. Prop. 2.3.10ff.:

> lilia non domina sint magis alba mea;
> ut Maeotica nix minio si certet Hibero,
> utque rosae puro lacte natant folia ...

It also recalls (b) Catullus' epithalamium, Catull. 61.185ff.:

> uxor in thalamo tibi est,
> ore floridulo nitens,
> alba parthenice uelut
> luteumue papauer.

The type of imagery was perhaps conventional in epithalamia. If it was,
it would explain the way 'Lygdamus's' thought moves in the following ([Tib.] 3.4.30ff.):

> ... et color in niueo corpore purpureus,
> ut iuueni primum uirgo deducta marito
> inficitur teneras ore rubente genas,
> et cum contexunt amarantis alba puellae
> lilia et autumno candida mala rubent.

These are, I think, the most relevant parallels for our simile,[18] and
they seem to me to guide its interpretation. It seems (a) a simile
appropriately uttered *by* someone in love; it seems too (b) a simile
appropriately uttered *of* somebody in love – by someone relatively detached. The erotic connotations, at least, seem indisputable; and the
simile has I think a twofold suggestion, and a twofold 'subjectivity'.
We detect quite distinctly I think (prompted by parallel (b)) *Vergil*'s
description of a girl in love; we detect too (following parallel (a))
Turnus' feelings for the girl he loves. That suggestion is confirmed
by the next movement of the text: *illum turbat amor*. But I should like
my emphasis to be on the first point: in the second simile, as in the
first, Vergil suggests the love of Lavinia, Lavinia's love for Turnus.

illum turbat amor ... The reference of *amor* is, I am inclined to think
(in view of the above), ambiguous: Turnus' love for Lavinia – and
vice versa. There is a point to be drawn out of this. *illum turbat amor
figitque in uirgine uultus; ardet in arma magis* ... In the opinion of
Plato's Phaedrus love inspires bravery in a warrior.[19] Our text suggests
a kindred idea, but with characteristic Vergilian colouring: passion
inspires violence. And Phaedrus specified that not only loving,
ἐρᾶν, but *being* loved, ἐρᾶσθαι, was inspiring.[20] Our ambiguity
suggests the same sort of point in the new context.[21]

Appendix

I collect here some comments on Lavinia in general and our passage in particular. Johnson's (12) is the most thoroughgoing, and has points of contact with my interpretation as well as radical differences from it.

(1) Servius ⟨auct.⟩ on 12.66: IGNEM SVBIECIT RVBOR 'hypallage est pro "cui ignis animi subiecit ruborem". mouebatur autem, intellegens se esse tantorum causam malorum, sic ⟨ut⟩ supra ⟨ipse⟩ [11.480] causa mali tanti, oculos deiecta decoros.'

(2) Tiberius Claudius Donatus on 12.65: 'Lauinia, inquit, uocem matris lacrimantis accepit et uirginalis uerecundiae signa ipsius uultus sui permutatione monstrauit. nouerat enim se propter illa omnia geri ...' (Donatus notices the stained ivory simile – 'admirabilis parabola' – but has nothing to say – beyond enthusing and paraphrasing.)

(3) C. G. Heyne, in the Heyne-Wagner edition of Vergil (1833) on 12.64–69: 'Praeclare τὸ ἦθος in virgine servatum. Erubescit illa; animi sensa non eloquitur. Quandoquidem autem sive ex antiqui aevi more, sive ex carminis oeconomia, Laviniae nullae praecipuae partes esse in rerum actu poterant: multo magis in rubore puellae acquiescere debuit poeta ... Erubuisse autem putanda est, cum praesente Turno nuptiarum esset facta mentio, quas mater cum ipso, non cum Aenea, factas esse vellet. Nam de amore Laviniae, in utrum illa animo inclinaret, nihil usquam, si bene memini, poeta meminit.'

(4) J. Conington, in the Conington-Nettleship edition of 1883 on 12.64: 'As Heyne observes, Virg. never informs us what were the feelings of Lavinia.' (As far as Heyne is concerned this is a little misleading.)

(5) R. Heinze, *Virgils epische Technik* (3rd. ed. Leipzig, 1914), p. 460: '... kein Versuch gemacht wird, Lavinia aus dem Hintergrunde hervorzuziehen und zu einer handelnden Figur zu machen; die Ereignisse am Hofe des Latinus sind so gerade kompliziert genug, und der Dichter bedient sich gern des Vorwandes, dass die altrömische *filia familias* keinen Eigenwillen hat ... Lavinia soll den Leser gar nicht als Individuum, sondern lediglich als Tochter des Latinus interessieren, mit deren Hand das Königreich vergeben wird.'

(6) W. Warde Fowler, *The Death of Turnus* (Oxford, 1919), p. 49: 'Once and again Virgil has carried the Homeric simile of fact into the region of feeling and character; the blush reveals Lavinia as she is nowhere else revealed ...' (But nothing more of substance is added.)

(7) Schur in *RE* XII.1.1006.45ff. (article 'Lavinia', 1924): 'L. selbst

ist bei dem ganzen Kampfe völlig passiv, wird nicht um ihre Meinung gefragt und lässt alles willig über sich ergehen.'

(8) V. Pöschl, *The Art of Vergil* (English translation: University of Michigan, 1962), p. 201 n. 43 (= *Die Dichtkunst Virgils*, Innsbruck/ Wien, 1950, p. 145 n. 211): 'Lavinia's charm, doubled by her grief (XII.64f.), is one more reason for Turnus to fight. His love for Lavinia is treated with the same restraint as that of Aeneas for Dido.'

(9) M. C. J. Putnam, *The Poetry of the Aeneid* (Cambridge, Mass., 1965), p. 159: 'Lavinia's blush, prompted by Amata's speech, is caused by Turnus' love for her.' (There is further comment on our lines, part fanciful, part stimulating.)

(10) F. Klingner, *Virgil* (Zürich/Stuttgart, 1967), p. 591: 'Ein einziges Mal wird Lavinia als schönes Wesen gegenwärtig, das Liebe zu erregen vermag, dort, wo Turnus zum letzten Kampf aufzubrechen im Begriff ist (12,64–70). Lavinia ist nicht eine betörende Beute für den kühnen Mann, sie ist Macht und Anrecht, und Ursprung einer Ahnenreihe.'

(11) W. S. Anderson, *The Art of the Aeneid* (Englewood Cliffs, N. J., 1969), p. 116 (a footnote on lines 64–70): 'Vergil never interprets Lavinia's feelings towards Turnus or Aeneas. It is clearly possible to explain her blush in several fashions, indeed to attribute it to her affection for Amata alone. We see how Turnus is moved, but his wild emotions may completely misinterpret the situation.'

(12) W. R. Johnson, *Darkness Visible, A Study of Vergil's Aeneid* (University of California Press, 1976), p. 56f.: 'But why does she blush? What is it that her mother says that conjures up this manifestation of simple embarrassment or of delicate, shy, turbulent eroticism? *Ardentem generum/generum Aenean*? We know nothing whatever of Lavinia's conscious thoughts, much less of her private fantasies. Does she respond to the passion of Turnus? Has she toyed with notions of the glamorous Asiatic barbarian ...? One may speculate, but Vergil has seen to it that such speculation is as fruitless as it is boring. We are given nothing but a fleeting, tantalizing vision of possible erotic excitement, but that vision is as incisive and as artistic as anything Vergil wrote. Yet it was not imagined in order that we might understand something about Lavinia; it was imagined in order that we might understand something about Turnus ... My point here is that we see Lavinia blush through Turnus' eyes, and it is Turnus' passion and his point of view that cause Vergil to select *uiolauerit* ... *Violauerit* echoes the *uiolentia* of Turnus ... The flawlessly mixed simile describes the confused manner in which Turnus see[s] Lavinia's blush ...'

NOTES

1. In an appendix I have collected together a range of comments, on Lavinia in general and our lines in particular. In an effort to keep my paper succinct and clear I have refrained from expressing agreement or disagreement with this or that aspect of this or that interpretation.

2. Cf. Aristotle, *Poetics* 1450 a 37–b2.

3. This seems to me a reasonable description of Aeneas' killing of Turnus. His own understandable desire to avenge the death and dishonour of Pallas has been reinforced by the compelling and touching plea of Evander: 11.177–81. Evander, at any rate, feels Aeneas has a *duty* to him in this respect. Note too that while it is part of heroic and indeed Roman ethics to despoil a defeated enemy (cf. Pallas at 10.449, about to fight Turnus), the *wearing* of spoils breaks what one might call a taboo: cf. S. Reinach, *Cultes, Mythes et Religions*, tome III (Paris, 1908), pp. 223ff.; also *Aen.* 8.562, 11.5–11, 83–84, 193–96. Aeneas, we could say, has honour on his side – and piety, and perhaps other things. But once more piety conflicts with Piety. Turnus is *subiectus* and no longer a threat to *pax*; from the grand point of view of Anchises (6.851–53) he should have been spared.

4. See my note on *Ciris* 293–94. The sentiment belongs most naturally to a parent or equivalent who loses or has the prospect of losing an only child. Amata exaggerates emotionally. The death of Turnus would not signify for her an ὀρφάνιον γῆρας.

5. There are no other examples of an appeal *per has lacrimas* in Vergil.

6. How useful for the modest Lavinia, and for Vergil! The fact that Amata is a plausible character speaking with plausible psychology does not of course *prevent* her advancing other people's action.

7. Cf. Callimachus fr. 80.10 with Pfeiffer ad loc., Musaeus, *Hero and Leander* 160–61 with Kost ad loc. (Apoll. 3.297–98 (see below) is a little different.) Bömer collects many other blushes in his note on *Met.* 3.423. It is interesting that Ovid depicts *rubor* on the face of the virginal Daphne (*Met.* 1.484), and that his Phaedra perceives it on the face of Hippolytus (*Her.* 4.72). Ovid may possibly mean to suggest that the two are virginal *in reaction* to stimuli they have at some time felt, or do in some way feel – they are not abhorring a completely unknown quantity. That would obviously be correct psychology; and the potential connotations of *rubor* would on this reading be fully exploited. I do not know whether *Met.* 1.469–71 works against such an interpretation; note too that Ovid does sometimes (as some of Bömer's passages show) simply use *rubor* for the 'roses' part of a natural, unstimulated 'milk-and-roses' complexion. (Jasper Griffin reminds me that blusing is not Homeric. Vergil colours the epic according to a later sensibility. But note Enn. *Ann.* 352, *et simul erubuit ceu lacte et purpura mixta*.)

8. Cf. Ovid, *Am.* 1. 2. 32, *Ars* 1. 608, etc. for *pudor* as an obstacle to love.

9. This is not an example of hypallage, pace Servius (Appendix (1)), who seems to have had influence on, among others, T. E. Page ad loc. Cf. Heyne on 64–69: 'non est hypallage ... utrumque dici et animo repraesentari potest; ut et ignis h. calor sanguinis ruborem faciat, et rubor, sanguine moto, calorem.' A. J. Bell's interesting discussion of Vergilian hypallage (*The Latin Dual and Poetic Diction*, Oxford, 1923, esp. p. 320) does not, incidentally, include a subject-object interchange.

10. *Rhet. Her.* 4.67: significatio est res quae plus in suspicione relinquit quam positum est in oratione (cf. Cic. *Orat.* 139, significatio saepe erit maior quam oratio); Quint. 8.3. 83, amplior uirtus est ἔμφασις, altiorem praebens intellectum quam quem uerba per se ipsa declarant.

11. R. Rieks, 'Die Gleichnisse Vergils' in *Aufstieg und Niedergang der römischen Welt* 31, 2 (Berlin/New York, 1981), p. 1087.

12. G. N. Knauer, *Die Aeneis und Homer* (Göttingen, 1964).

13. Knauer, pp. 317–20.

14. A neutral sense 'stain', 'dye', is a figment of lexicographical imagination (this point is pressed upon me by D. P. Fowler). It is *not* illustrated by Heliodorus 10.15, pace LSJ; and in *Iliad* 4.141ff., μιήνῃ (141) is surely an example of 'intrusion' by a 'tenor' term (cf. 146, μιάνθην αἵματι μηροί) into the 'vehicle': cf. M. S. Silk, *Interaction in Poetic Imagery* (Cambridge, 1974), pp. 138–42. For other uses of μιαίνω in Homer, see *Iliad* 16.795, μιάνθησαν δὲ ἔθειραι/αἵματι, 797, 17.439, 23.732: a sense 'sully' is clear in all of them.

15. See Lewis and Short sub voc.; *Aen.* 11.277, 591, 848, 12.797.

16. *sanguineus* might also be interpreted as the intrusion of 'tenor' terminology (the blood in Lavinia's cheeks) into the 'vehicle' (cf. n. 14). But this certainly does not preclude, nor is it as important as, the interpretation offered above.

17. Cf. Brooks Otis, *Virgil* (Oxford, 1963), pp. 70ff.

18. But note too the interesting passages cited by Enk on Prop. 2.3.11–12; also some of the passages listed by Bömer at Ov. *Met.* 3.423. It should be observed that such imagery sometimes applies to a stimulated effect (Lavinia, Catullus' *uxor*), sometimes to a natural 'milk-and-roses' complexion (Propertius' Cynthia). But I do not think the distinction affects the point I am making, and so I have not encumbered the text with it.

19. Plato, *Symp.* 179A and following.

20. Note the case of Achilles, *Symp.* 179E–180B.

21. My best thanks are due to D. P. Fowler and Jasper Griffin for helpful contributions and criticisms.

ADDITIONAL NOTE (1989)

Page 158 line 28
For 'it would be misleading' read 'it might be misleading'

Page 165 line 33
For 'blusing' read 'blushing'

CRITICAL APPRECIATIONS II
VIRGIL, *AENEID* xii. 843–86

By R. D. WILLIAMS *and* C. J. CARTER

I

The following is the second of a series which began in *G & R* xx (1973), 38 ff. and 155 ff.

His actis aliud genitor secum ipse uolutat
Iuturnamque parat fratris dimittere ab armis.
dicuntur geminae pestes cognomine Dirae,   845
quas et Tartaream Nox intempesta Megaeram
uno eodemque tulit partu, paribusque reuinxit
serpentum spiris uentosasque addidat alas.
hae Iouis ad solium saeuique in limine regis
apparent acuuntque metum mortalibus aegris,   850
si quando letum horrificum morbosque deum rex
molitur, meritas aut bello territat urbes.
harum unam celerem demisit ab aethere summo
Iuppiter inque omen Iuturnae occurrere iussit:
illa uolat celerique ad terram turbine fertur.   855
non secus ac neruo per nubem impulsa sagitta,
armatam saeui Parthus quam felle ueneni,
Parthus siue Cydon, telum immedicabile, torsit,
stridens et celeris incognita transilit umbras:
talis se sata Nocte tulit terrasque petiuit.   860
postquam acies uidet Iliacas atque agmina Turni,
alitis in paruae subitam collecta figuram,
quae quondam in bustis aut culminibus desertis
nocte sedens serum canit importuna per umbras—
hanc uersa in faciem Turni se pestis ob ora   865
fertque refertque sonans clipeumque euerberat alis.
illi membra nouus soluit formidine torpor,
arrectaeque horrore comae et uox faucibus haesit.
    At procul ut Dirae stridorem agnouit et alas,
infelix crinis scindit Iuturna solutos   870
unguibus ora soror foedans et pectora pugnis:
'quid nunc te tua, Turne, potest germana iuuare?
aut quid iam durae superat mihi? qua tibi lucem
arte morer? talin possim me opponere monstro?
iam iam linquo acies. ne me terrete timentem,   875
obscenae uolucres: alarum uerbera nosco

letalemque sonum, nec fallunt iussa superba
magnanimi Iouis. haec pro uirginitate reponit?
quo uitam dedit aeternam? cur mortis adempta est
condicio? possem tantos finire dolores   880
nunc certe, et misero fratri comes ire per umbras!
immortalis ego? aut quicquam mihi dulce meorum
te sine, frater, erit? o quae satis ima dehiscat
terra mihi, Manisque deam demittat ad imos?'
tantum effata caput glauco contexit amictu   885
multa gemens et se fluuio dea condidit alto.

II

This passage follows immediately upon the resolution in heaven of the
conflict between Trojans and Italians, when Jupiter and Juno agree to the
conditions under which Aeneas shall be triumphant over Turnus. The
Italians are to become dominant partners in the racial alliance destined to
lead to the emergence of the Romans as rulers of the world, but Aeneas
and the Trojans must start the process. In the passage we are considering
Virgil conveys with power and poignancy the helplessness of those who
misguidedly oppose the divine destiny.

The first section of our passage concentrates the attention on the fate of
Turnus, deprived as he now is of the help of Juno. The second section
switches to Juturna, and her misery at being prevented from helping her
brother. After our passage comes the rest of the narrative of the single
combat between Aeneas and Turnus—now that Jupiter and Juno have
agreed, and Juturna has been forced to withdraw, all the characters of the
poem have finished their roles except only for Aeneas and Turnus.

The passage begins with two matter-of-fact lines as Jupiter plans the
outcome on earth, an easy matter for the king of the gods now that he has
dealt successfully with the opposition of Juno; *secum ipse volutat* conveys
that he and he alone will plan the outcome. *Aliud* almost means 'the next
item on the agenda', and 844 is stated in straightforward and precise
terms, defining the action Jupiter proposes to take in the simplest possible
way. But this clarity and brevity are succeeded by lines densely packed
with pictorial elaboration and horror, set in the form of an ecphrasis. The
description of the fiends is introduced at 845 ff., with no indication of their
relationship to the narrative until the pronouns *harum unam* (853) establish it.[1] The twin Furies (*Dirae* is used by Virgil several other times[2]) are
Allecto and Tisiphone, oddly here separated from their sister Megaera: we
are not told which of them is chosen by Jupiter, but it can be assumed that
it is Allecto, already an agent of disaster in Book vii. 324 ff. where her
gruesome and horrible nature was described in full. Their location in
Tartarus is frequently alluded to by the poets,[3] and their parentage as

daughters of Night makes them primitive and primordial in the highest possible degree. The epithet *intempesta*—a word taken from Ennius (*Ann.* 102) which occurs also at iii. 587—adds a kind of supernatural quality to Night, placing it outside time. The strange scansion of e͞ode͞mqu͞e (cf. x. 487) adds to the eerie effect, and the spondaic movement and alliteration of *s* in 848 rounds the description with words which emphasize the horrid qualities of these grim monsters.[4] The description might here be thought to be finished, but Virgil pauses for four more lines before coming out of his ecphrasis back to the narrative: the word *saevi* (Jupiter in his angry mood) anticipates 851 f.; a sonorous and archaic effect is achieved by the Homeric phrase *mortalibus aegris* (δειλοῖσι βρότοισιν), by the formulaic monosyllabic ending of 851, and by the extremely powerful alliteration of the menacing letter *m*, first lightly in 850 *metum mortalibus* and then more powerfully in 851–2 *morbosque* ... *molitur, meritas* ... The colourful verb *molitur* (here 'wreaks') is a favourite with Virgil.[5] The word *meritas* is given emphasis not only by this alliteration, but also by its position before the world *aut* which introduces the clause: Virgil is emphasizing that this kind of horror is not sent by Jupiter unless it is deserved.

As the narrative resumes (853 ff.) after the descriptive digression the movement becomes rapid with dactyls and a trochaic break in the fourth foot. The instructions of Jupiter are given some vividness by the use of the preposition *in* to express purpose—*inque omen*, 'to be an omen'—but they are brief and precise, and the action of their fulfilment in 855 is even more brief and precise. Now Virgil again uses the technique of descriptive elaboration on a briefly expressed narrative, this time with a simile: the structure of 853–5 and 856–9 thus balances with the short lines of narrative (843–4) followed by the descriptive ecphrasis (845–52). The simile builds up its points of resemblance: it starts with the idea of speed (*impulsa*), picking up *celerem* in 853 and *celeri* in 855; then it passes to the image of destruction with the mention of poison and inevitable death, *telum immedicabile*; finally it exploits the notion of unexpectedness—the arrow is not seen as it swiftly seeks its mark, nor is the Fury. The diction of the simile is noteworthy: the patterned line 857 has an adjective before the third foot caesura agreeing and rhyming with the noun at the line-ending; emphasis is given to the Parthians by the repetition of *parthus*;[6] and the area of reference is widened by the inclusion of the Cydonians,[7] another people famed for archery. *Immedicabile* is a sonorous adjective of the kind favourite with Virgil in this position;[8] great stress is put on *stridens* as it fills the first foot, a relatively rare rhythm in Virgil and often used for special effect,[9] and here anticipated in the preceding line (*Parthus*) and repeated in the summarizing line which follows (*talis*).

The atmosphere of terror and death now becomes more overpowering. Line 861 is preparatory and indicates the moment for action; but the fulfilment of the action does not come until the main verbs of 866, being held in suspense by a number of descriptive clauses. Line 862 is frightening with its lack of specification—we are not told what kind of bird the Fury turns herself into (notice the middle use of *collecta*), and the idea of shrinking conveyed in *parvae* and *collecta* is eerie and weird. The next lines indicate that the bird is an owl, a bird always associated in literature with ill-omen and here located on graves or lonely rooftops. We are reminded of the terrible scene (iv. 460 f.) where Dido, visiting her dead husband's memorial shrine, is haunted by the sound of his voice amidst the hooting of owls. The rhythm of 863 is utterly unusual with its spondaic fifth foot and trisyllabic word-ending. Virgil employs a spondaic fifth foot only some thirty-five times altogether, generally with Greek nouns; the nearest parallels to this one are *Geo.* iii. 276 *depressas convallis*, *Aen.* vii. 634 *lento ducunt argento*. Both of these clearly aim at and achieve very special rhythmical effects. Finally the note of ill-omen is stressed with the long menacing word *importuna*: 'It was the owl that shriek'd, the fatal bellman, which gives the stern'st good-night.'[10]

The long description is now broken off with a slight anacoluthon as the sentence is summarized with *hanc versa in faciem*: we are required to concentrate our attention on visualizing the shape of the transfigured Fury. Then the narrative turns to the victim with the word *Turni* and the strange use of *ob*; the expected phrase would be *ante ora* or *in ora*, but *ob* adds an extra hostility. When the main verbs of the sentence come at last in 866 they convey the insistence of the apparition by means of the trochaic caesuras which come after *-que* in the first and second feet,[11] and virtually in the fourth foot as well until the elision is made. Finally the picture concentrates fully on Turnus, first with an echo of the rhythm of a spondaic first word (*illi*), then with emphasis on the effect on him (*novus . . . torpor*, 'a strange numbness'). We are reminded of the earlier description of Turnus' utter confusion in these final moments,[12] but this time the hand of divinity is even more clearly recognizable, and Turnus' pitiable state is even more obviously portrayed.

So much for the unhappy Turnus; his imminent fate is now held in suspense as Juturna makes her exit from the poem. She is half divine, daughter of Jupiter and a nymph, and she recognizes more clearly than Turnus the precise significance of the divine intervention. She is aware that the bird is a manifestation of the Fury from the underworld, and she realizes that she can no longer aid her brother. She tears her hair in her grief and distress, and Virgil links her sisterly agony with that of Anna for Dido by repeating (871) the exact words of iv. 673, a repetition made particularly significant by the presence of the word *soror*. Thus the tragedy of Turnus is linked with that of Dido: the two great opponents of the Roman mission both win sympathy from the reader as they come to disaster, and the sympathy for Turnus is greatly increased by the reminiscence of Dido's death—a reminiscence strengthened by Juturna's wish to be swallowed up in the depths of earth (883–4, cf. iv. 24 f.), and by her words in 879 ff. which recall Anna's lament that she too could not die when Dido died.[13]

Juturna's speech begins with monosyllables giving an effect of broken rhythm, and strong alliteration of *t* in a line (872) which expresses in the simplest possible way her agonizing plight. The juxtaposition of *te tua* reinforces the feeling of sisterly obligation which is picked up again by *durae* (873, 'hard-hearted as I must be now'). The rhetorical question is echoed by three more in the next two lines, staccato, indignant, yet useless, as she recognizes when she collects herself to say *iam iam linquo acies*. The paradox, reinforced by harsh alliteration, *ne me terrete timentem*, is followed with the strongest word of loathing available in the Latin language, *obscenae*.[14] Midline stops (used with the rhetorical questions in 873–4) continue in the next few lines, and are taken up again in the new series of rhetorical questions (878–80) and again in 882–4; the effect is one of agitation and of the breathless blurting-out of all the thoughts that come to her. This is reinforced by the irony—*magnanimi Iovis* and *haec pro virginitate reponit*—and by the unfulfilled sentence about what she might have done now had she not been prevented by her immortality. She prays for the earth to swallow her and to receive her with the shades of the dead, goddess though she be. Yet she knows all her complaints are vain, and when she has uttered them she accepts her immortality, as she must, veils herself from sight and hides herself in the river sacred to her.[15]

Thus the helpless plight of Turnus, and the agony of his last ally, his sister Juturna, as she is forced to leave him, are portrayed with such power as to induce a feeling of sympathy and sorrow which overshadows the victory of Aeneas. Turnus was in the wrong—he had opposed the fates and he had killed Pallas with arrogant violence; yet in this passage, as we see him brought low by supernatural agency, and as we see his sister removed from his side, we are prepared for the sorrow and perplexity with which the poem ends, when Turnus begs Aeneas for mercy but receives none, and his life with a groan departs complaining to the world below: *vitaque cum gemitu fugit indignata sub umbras.* The reader echoes the protest of *indignata*.

III

First, the situation as it divides into the architectural framework of the whole. Opening 2 lines—evolution of Jupiter's plan for Iuturna's 'dismissal' from her brother's fighting cause. Then a fluent scene of 24 lines (845–68)—Jupiter's plan in action, its agent the terrifying Dira, one of the three

Sisters of Doom (845–52); its climax (867–8), the unhinging not of Iuturna herself but her brother Turnus, commander of the troops massed against the Trojans (861). *At procul* 869—superb camera-shift to Iuturna, closing the focus on her reaction; 18 lines (869–86) indicate her utter despair and impotence, dominated by 13 lines of direct speech; she knowingly abandons her brother to death (873–4; 877; 881) and departs to her river-home (886).[16] The 'dismissal' is indeed the final separation implied by the opening *dimittere* (844), widely used in Latin of disbanded armies, dismissed assemblies, renunciation, loss, divorce.[17] We have then an apparently self-contained drama in two acts, the extremities of the plot deftly outlined in a prologue-couplet. The quiet neutrality of *aliud* and *parat* sinks into a pit of horror and panic, one of many implicit links between two superficially very different scenes (i.e. action/reaction: 3 + 3 people/one person: use of direct speech, simile and comparison, etc.). The dramatic situation is the denial under appalling stress of a profound human relationship, sister–brother.

Turnus' panic is clear enough. Iuturna's also; more obviously in the direct agony of 870–1 and the more subtle grandeur of the closing funerary imagery (*caput ... contexit amictu, gemens, se ... condidit*), together framing the less obvious, perhaps, but still more effective panic of her speech, i.e. her sequences of panic-questions, like a rat caught in a trap, cross-set like Donne in distorted line-rhythms; her leaping from subject to subject, cancelling every possible aid or comfort in its very expression; the diverse economy of language, which is common to every facet or theme one explores in the whole 44 lines and an index to its quality; the patterned insistence of *te tua, Turne, potest germana, mihi/tibi, me/me* broken by the concentrated terror of *ne me terrete timentem*, to resume only in the disorder and horrid irony of *misero fratri, ego, mihi, meorum*,[18] *te sine, frater, terra mihi, deam demittat, dea*; and so on. All this panic can be further pursued in its own right,[19] but the direct or indirect cause is the same, the Dira. Since she preconditions everything and looks more colourful anyway, let's see how the poet makes her work and how effective he makes her seem. If she's no better than the conventional horror-film monster, we shall end up bored, impatient, or laughing, and it won't be very good poetry, no matter who wrote it. If we end up as frightened as Turnus and Iuturna seem to be, if the poet makes us imaginatively identify with his human victims, then he will have done the job properly and it will be exciting to see how and why. That's what critical appreciation means.

The Dira terrifying? She seems vast, but the only size-word in the whole passage is *parvae* (862). She seems hideous but the only details about physical appearance come in 848, remote from her contact with Turnus—though the line repays close attention since it paradoxically contains both a lot less and a great many more snakes than the snake-hair cliché of an over-hasty reading. And when she terrifies Turnus (867–8), she does so *alitis in parvae ... figuram* (862). If she had to undergo a transformation, isn't a 'small bird' a huge let-down? And aren't the next two lines a desperately weak attempt to rescue some atmosphere by connecting her with a *quondam* night-owl sitting on a tomb? Even so, why doesn't she tear at least one of Turnus' eyes out with gory beak and dripping claws? 'Contact with Turnus' is strictly incorrect—isn't it amazingly feeble that she only goes to-and-fro, flapping and fluttering *in front of* or *up to* his face (*ob ora* [865], correctly in our text),[20] that the only thing she 'contacts' is the toughest thing about him, his shield? As Jupiter's agent, wouldn't 'a *fierce* eagle with *vast* wings and *vicious-looking* eyes and *big hooked* talons, *ripping* his face to *bloody ribbons*' have been more effective? Perhaps our Dira isn't so terrifying after all?

But she is, for the reasons implied by the italics. Bad art is only superficially impressive. It fails sooner or later because it's too explicit and doesn't know when to stop. Our poet isn't, and does. It's not explicit reference but dramatic atmosphere which makes the Dira and the incredible plot convincing, creating the impassable gulf which finally separates Iuturna and Turnus.[21] It's that age-old question of Art and Illusion. This passage is a masterly study in the art of controlled suggestion, a miniature piece of Alfred Hitchcock at his best. Our Dira becomes a 'small bird'; birds are nice and bats are nasty, but Hitchcock, like Virgil here, can deliberately turn his back on the clichés of the genre and create an *atmosphere* in which the mere sight of a single bird, or just the sound of its wings, becomes in context the most terrifying thing on earth, leaving Dracula jogging merrily along in the rear.

Our Dira's not a bug-eyed monster of the more conventional sort, like Fama in *Aeneid* iv (cf. esp. 180–3) or worse still Statius' Sphinx.[22] What, exactly, makes her terrifying? Not a liberal sowing of familiar emotive adjectives applied direct or implicitly.[23] Nor superlatives and green teeth, which don't occur either. The answer is a complexity of words, sounds, and rhythmic control, small-scale and large-, i.e. the *whole* poetic texture and quality of the drama: which sounds vague and puffy. Detailed appreciation will prove it to the hilt, but, briefly, her terror is not conveyed in ghastly visual close-ups, the technique of a second-rate writer or film-director. She is faceless throughout, just something with wings.[24] But so much is wrapped emotionally and almost exclusively *by implication* around her that she becomes a THING. The only simple terror-adjective she herself bears is her surname/nickname/derived name, Dira—and when you look closely in context almost all the natural horror of both *Dira* and *dirus* has been attracted out by more significant words near by. No, the essence and power of this THING named Dira (*dicuntur ... cognomine*

[845], occupying half the line) expands imaginatively in the mind as we hear and see her primeval birth in the abyss (845–8); what she can and already has done in concert with her three Sisters (849–52)—simple numerical intensification, but disguised here;[25] how and literally in association with what she descends on this mission (853–64); and finally of course her effect on Turnus. All this acquires a momentum from 845 onwards, carefully directed by the rhythm of individual lines and their strategic grouping: and it's this final accumulation of rhythmic and verbal forces, suddenly and unexpectedly gathered and concentrated (*subitam collecta* [862]) into the small but highly 'volatile' confines of a bird which makes her impact on Turnus and listener alike not bloody and ineffective, but physically and emotionally shattering. Turnus' panic gets only two lines. A lesser poet would have given it lots more, elaborating for elaboration's sake. It's only two lines here *not* because Iuturna is the immediate heroine and we have to be hurried into Act 2 before we lose the discreet effect of 844 and 854.[26] That is only part of the reason—the smaller part: the author could have made Iuturna herself the Dira's direct victim and cut Turnus out altogether had he wanted—and again, wider context or no, a lesser poet would. We get only two lines because at 867–8 we need only two lines' convincing of *anybody's* panic confronted by *this* Dira. It's in all senses a *tour de force*.

Let's take it in more detail from 853, the start of her mission. We already have a forcible impression of her general horror, mostly by implication—*pestes, Dirae, Tartaream, Nox intempesta,*[27] *serpentum spiris, ventosas alas, saevi . . . regis,*[28] *apparent* (sc. lictors, with scourging rods and beheading axe—wonderful poetry in context in an 'unpoetic' word), *acuunt metum* ('whetting the axes of terror'), *aegris, letum, horrificum, morbos, rex, bello, territat*. It's a fine selective range, twice as many nouns as adjectives and three striking verbs, and only *pestes, Dirae, Nox*, and *alas* will be used again, in different form, for deliberate connective effect. All by extension of one sort or another belong to her,[29] the words which correlate most to form our mental image in 845–52, Jupiter adding a perverted sublimity as a veritable Genghis Khan. Rhythm is also important, highlighting the most emotive words, and at the end of 852 we are pointedly slowed to the full stop by the recited rhythm of the last three words, directed by their solemn weight of meaning and self-containment in the last three metrical feet—|*bello*| |*territat*| |*urbes*|—verse-beat and natural word-stress are normally 'coincident' in two of these feet, but the self-containment here throws a heavy dragging stress on each opening long syllable and pulls the voice back on the grim significance of language. It's even more effective because *molitur* has already applied several harsh brakes right at the start of the line. Drawn by all this to a reflective halt, high above a panoramic vision of the worthy (*meritas,* a deliberate ambiguity) cities of the earth in apocalyptic agony, we meet the Dira face-to-face as an individual for the first time. Except it's not a face-to-face meeting because she's already off—*harum unam celerem* . . . (853). Sudden speed is the essence of the next ten lines. Mix speed with fresh horror and destructive energy and you get panic, the recipe of 853–62. Her descent becomes panic itself, whirling down with poisoned precision and an unnerving shriek on its unknowing human target.

celerem demisit ab aethere summo lurches us forward after the heavy braking of 852—a sudden plunge from the heights of nowhere. There's only one more dactyl than 852, but it's at the beginning of the second half of the line, the crucial fourth foot: the two speed-words and thin air do the rest. 854 makes her sublimely 'ominous' (*Iuppiter inque omen*) and intro-duces the shock of what is clearly to be a sudden hostile 'run-up to' (*occurrere*). *illa volat celerique* (855) accelerates her and *turbine* feeds in destructive energy as well; its funnelling whirl, delicately reinforced later by *torsit* (858), not only narrows her descent to a fine point of contact with earth but pinpoints in a word the over-all rhythmic momentum of 854–62. We must also appreciate that 855 is a faster line than 853 with the same number of dactyls,[30] and that |*terram*| |*turbine*| |*fertur*| doesn't have the same brake-power effect as |*bello*| |*territat*| |*urbes*| for several obvious reasons which close comparison will extract. In fact 855 falls very fast *ad terram turbine* through the poetic vacuum of *fertur* (cf. *urbes*) and stops very short on the full stop. We're thrown—or rather shot—into the 4–5 line sweep of the arrow simile.

By definition the arrow's velocity becomes hers—*nervo impulsa, Parth-us,*[31] *Parthus sive Cydon, torsit, celeris, transilit,* the basic fabric of the simile: *celeris* makes the link with the Dira explicit. *per nubem . . . umbras* (rightly in our text) frames the scene in disconcerting uncertainties of light, which are effective within the simile (and necessary: not even Parthians could shoot with unimpaired accuracy in pitch-darkness) and prepare a sinister way to *petivit . . . videt* (860–1). They also leave undisturbed at a more potent depth the reverberating artistry of *Tartar-eam Nox intempesta* (846), *Nocte* (860), *nocte* (864). From the emphatic repetition and extension *Parthus . . . Cydon,* the Dira acquires deadly precision of aim, unexpectedness and fell human intent to an intense degree, the identification braced by the triple rhythmic sequence |*Parthus*| |*stridens*| |*talis*|, another piece of magnificent orchestration.[32] The premed-itated horrors of a poisoned barb are injected by a cluster of three word-pairs, interwoven with *Parthus . . . Cydon.* Together they permeate the body of the simile until everything concentrates in *torsit stridens,* and the literary critic gives up in blissful despair that so much diverse intensity can be packed into two words put 'simply' side-by-side in a context. The unnerving climactic sequence *torsit stridens . . . celeris incognita*—perhaps analogy is the last refuge of critical appreciation at such junctures, driven by a simile to similes of its own time: to us, the inhuman scream of a bomb, falling *ab aethere summo . . . per nubem . . . et umbras* from a formation of high-level bombers; or cowering under heavy artillery bombardment, hearing the whine of each shell (*torsit | stridens et celeris incognita transilit umbras*) as it approaches, the screams of the maimed in counterpoint. Outward things change: fear and pain and terror are gauged from within, have elemental identity. Poisoned Parthian arrows or armoured high explosive, the effect on the human mind and imagination is the same.

The riches of the simile are far from exhausted. *armatam saevi Parthus*: word-position clearly dominant over mere grammatical inflexion in the logic of poetic order. The precise nastiness and horror which blossoms from *felle*: wrenching bitterness; greeny-yellow inner-organ slime or blackness; proximity to the stomach; wrath; raging insanity. The tantalizing voice-inflexion *immedicā-bĭle* in this context—a knowing reader, silently or aloud, can harness it for a functional effect (cf. my deliberate 'bloody and ineffective' above). There may be no orator's superlatives and perfect infinitives spitting aural venom, here or anywhere in the piece, but the s's are there all the same working away at our subconscious at more magically effective levels: *sagitta . . . torsit stridens* inside the simile and *talis se sata* just outside it can take us forward and back in fascinating patterns of sound. T's likewise. Sooner or later one appreciates the opening prominence of *nervo*: 'hamstrung' is the nearest an English 'bowstring' gets to everyday physical anatomy. Romans drew and plucked a tense, taut *nervus* to give an arrow impulse. It's context which determines relevance of implied meaning; and we often respond subconsciously and put it down to the 'mystery of art'. Even the motley *non secus ac* (856) has something in sound and controlled association to offer the context which *haud secus ac*, *ut veluti*, *ceu* or even *qualis* cannot fully match. And then there are rhythmic felicities . . .

Twenty-six words, a 'typical' Virgilian simile. The minimum of small grammar-words to obviate clutter and allow the significant poetry to emerge, working the language to its natural and contextual utmost. It arms the Dira with immensities of charge. Miraculous writing, which *talis se sata Nocte* (860) sweeps rhythmically on, backed by a superadded thrust of her primeval horror (cf. 846–7). In the one simple word *petivit* she looks for and at once finds the earth's features, and in the dactylic run of 861 narrows her sights progressively on Turnus. Then comes that line of pure poetry, her sudden concentration into a small feathered bundle with the reactive potential of a galactic implosion—and not one 'poetic' word in its whole length. Two lines (863–4), a sinister spreading evil at a still point of immanence, the final two spondees of 863 eerily tilting the lines and *nocte . . . per umbras* quietly gathering everything which stretches back from 860 and 859 right to the beginning of Time and the time that was before Time (845 ff.)—and the Dira attacks in shock. *illa* (855) is drawn to *illi* (867) and it's all over. Her terror is absolute.

I have used the phrase 'in context' a great deal in a necessarily brief study which deliberately confined itself to the self-contained world of the episode. But as the harrowing of Turnus and 'dismissal' of Iuturna imply, Turnus is the figure of ultimate interest in the narrative which will ensue. And his death is near. The horror and terror of the Dira is the horror and terror of the final stages of the *Aeneid*, foreshadowed and predetermined. Behind the passage stretch the vast recesses of the rest of the *Aeneid*, and as words and phrases have been seen to echo and link across the smaller limits of the passage, so this passage too as a whole draws structural threads and thematic links from what has passed. But it would take an article at least as long as this again to broach and appreciate the other half of its wonder. For in critical appreciation:

> On a huge hill,
> Cragged, and steep, Truth stands, and he that will
> Reach her, about must, and about must go.[33]

They said that Virgil wrote at an average rate of three lines a day, and it was his native language. He is not lightly to be dismissed or the *arcana* of his art easily unlocked, but for those with patience, a good ear, and an imagination controlled by a good Latin dictionary, the rewards are infinitely satisfying.

NOTES

1. For other examples of this type of ecphrasis in Virgil cf. *Aen.* i. 159ff., iv. 480 ff., vii. 563 ff. It is a favourite device of Milton's, e.g. *P.L.* i. 670 ff., x. 547 ff.

2. e.g. iv. 473 and 610, viii. 701.

3. e.g. *Aen.* vii. 328.

4. For the snaky hair of the Furies cf. vii. 329; the use of *spiris* recalls the terrifying serpents which killed Laocoön (ii. 217).

5. Cf. vii. 127, x. 477.

6. Cf. ix. 774 f., x. 200 f.

7. Cf. *Ecl.* x. 59.

8. Cf. vi. 425 and 438, x. 467, xii. 816.

9. Cf. iv. 185 and 190, ix. 419.

10. *Macbeth* ii. 2.

11. Cf. vi. 122.

12. xii. 665 f., 'obstipuit varia confusus imagine rerum | Turnus et obtutu tacito stetit . . .'.

13. iv. 677 f., 'comitemne sororem | sprevisti moriens? eadem me ad fata vocasses . . .'.

14. Cf. iii. 262, where it is used of the Harpies.

15. Cf. 138 ff.

16. In context, *se fluvio . . . condidit alto* is meant to suggest death and burial, but *dea* (cf. 884; 882; 879) blocks any thought of real suicide in the nearest stream. Hence the *internal* logic of going home.

17. Cf. Lewis and Short and *Oxford Latin Dictionary*, indispensable modern aids to critical appreciation and the 'feel' of Latin. More sensitive Romans were better off, the poets especially knowing the language inside out, intuitively.

18. Sc. *cognatorum, consanguineorum,* as Henry rightly observes.

19. e.g. the economic range, distribution, and personalizing crescendo of the only explicit fear/terror words: *metum-horrificum/territat; formidine/horrore; me terrete timentem*—magnificent orchestration of language. The full significance of *formidine* in *this* context must be appreciated too, viz. *alas, sagitta, alitis,* 863, 864, 865, 866, *everberat alis, formidine*: or cf. (via Lewis and Short) Seneca *Dial.* iv. 11. 5 and *Aen.* xii. 750, no more than ten minutes recital-time before!

20. It's the sound-pattern and dactylic rhythm of *fertque refertque* which make it flap and flutter in this context: *versa* and *alis* support it to flood the line and intensify into the huge batter of its climax.

21. *At procul* (869); *te sine, frater, erit* (883) are the only two explicit separations (and again the economy, simplicity of language, and timing are magnificent) and the most effective thing about Iuturna's exit (*condidit*) is its implied meaning. There is an explicit 'gulf' (*dehiscat* [883])—an imaginary one denied Iuturna! *Terra/fluvio* is more, neat pointing of implied effect—a never-ending river flowing into oceanic infinities of mystery, horror, and gloom, esp. for Romans, and a far longer way to the Underworld.

22. *Thebaid* ii. 505 ff. In context, the 'pictorial' physical features of Fama are, of course, functional. But as imaginative writing, compared to the Dira here the whole Fama episode seems to me more obvious and crude—though that could arguably be deliberate too. Nothing's beyond a really great artist if it's controlled and supported by the context and functionally effective. Art is the exercise of controlled imagination after all.

23. Sooner or later, one suddenly notices that *celerem* (853) and *parvae* (862) are the only two adjectives applied to the Dira direct—the sort of realization which indicates either that the author is an idiot, to dispense with the obvious so utterly, or a genius. Her adjectival horror starts at first or second remove (*ventosas, obscenae, letalem*) and is most in evidence at the third (e.g. *horrificum* [851]). A list of the terror/general nastiness words *not* used in this passage is instructive and can quickly be compiled from Lewis and Short; it's useful for Fama and the Sphinx, etc. too.

24. Leaving most if not all the snakes behind in 847–8, in childhood or otherwise (cf. Lewis and Short s.v. *revincio* and in some senses the preceding *tulit partu*).

25. i.e. no *tres, tertia,* etc., one way of first appreciating that family relationships elsewhere in the piece are indirectly used to enhance the family/human feeling between Iuturna and Turnus: cf. *genitor, fratris, geminae, cognomine, uno eodemque tulit partu, paribusque revinxit, addidit,* etc., *soror, germana, mihi, tibi,* etc., *fratri, frater.* By '*addidit,* etc.' I mean other join/unite words, culminating in the sublime irony of *contexit, condidit.* 'But Iuturna and Turnus weren't twins, were they?' is as irrelevant a question as the notorious 'How many children had Lady Macbeth?': the poetic issue is unaffected.

26. Beautifully sparing in the Act 1 context and designed to mislead the reader; everything which 'suddenly surprises' is functional.

27. Cf., in context, the impact of the *Revised Version* 'there shall be time no longer' (Rev. 10. 6) or Messiaen's *Quartet for the End of Time* which it inspired.

28. 'A very odious name in the time of the Republic, i.q. tyrant, despot' (Lewis and Short s.v. *rex*); cf. *rex sacrificus, rex Nemorensis* (ibid.). Words don't change their emotive connotations overnight, except in Orwell's *1984.* Octavian's victory if anything heightened the implicit horror of the word for a decade at least—and both Virgil and Horace were too intelligently sensitive to language not to exploit its razor-topicality. Properly appreciated (cf. my paper 'God, King, Law—and Augustus?—in Horace *Odes* I–III' delivered to the 1973 Class. Assoc. A.G.M.), *neither* was the weak-kneed tout portrayed by traditional commentators on their respective 'politics'.

29. The horror of *Megaeram, partu, revinxit* likewise, which will 'need' explaining in their different ways if the context is insensibly felt *not* to be self-explanatory.

30. i.e. relative order + emotive language matters more than crude metrical statistics. There are five lines in the passage with more dactyls than 853 or 855. Three have little or no atmospheric speed from the dactyl-count itself (878; 883; 886) and 866 suggests rapid fluttering to and fro, not motion hurtling forward. 861 certainly patters rapidly overhead and down onto Turnus, but is arguably less precipitate than 855's whirlwind plummet to the ground.

31. Parthians are Antiquity's Red Indians, as a response to the rest of the simile will finally suggest to even the weakest pupil/student of Latin, *experto credite.* Otherwise Lewis and Short provides the horses and insidious 'retreat' at unnerving death-dealing gallop. The emotive

historical implications of *Parthus* ... *Parthus*—the horror of Crassus' defeat, the Parthian prisoners, etc. (cf. 'Jap', 'Nazi', *'goum'*, 'Angry Brigade', etc.)—do have to be supplied from outside the piece, either from history text-books (e.g. Scullard's *From the Gracchi to Nero*, ch. vi. 8) or from commentators elsewhere: commentators on this Virgil passage itself are not specific or helpful enough.

32. There does not seem much point in the repetition of Parthus, though it is in Virg.'s manner' says Conington ad loc.! Cf. note 31 above. One wonders whether Conington, *et al.*, understood how English poetry works, let alone Virgil.

33. Donne, *Satyre* iii. 79 ff.

WHAT SORT OF TRANSLATION OF VIRGIL DO WE NEED?[1]

By D. E. HILL

Our first need is to define closely the sort of people for whom we intend the translation. Then we must be clear as to what we aim to achieve with them and it. Our audience, presumably, consists of young people many of whom have a primary allegiance to some other Arts discipline, chiefly English, Modern Languages, or History. Almost all will have some experience of studying literature in their own tongue, some will be familiar at first hand with foreign literatures, few will have more than a nodding acquaintance with Latin. By and large they will be used to taking a text and pressing it so as to establish a close understanding of it. Unhappily, if they attempt that with any translation known to me disaster will inevitably ensue. At this point, many readers will no doubt feel that all their doubts about the wisdom of attempting to teach Virgil through translation are being vindicated, while, in my experience, those who wish to defend the practice will tend to do so by granting the proposition that much will inevitably be lost in translation, conceding that students must learn not to press translations, and then making a number of ill-defined generalizations on what can be achieved. What I wish to argue is that none of the popular Virgilian translations was composed with our needs in mind, all make certain assumptions which were possibly quite proper for their audiences but which render their work unsuitable for ours. I shall argue further that we are far too lenient in the demands we make of our translators.

The discipline with the longest history of using translations for serious study is Theology. Of course, most churches do still require small Greek and less Hebrew for their ordinands and real linguistic expertise in their scholars, but at the same time, the Judaeo-Christian tradition has long felt the need for translations that can be pressed, witness the Septuagint, the Vulgate, and the Authorized Version, all of which I note in passing were the work of committees, and all of which strove for detailed accuracy, while at least one displays real literary values. Scholars and the devout have been able, by and large, to press these texts without committing the sort of blunders into which our students are so often enticed. Furthermore, in the theological tradition, a vast literature has grown up to help in detailed exegesis of these translations, an aid so far denied to our students.

There is an assumption behind most modern translations that is, I believe, particularly unhelpful in our context. It runs somewhat like this. To Virgil's audience the *Aeneid* would be an up-to-date poem with an immediate appeal. Accordingly, our translation should appear up to date to the modern reader; if it seems foreign or archaic it will give a false impression. Now, in so far as that is an appeal against deliberate archaizing it is indeed justified; but nowadays it means more than that. In a previous article in this journal,[2] Dr. Bryn Rees gives us some very illuminating observations on the whole subject of translation. He has, however, one disturbing but very revealing passage. He is arguing that verse translations are not necessarily to be preferred for verse authors.

Those who arbitrarily dismiss prose translations of classical poetry may still be thinking of a clientele of scholars, teachers, parsons, and civil servants, educated and cultured, sensitive to every nuance of meaning and appreciative of every trick of style; our contemporary audience is cast in a different mould, impatient of rhetoric and elegance, demanding clarity, movement and 'story line'.

E. V. Rieu, in his introduction to his translation of the *Odyssey*, alleges that the novel is the modern equivalent to that poem and that, accordingly, the form of the modern novel is the appropriate form for his modern translation. There may well be an audience such as Dr. Rees describes and techniques of the sort employed by Rieu may well be suitable for them. Neither that sort of audience nor that sort of technique can have any rightful place in a serious study of literature. A student should read Virgil to find out what is there and to understand how and why it is all achieved. He cannot do that if he is unwilling to tolerate anything that is alien, anything that is unclear at first sight. One of the most important things about Virgil is his distance from us in space and time. A translation which seeks to conceal that has no place in our courses, and, to a greater or lesser extent, all the popular translations of Virgil do just that. Consider the end of Jupiter's prophecy to Venus, *Aeneid* 1. 291–6. Here is the text and three modern translations:[3]

> aspera tum positis mitescent saecula bellis:
> cana Fides et Vesta, Remo cum fratre Quirinus
> iura dabunt; dirae ferro et compagibus artis
> claudentur Belli portae; Furor impius intus
> saeua sedens super arma et centum uinctus aënis
> post tergum nodis fremet horridus ore cruento.

> The bitter centuries of war shall cease then,
> *the world* grow mild *at last*. And white-haired Faith,
> Vesta, and Romulus with his brother Remus
> shall make the Laws and the grim, iron-bolted Gates
> of War shall be closed and within them the fiend of Fury
> throned upon weapons lethal *as himself*
> rage *impotently, his arms and his hands* pinioned
> behind his back with a hundred brazen shackles,
> *roaring* from his blood-boltered throat *in vain*.

Then shall our furious centuries lay down their warring arms, and shall grow kind. Silver-haired Fidelity, Vesta, and Quirine *Romulus*, with his brother Remus *at his side*, shall make the laws. And the terrible iron-constricted Gates of War shall shut; *and safe* within them shall stay the godless *and ghastly* Lust *of Blood*, propped on his pitiless piled armoury, and *still* roaring from gory mouth, *but* held fast by a hundred chains of bronze knotted behind his back.

> Then shall the age of violence be mellowing into peace:
> Venerable Faith, and the Home, with Romulus and Remus,
> Shall make the laws; the grim, steel-welded gates of War
> Be locked; *and* within, on a heap of armaments, a hundred
> Knots of bronze tying *his hands* behind him, shall sit
> Growling and bloody-mouthed the godless *spirit of* Discord.

The first, Dickinson's, is little more than a paraphrase. In all the versions I have italicized the words that cannot be supported directly from the text; Dickinson has most such words. I would not necessarily deny that the expansions can, generally, be inferred from Virgil's text. My point is that they could be just as easily inferred from a straight translation, and a translation that *states* what an author only *implies* is not an honest translation. His language is bizarre, the most obvious example being 'blood-boltered' for *cruento*. I do not deny that Virgil sometimes gives us bizarre words but that does not justify the inclusion of a bizarre word where Virgil has a common one. As Dr. Rees points out, Dickinson's is a prose translation arranged in lines; that is at best a dishonest procedure.

The second version is in honest prose; it is, of course, Jackson Knight's. It is, interestingly, the one preferred by Dr. Rees. Here too there is much elaboration, much that is paraphrase.

The third translation, that of Day Lewis, appears at first sight to be the most literal as well as the most mellifluous. The impression is, however, to some extent misleading. Day Lewis does not add, he suppresses. 'Into peace' seems very inadequate for *positis bellis*; 'steel-welded', even if we concede the anachronism, is hardly enough for *ferro et compagibus artis*.

That in line 291 Virgil is referring not just to the immediate past but to the whole sad tale of human cruelty and folly I take to be obvious. Dickinson, and Day Lewis too perhaps, makes the point clear; Jackson Knight does not. Day Lewis treats the end of warfare only by inference, Dickinson spoils the structure by the gratuitous addition of 'the world'. Dickinson and Day Lewis abandon *Quirinus*; Jackson Knight, with his 'Quirine Romulus', gets the worst of both worlds. Either the reader knows what *Quirinus* is, in which case 'Quirine Romulus' merely changes the Virgilian balance, or the reader does not, in which case 'Quirine Romulus' adds obscurity to adaptation. If Austin can give a note on *Quirinus*, why should not our translation? Day Lewis is here faithful to the principles stated in his introduction.

There are many passages in this epic which cannot appeal to the modern reader as they must have done to the Roman. The antiquarian aspect of the *Aeneid*—the frequent place-names and family names, some of the customs and legends even, which Virgil introduced to glorify the Roman people and its history—can be of interest only to scholars nowadays: I found it almost impossible to reproduce such passages without causing the narrative to lose grip.

Are we then to look forward to new editions of *Paradise Lost* stripped of all its Biblical and Classical allusion so that the reader should not have his attention distracted from the plot? The object of our courses is not to make Virgil seem like a modern but so to attune our sensibilities to him and to his time that we feel some sense of comprehension of that alien world and thereby, one hopes, a deeper understanding of our own. All the translations change the structure of the last sentence of this passage. But there is surely no advantage in subordinating the notion of 'roaring', certainly none in making *sedens* the main verb.

But the most unhappy feature of all these translations is the treatment of *Furor impius*. What is anyone to make of 'fiend of Fury' with its echoes of the *Eumenides*, or 'godless and ghastly Lust of Blood' with its suggestion of Bram Stoker, or 'the godless spirit of Discord', which is far more faithful to the sense of the context but which utterly suppresses the fact that we have here a reference to the conflict between *Pietas* and *Furor*, one of the great themes of the *Aeneid*? The problem with such words is, of course, notorious but the accepted solutions are absurd. Translators correctly observe that the Roman concept of *pietas* as an essentially single and coherent virtue is missing from our experience and therefore from our vocabulary. Our words, 'piety', 'duty', 'patriotism', etc. have inadequate as well as inappropriate associations. So, the translator chooses the best fit he can for each context, thus totally concealing the fact that the *Aeneid* is at least partly about *pietas*. It is important to understand at this point that while there really are features of Latin literature that require a knowledge of Latin to comprehend, this is not the sort of problem that linguistic skill helps at all. Indeed, sometimes a knowledge of Latin can be a positive impediment. The Latin student, armed with a few dictionary definitions of *pietas*, may feel that he understands the concept without further ado; the translation student, confronted by a translation which treats the word consistently but warns him in a note that this is an alien concept that he can understand from its contexts alone, has a much better chance of success. When an author alludes to a concept unknown in our society, the translator has two honourable choices. Either he takes one of the inappropriate English approximations, uses it consistently and gives a footnote to explain the problem, or he simply preserves the Latin word, again with an appropriate footnote. In either case it might be helpful to italicize the chosen word. As a rule, the English approximation probably works better in verse, the preservation of the Latin word in prose. No translator of

Tacitus should translate *imperium* or *potestas* any more than he should render *consul* as 'prime minister'.

In general, particular Latin words should be consistently rendered by particular English ones, and care should be taken to ensure that the same English word is not repeated, especially in close context, if the Latin employs different words. Carelessness by translators on this point frequently leads better students into real errors. It is not, of course, quite as easy as that. All languages have certain words which cover a wide range of meanings and it is rare indeed for another language to have a word with just that same range. For instance, few translators would feel constrained to render *moles* consistently in 'tantae molis erat Romanam condere gentem' and 'et molem mirantur equi', and they would be right not to try since it is hardly arguable that Virgil sees here some unitary concept. On the other hand, when an author is self-consciously developing a theme based on particular concepts to which he consistently alludes with identical or cognate terms, it is quite irresponsible to suppress the fact.

One of the most unhelpful and misleading concepts normally encountered in debates on translation is the traditional distinction beween literal and literary translations with the unspoken assumption that the former must be pedestrian and unfaithful to the spirit of the original, while the latter, released from the shackles of pedantic niceties, can soar into a close spiritual affinity with the original. But a translation is not literal in any helpful sense if it is ugly where Virgil is mellifluous, prolix where Virgil is concise, flat where Virgil is elevated. Similarly, a translation freed from the text and soaring into literary beauties may indeed be *magnifique, mais ce n'est pas la guerre*. It is my contention that we have been too quick to assume that we cannot render Virgil faithfully. I do not, of course, mean to suggest that nothing will be lost in translation, I mean rather that we have allowed our perception that something will be lost to make us tolerate a degree of loss that is quite unnecessary. Good translation is a slow, painstaking exercise in which the characteristics of the translator should entirely vanish. With a few honourable exceptions translation has been regarded as unworthy of the best scholars. Half the effort required to produce a scholarly edition could bring us wonderful translations but we seldom get half the effort, we get one-tenth of the effort. There is something wrong with our sense of values when a man can dash off a translation of Lucan in six months, deliberately and openly substituting his own notions of what literature should look like since he disapproved of the taste of his author; such a man should not find a publisher.

The Americans have had much longer experience than we have had of teaching classics in translation and it is, accordingly, not surprising that they have had far more success than we have had in the preparation of translations suitable for academic contexts. Men like Lattimore and

Grene[4] know what it is to teach literature in translation; small wonder, then, that their translations work so much better for our purposes. Latin has been much less well served, but there seems no reason why the techniques that have worked so well for Greek should fail in the case of Latin. Combine the self-effacing care of a Lattimore with the annotated approach of the new Prentice-Hall series and you have the recipe for success.

For too long we have so stressed the inadequacy of translation, as a device to persuade people of the value of our discipline, that we have been deceived by our own propaganda. The danger is that society may decide that if it is all that difficult they will not bother at all. Inadequate translations will serve only to replace the prejudice that it is all too difficult with the worse prejudice that there is nothing of worth there anyway. Ideally, a translation will impart a real and honest appreciation of the value and importance of classical literature. It will inspire some of our students into language study, it will give all of them a respect for the values of our discipline.

In an attempt to illustrate my proposition that we have in the past abandoned the aim of real fidelity too easily, I have prepared a specimen version for the passage discussed just now and also for the beginning of the second book of the *Aeneid* (verses 1–39). When I was taught verse composition I was constantly struck by the contrast between the fidelity we were supposed to aim for in turning Milton into Latin hexameters and the freedom with which many translators of Virgil treated their subject. A translator needs not the inspiration of a poet but the discipline and craftsmanship of the master of verse composition.

Before we go any further I want to make it plain that I am not putting forward my versions as a solution or fair copy. They are intended to illustrate an attitude of mind, to be a shadow, with luck a foreshadowing, of the translation I should like to see. Treat them as the first tentative draft for the committee to work on, for I see this task as one that lends itself to a committee. My aim has been a line-by-line rendering, changing the word order only when driven by syntactical compulsion. Sometimes it is possible to preserve Virgil's word order by changing his syntax, sometimes one can do the reverse. In each case I have tried to decide which is the more significant. More frequently than you might suppose it is possible to preserve both.

There is no way of giving an adequate impression of Virgilian metre. The fact that Virgil uses two distinct features of language, quantity and stress, to achieve his effects is enough to preclude anything but the palest shadow in English. I have accordingly followed the technique of Lattimore and Day Lewis. I have avoided harsh rhythms and have placed six strong beats in each line. Incidentally, the line-by-line arrangement has the great merit of allowing students to relate the translation to the traditional line numbering system and thus to derive far more benefit from the secondary literature. I have striven to preserve the balance of the original by giving strong, heavy words where Virgil does, and by avoiding them where he does. I try to preserve enjambment, run-on lines, end-stop lines, and heavy syntax break in mid-line. I give notes where they seem necessary. We profess a belief in the proposition that only our language students can really understand, but it is to them that we give the annotated texts. Our translation students are expected to rub along with their unaided wits. 'For he that hath, to him shall be given: and he that hath not, from him shall be taken even that which he hath.'

Aeneid 1. 291–6

> Then with warfare laid aside, the harsh centuries will soften; | white-haired Faith and Vesta, Quirinus with his brother Remus | will give the laws; the grim gates of War with its tight | iron construction will be closed; impious Passion within | sitting upon its savage arms and bound with a hundred brazen | knots behind its back will rage hideously, with gory mouth.

292 Quirinus: the name by which Romulus was known after his deification.

293–4 When Rome was at peace the gates of the temple of Janus were closed. Augustus made much of the fact that he had been able to close these gates in 29 B.C. for the first time since the First Punic War.

294 impious Passion: *Furor impius*, untranslatable because it alludes to two very Roman notions which are quite unfamiliar to us. *Pietas* (piety) is one of the most important virtues that a Roman could display and the word has none of the overtones of sanctity and other-worldliness associated with our word. Loyalty to state, family, and religion were regarded as but different aspects of essentially the same virtue, *pietas*, and we are made to see that Aeneas, who is frequently called *pius* (pious), exemplifies all three aspects. *Furor* involves the madness that comes upon us when we lose our self-control. Both Dido, who gives way to a singularly ill-advised sexual passion for Aeneas, and Turnus, whose weakness is bloodlust, are types of *furor*. Passion is a woefully inadequate translation but at least it is a word which does not absolutely exclude one or other of the important contexts in which *furor* is to be found. One of the important themes of the *Aeneid* is, without doubt, the triumph of *pietas* in the person of Aeneas over the forces of *furor* represented especially by Dido and Turnus. Accordingly, it is not insignificant that Jupiter's prophecy should end with the conquest of *Furor impius*. In this particular context there is clearly also an allusion to that most impious of all human activities, civil war.

Aeneid 2. 1–39

> All fell silent and held their gaze intent upon him.
> Then, from his high couch, father Aeneas thus began:

'Unspeakable, O queen, is the pain you ask me to renew,
how the riches of Troy and the piteous kingdom
were destroyed by Danaans, both the miseries I saw myself   5
and those in which my part was great. In speaking of such things
which of the Myrmidons or Dolopes, what soldier of hard Ulixes
would refrain from tears? But now damp night is rushing
from the sky and the setting stars urge rest.
Yet, if there is desire so great to know of our calamities   10
and briefly to hear the last toils of Troy,
although my mind shrinks from the memory and starts back
   in grief,
I shall begin.
               Broken by war, by fate repulsed,
the leaders of the Danaans, as now so many years slip by,
with Pallas' art divine construct a horse of mountain   15
size—they weave its flanks with boards of pine.
They pretend it is a vow for their return, that is the tale that
   goes about.
They pick choice specimens of men and secretly
enclose them in the blind recesses, filling up tight
the huge and cavernous womb with armed soldiery.   20
    There in full view is Tenedos, an island renowned
in story, rich in resources while Priam's rule remained,
now just an inlet and a treacherous anchorage for ships:
here they proceed and hide themselves on the deserted shore.
We thought that they were gone, that they were sailing for
   Mycenae   25
So all of Teucer's land shakes free from its long grief:
the gates are opened wide; it is a joy to go into the Doric camp,
to see their sites deserted and the abandoned shore:
here was the band of Dolopes encamped, and here the cruel
   Achilles;
their ships were here, and here they used to fight in battle-line.   30
Some gape at the deadly offering to the unwed Minerva
and marvel at the horse's bulk; Thymoetes first
suggests that it be led within the walls and on the citadel installed,
perhaps through treachery, perhaps the fates of Troy already
   leant that way.
But Capys, and those with better thoughts in mind,   35
tell us to hurl the Danaans' trap, their suspect gift,
into the sea or have it burnt with flames beneath,
or bore and probe into the hollow hiding places of its womb.
The unsure people split into conflicting factions.

5 Danaans: Greeks. The word is used particularly of Greeks besieging Troy. It is a particular favourite of Virgil's.

7 Myrmidons: the Greek tribe led by Achilles.

Dolopes: the Greek tribe led by Achilles' son, Neoptolemus.

Ulixes: the point of this line is that even those Greeks whose hostility to Troy was especially implacable would find the sufferings of Aeneas pitiable. That Ulixes was the Trojans' most hated adversary is a point of which much is made during this book.

17 Vow: the purposes both real and alleged for the horse are at this point kept deliberately vague. A *uotum* (vow) is either something you promised to a god when you were in difficulties, or an offering to a god in the hope of receiving some particular future gain.

19 Blind: *caecus*, the ordinary word for 'blind'; unlike 'blind', however, the word can also readily convey the sense of 'dark' as here. We may compare our 'blind alley'. I have kept the word 'blind' so as not to lose the particular emotional overtones of *caecus*, a word that vividly suggests the blindness of the men inside the horse.

30 Ships: *classes*, a word which normally means 'ships' but which is occasionally used to mean 'cavalry'. Servius and others have argued that this is the meaning intended here.

34 Perhaps through treachery: there was a story that Priam had had Thymoetes' wife and son killed, so the question arises as to whether Thymoetes was acting from motives of revenge.

NOTES

1. This paper is slightly amended from a paper read to the conference of the Council of University Classical Departments held at St. Edmund Hall, Oxford, in January 1976. A short version appeared in the Council's fifth *Bulletin* (London, 1976). I am indebted to Professor W. J. N. Rudd, the editor of the *Bulletin*, for his kind permission to allow this longer version to appear in *G & R*. The *Bulletin* also includes a summary of a paper on the same topic by Professor R. D. Williams as well as a brief report of the discussion at the time.

2. *G & R* 21 (1974), 111–27.

3. P. Dickinson, *The Aeneid* (New York, 1961); W. F. Jackson Knight, *The Aeneid* (Harmondsworth, 1956); C. Day Lewis, *The Eclogues, Georgics and Aeneid of Virgil* (London, 1966).

4. Professor Richmond Lattimore is perhaps best known for his magnificent translations of the *Iliad* (Chicago, 1951) and of the *Odyssey* (New York, 1967). He and Professor David Grene are joint editors and most significant contributors to *The Complete Greek Tragedies* (Chicago, 1959), a series familiar to all who have made any serious attempt to teach Greek tragedy in translation.

ADDITIONAL NOTE (1989)

For a provocatively different view on Lattimore, see now A. G. Geddes, *G & R* 35 (1988), 1–13.

SUBJECT INDEX

INDEX OF PASSAGES